ON THE HOUSE

ON THE HOUSE

Harry Greene's

D-I-Y HANDBOOK

BBC BOOKS

Dedicated to Marjie

Cover photographs by
Guglielmo Galvin

Illustrations by
Kevin Maddison, Jim Robins and Paul Williams

Published by BBC Books
A division of BBC Enterprises Ltd
80 Wood Lane, London W12 0TT

First published 1987

ISBN 0 563 20569 5

Typeset in 9/11 pt Univers light/bold
by Phoenix Photosetting, Chatham
Printed in Great Britain by
Mackays of Chatham

CONTENTS

ACKNOWLEDGEMENTS

Exactly thirty years ago, my new young wife, actress Marjie Lawrence, displayed a remarkable degree of perception and foresight. She conceived an idea based on the renovation of our first flat. 'Show television viewers how they can do-it-for-themselves', she said.

So, in 1957, we devised, wrote and I presented on television, DIY, for the first time in Britain. My credits read 'Harry Greene, being handy around the home'. Marjie's commonsense approach and guidance throughout our partnership has ensured that, whatever craft I talk or write about, it is simplified with no jargon! Together, we're still 'being handy around the home'.

Thank you Stephanie Silk and Andy Miekle of BBC TV Pebble Mill, for making this book and the television series possible for me. Talia Rodgers and Gillian Shaw, of BBC Books, have advised me and applied their expertise and knowledge in the production of this book; I owe them both a special debt. Thanks, also, to Beryl Drinkwater for typing into the early hours; to Robin and Laura; Len McIntosh; Keith Haslewood; Geoff Hayes; Glen Roberts; Terry Hackney; Lesley Barker and Gordon Grant: experts and friends who have freely given their help and advice, whenever it was needed.

Harry Greene
London 1987

INTRODUCTION

How many times have you heard the expression 'I'll do that tomorrow' or 'I must get somebody in to fix that before someone has an accident'? Today, more than ever before, there is a need to be able to tackle the countless repair and maintenance jobs which crop up in every household. Most people make one major investment in their lives: they buy a house. Treat a house with reasonable care and attention and it quickly becomes a home. It not only looks better but will have a longer life and will improve in value. Lots of people are worried by the cost of maintaining their home, or bothered by not quite knowing how to tackle a job. It would be ideal if each and every household had a DIY'er experienced in all forms of repair and maintenance, so that all the repair work could be left to them, but life, of course, just isn't like that!

Most jobs related to 'do-it-yourself', however, can be done very well and with a great deal of satisfaction by most householders. No matter how unskilled you believe yourself to be, providing you have a basic tool kit, you carry out the correct preparation work and take each job step by step, it's possible to cut through the myths and mysteries and 'do-it-yourself' successfully.

In every home, in fact in practically every room, you can find something that is faulty, damaged, cracked or broken. To put things right is often a very simple matter indeed, but it is even easier to avoid actually doing them. A cracked window; a drawer which sticks; a chipped wall tile; a loose hinge; a dripping tap; blocked drains; there are hundreds more! Doing a good job in your own home is satisfying and obviously saves you money. We all have to become home handypersons. Self-sufficiency is the goal of every DIY enthusiast: this book aims to help you translate your passion into action! It is worth remembering, however, that circumspection is the best practical approach. A healthy fear of error will give the DIY'er the vital care in planning every move. Confidence comes as you proceed, as you drill more holes, lift more floorboards or hack off more plaster. Gradually the simple secrets of doing the job properly are unveiled! All you need to do is get to know how the home works. New techniques of plumbing in copper and plastic are easy to understand and – even more important – easy to get right.

Whatever you do, don't be put off by thinking that you need a huge tool kit. Basic tools are all that are necessary. The more esoteric tools can be hired by the day; an inexpensive alternative which allows you to choose exactly the right tool for the job.

The ideal job for the DIY person to do is one where material costs are low, labour costs are high, and the skill required is minimum. Laying fibreglass insulation in a roof void or attic is a good example, as is decorating. We can save up to 80% of the cost of decorating a room simply by doing it ourselves. Most tasks can be undertaken by the ordinary man or woman helped by step-by-step instructions. Obviously professionals are quicker, but then we as householders are not usually in a hurry.

A BASIC TOOL KIT

The maxim 'You get what you pay for' is certainly true when selecting the surprisingly few tools that you need for your work around the home.

Don't skimp on the essentials; you really should buy the best you can afford. A cheap screwdriver bought on a market stall will soon lose its 'flat'; 'Never-to-be-repeated', bargain-price tools are simply not a good idea. We are all limited to a financial budget, but the need to become equipped for the tasks involved in maintaining our homes has never been more evident than in today's economic climate. What we all need in order to carry out routine maintenance, repair and improvement jobs is a basic tool kit.

Ten important points for you to consider first:

1 Always buy the best that you can afford.

2 Choose good, household-name brands.

3 Decide on a place for each tool, whether it's a carpenter's box, a wall rack or a cupboard.

4 Use each tool for the purpose for which it was designed.

5 Learn the correct way of using each tool and always read instructions when provided.

6 Handle tools carefully and properly.

7 Always handle power tools with special caution.

8 Make sure that tools are returned, after use, to their designated place.

9 Keep all tools sharpened and in good repair.

10 Don't buy expensive, sophisticated tools when you can hire them.

Your best strategy is to start with a set of general-purpose tools. Later on, add to them as and when you need things like a sharpening stone, wire-strippers or a 'G' clamp. Choose, first of all, a versatile electric drill. (Black & Decker offer a good range, with a back-up service. Bosch offer a more sophisticated drill with the opportunity to purchase attachments later: their criteria are versatility and durability.) An electric power drill is certainly less work than a hand drill and easier to handle. You must remember to read the instructions carefully before using the electric drill and any attachments. A hand drill gets you into small spaces which are sometimes inaccessible to an electric drill, although a flexible drive shaft (a bendy extension for drilling in awkward places) is available for an electric drill. A hand drill with enclosed gears is best for your safety and protection.

A hammer's first job is to bang in nails. Its second job is to pull them out, so a **claw hammer** which combines the two is the answer. If a nail is too deep for it to be drawn out, try tapping it in further using a bigger, blunted nail and pulling it through the opposite side with pliers. If there's no opposite side to pull it through, tap it as far in as it will go and fill the hole with putty or plastic wood. If there's a fear that you're going to damage the wood by drawing a nail out, use a small piece of wood against the nail head as a sort of wedge and you'll find you'll need to use very little effort. For light jobs needing precision, not strength, use a smaller **cross pein hammer** instead.

The first saw you buy should be a 22-inch (550-mm) **panel saw**, which will suit your general needs. It should have eight points (the number of teeth to the inch). Always hold the saw with your index finger pointing along the direction of the blade; this gives you better control. Do use the whole length of the blade and never force a saw or put pressure on it. Let the saw do the work, applying light pressure on the downward stroke only. The **junior hacksaw** is a handy tool for cutting off nails and cutting through wire, cable and small pieces of metal. The **tenon saw** is for fine, small work where accuracy is important.

Standard screwdrivers are designed specifically for driving in or removing screws. Don't be tempted to use them for opening paint tins, forcing up bent nails or chipping off hardened cement. Buy a screwdriver that feels right for your hand. Slightly more expensive is a **pump screwdriver** with a range of interchangeable bits. This will cope with electrical work and 'Posidrive' screws with cross slot heads, as well as slotted screws, although you can, of course, buy separate screwdrivers for the different types of work.

A **steel tape**, apart from its job of measuring, serves as an excellent conversion device for

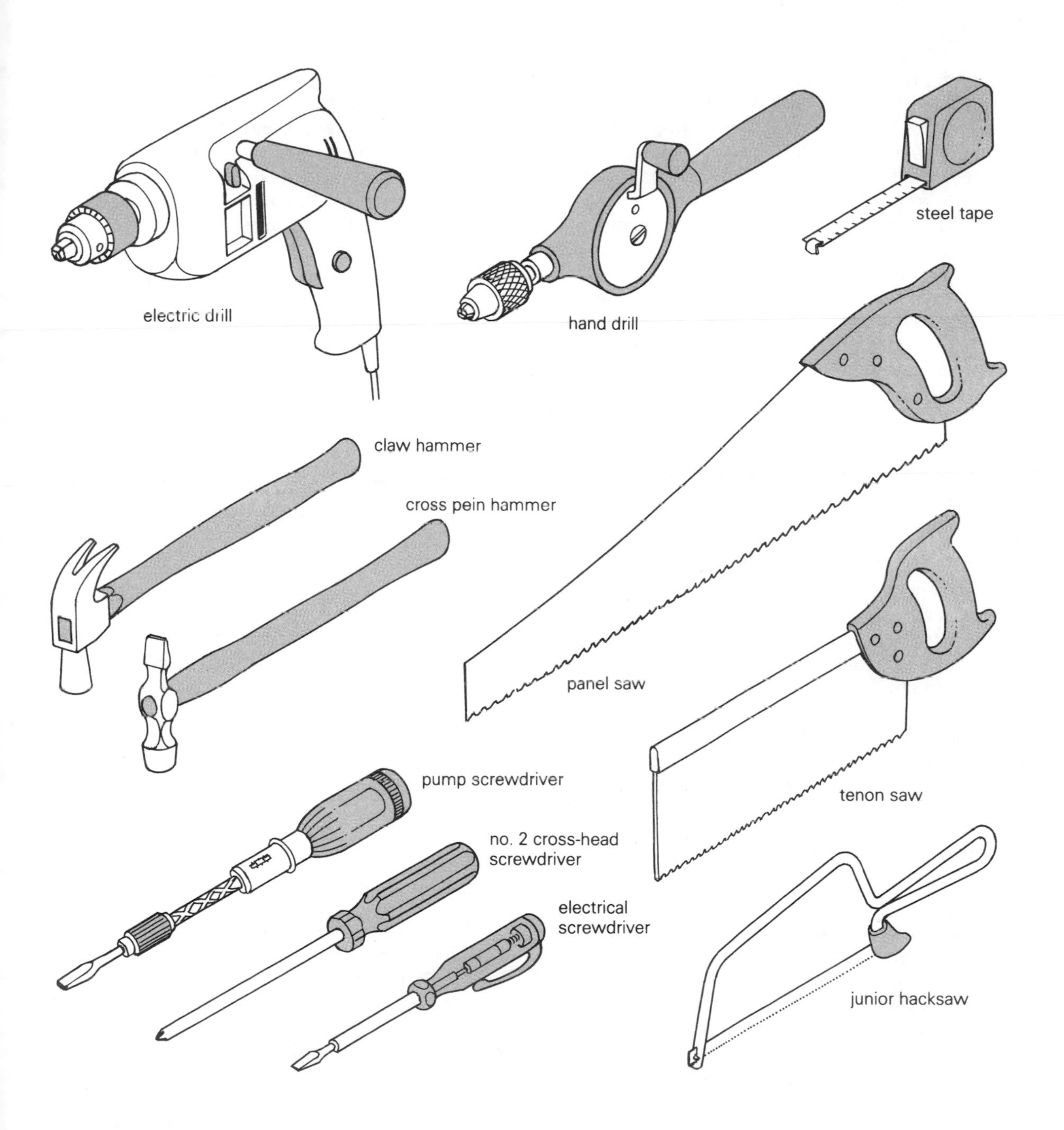

A Basic Tool Kit (see also page 11)

imperial to metric measures. Buy one up to 16 feet (5 m) long, which is ideal for measuring rooms, carpets, curtains, wallpaper and for the job of measuring before cutting wood. Do buy a steel tape that has a little arm which locks off the tape to any measurement.

Pliers are the ideal tool for holding small items. Long-nosed pliers are invaluable in electrical work, but be certain that the handles are insulated. Pliers will also cut wire and hold nuts whilst you unscrew a bolt. **Pincers** come into the same category, but are only used for gripping, not cutting. (Once you've bought and used a wire-stripper, however, which both cuts wire and strips off the insulation around it, you'll wonder how you ever did without one. We all have dozens of electric items which need plugs and the wire-stripper is a safe time-saver in this frequent operation.)

The **multi-purpose trimming tool** is available in lots of sizes. Replaceable blades are held by only two screws.

A **bradawl** is a useful tool for starting drill-holes for small screws, but make absolutely certain that you cut into the wood at right angles to the grain. If you don't, you run the risk of splitting small pieces of wood.

The first chisel that you buy should not be a wooden-handled one. For general-purpose work, a ¾-inch (20-mm) **bevelled-edge chisel** is ideal – the plastic shatterproof handle will withstand banging with a hammer if you don't possess a mallet. Make sure that you also get the protective plastic cap for the blade, to protect its sharp edge in your tool kit.

A **trimming knife** with a retractable blade is also an essential part of your tool kit and can be used for cutting through thin ply when used in conjunction with a straight steel edge and marking timber to get a more accurate saw cut. It will also cut carpets, vinyl and cork floor-tiles.

Keep an aluminium **step-ladder** (with an open leg-lock and non-slip feet) somewhere handy in the house. Make sure that you can reach your highest ceiling or the attic trap from it. A paint tray that locks onto the top of the ladder is a very useful accessory.

The traditional **work-bench** is a heavy and cumbersome piece of equipment, but its modern counterpart is flexible, lightweight, portable and strong. Once you've got into the swing of DIY and mastered some of the techniques, you'll probably find it's worth investing in a portable bench if you intend doing a lot of repair and home-improvement work.

The modern equivalent of the hammer and tack is the **staple-gun**, an invaluable tool for things such as small upholstery jobs; mounting thin ply or card onto the backs of picture frames; holding down carpet underfelt; fixing roofing felt to the underside of rafters and many other holding and fixing jobs around the house.

As you get more experienced, some of the tools that you'll be seeking to use will probably be: a steel combination square, a spirit level, a tenon saw, a smoothing plane, a flat file, a pointing trowel, a try square, and a brace and bit (or hand brace) with some auger bits for drilling larger holes in wood. (Remember that those bits need to be kept separately from the electric drill bits which come housed in a plastic case.)

All tools, of course, need to be maintained properly and it's no use owning a plane or chisel without having sharpening facilities and knowing how to use them. A double-sided oilstone with an inexpensive honing guide is a must. The hardest job that you will have to do in order to get an accurate cutting edge is to set the blade into the guide!

HIRING PLANT & TOOLS

A tool hire shop can be found on most high streets. Pop in, browse around and ask them for their catalogue. Do check their price lists, because hiring by the week can sometimes be much more economical than the daily rate. (Make sure you always get instructions with everything that you hire.) Did you know, for example, that you can do your own cleaning of carpets and floor-sanding? A small pneumatic

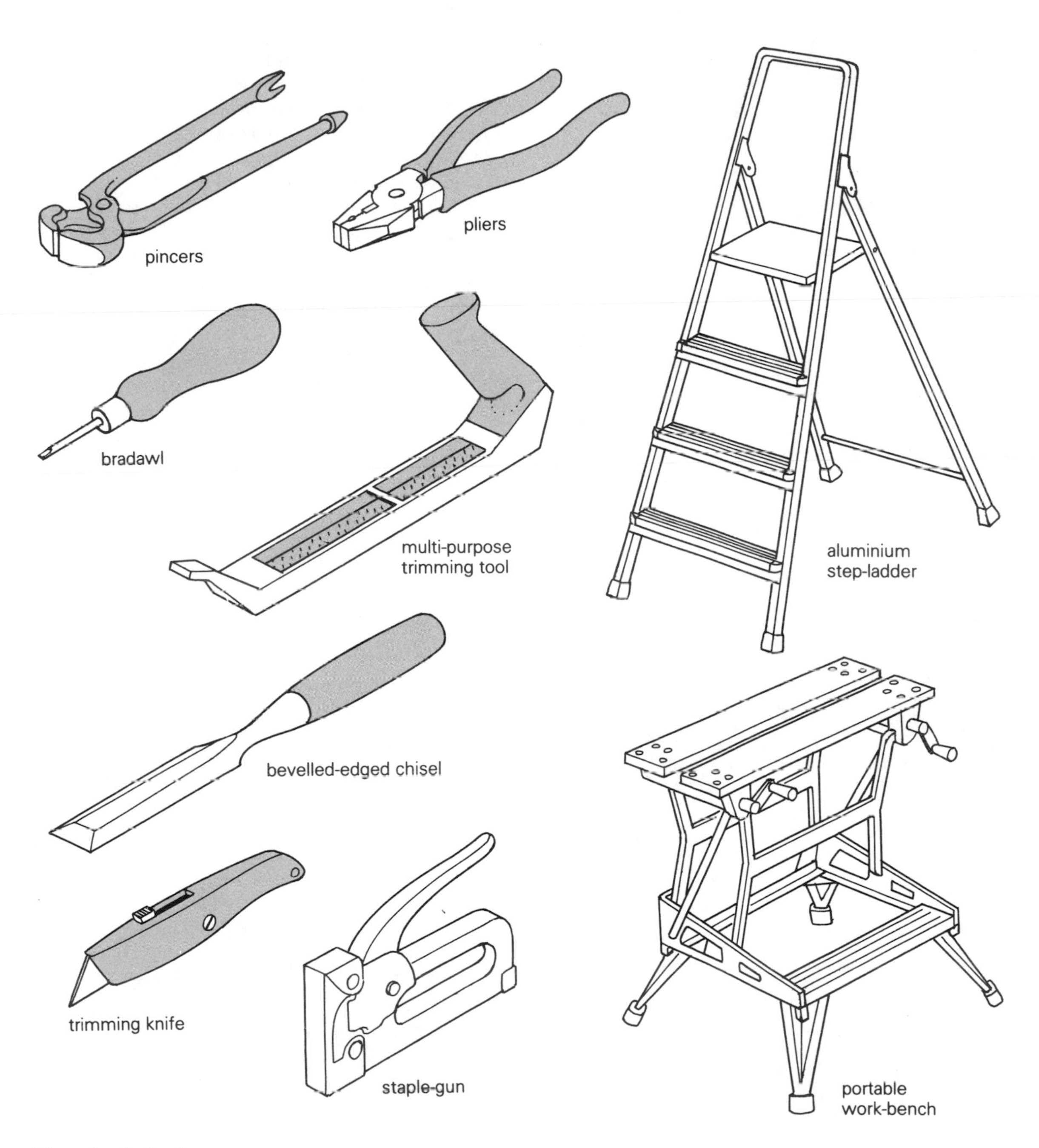

More basic tools

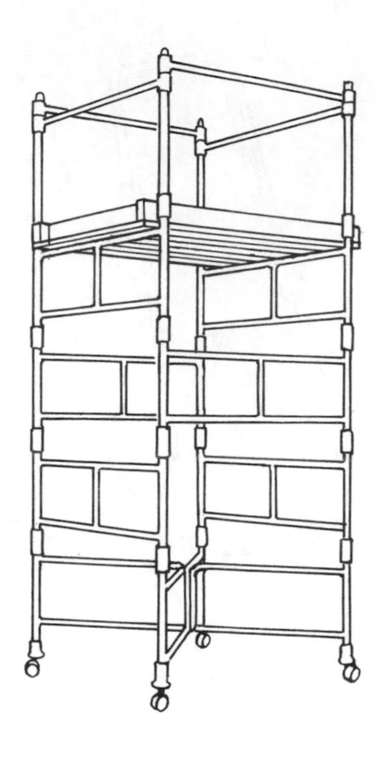

drill called a Kango can be hired for breaking up concrete and demolition work; a steam wallpaper stripper is an important innovation in the decorating area; concrete-mixers (which you simply plug in) will save hours of back-breaking mixing with a shovel. For work on the outside of the house a scaffold tower is easily erected, sturdy and very safe as long as you follow the instructions. Extension ladders made of aluminium are easily transported and lightweight to handle. Do, of course, make sure they are secure (see page 111).

Tower Scaffolding

When you buy or hire a lightweight scaffolding tower, you'll have explicit instructions as to its use and safety. The use of a tower can be the safest, most efficient and quickest way of redecorating the outside of your house, provided that you always have safety in mind. Lock the wheels before you start using it and ensure that it is made safe by tying off somewhere. If stays are provided, use them. Make sure that you are working at a comfortable height. Ensure that all joints are firmly locked. Use the toe board and the guard rail properly. Put a spirit level against the vertical poles and adjust them if necessary.

Large items can be hired by the day and delivered and collected by the hire company; Above left: Aluminium scaffold tower; Left: Portable concrete-mixer; Below: Builder's wheelbarrow

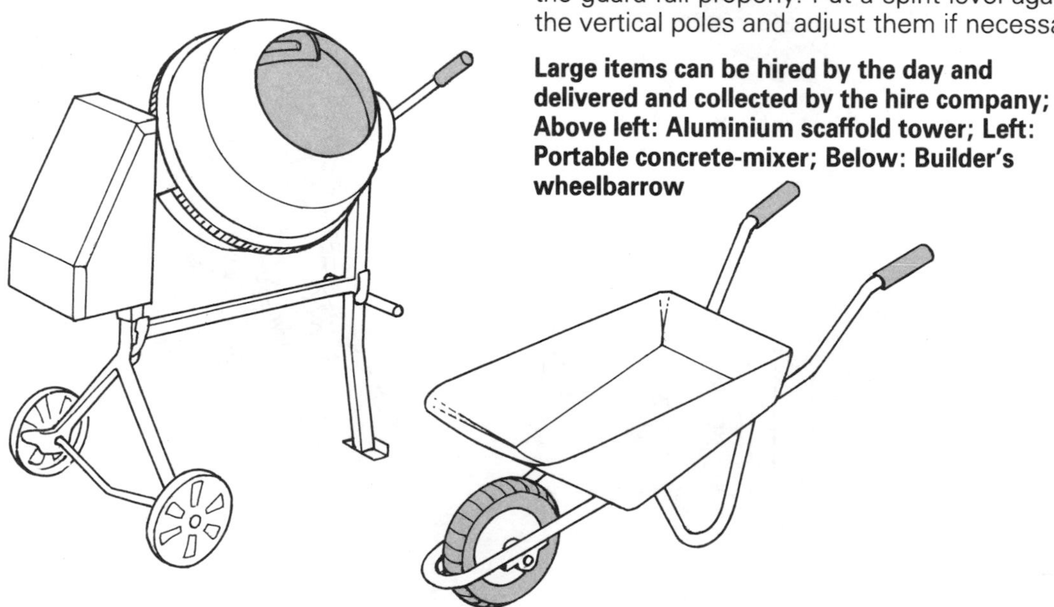

DECORATING 1

The techniques of painting and decorating are fairly easy to master and the materials are readily available, so with some application and determination you have all you need to begin! Do you realise that you will have completed 60% of the work of redecorating a room before you've even lifted a paint brush? I'm talking, of course, about the preparation. It's hard, physical work, but not beyond any householder's ability. The apparent tedium of preparation (or 'preparing the substrate' as it's often called) is not to be exaggerated, but there is no short cut to the success of this most rewarding of DIY jobs.

Of the total cost of redecorating a room, taking into account materials and labour charges, only 20% is chargeable to materials. Decorating, therefore, is one of the jobs on which you can save a great deal of money.

Pay particular attention to the planning and preparation stage. Before rushing out to buy a pot of paint and a brush, relax, sit down with your pencil and notepaper and begin to note all the preliminaries. Already you've begun on the first and most important part of the job! Do this properly and in the end you'll have a finished job you'll really be proud of.

A few notes and queries for you to jot down at this point: 1. Surfaces must be clean and dry (this can mean hours of scraping and rubbing). 2. Household dirt is mostly silica and carbon, found hiding as a coat of grease. All you need to do to get rid of that grease is to use an ordinary household cleaning agent. 3. What about the chimney – should you have it swept before you start? 4. Is there a window sill outside that needs a repair to stop water coming in? (Often cracked or missing putty on a lower bar will allow water to creep in and run down the inside of the window.) 5. It's worth removing strip-foam insulation from a door or window frame, especially if it's been on for some time. If it has, you'll find it has attracted dirt and even though you think that you have cleaned the frame, you'll be disappointed when you find grey streaks of dirt in your bright new paint. 6. Wipe off the tops of doors and windows; few people think about doing this before beginning to paint. 7. Vacuum dust out from keyholes and window latches – another source of dirty grey on your fresh coat of paint. Dust, of course, is the enemy to the painter, leaving grey streaks and a gritty surface to the paintwork.

STARTING FROM SCRATCH ON WOODWORK

After you've read through this chapter on painting and decorating you can then relate certain parts of it to your own decorating job. Make your notes. We're all impatient, we can imagine what the room is going to look like and we're too anxious to see the transformation! The best way to approach any decorating job is to look at it through the eyes of a professional. Not necessarily with professional expertise, but through the eyes of somebody unfamiliar with that particular room. Try this: leave the room and when you come back a little while later, try to look at the woodwork dispassionately. You'll begin to see blemishes, scratches, dull patches and edges of paintwork that could have been painted straighter.

Are you going to paint on new wood or onto

existing paintwork? If it's new wood you need to get it quite smooth. A good sanding down with first a medium-grade sandpaper and then a fine-grade one will give you a well-prepared surface. Always sand the wood in the direction of the grain. If you're working on soft wood there are no special primers to consider. If you've bought and are using special hard woods, check with the timber merchant who will be able to tell you what special primers are to be used (on, for example, teak and certain resinous West African timbers).

Any nails in the woodwork should be punched in and covered over with filler, in order to prevent them being rusted by the (water-based) paint and ruining your new paintwork.

Now that you're ready to start work on the wood, you'll first of all have to start preparing the room. Then, from the notes you've made, you'll be able to bring in all your tools and materials. Don't let the dust on the top of the lid spoil the paint inside the tin and don't try to open the tin with a screwdriver – you'll damage both the lid and the screwdriver. If it's a new tin of paint, read the instructions carefully and remember them. Make a note of whether it's a water-based paint or an oil-bound paint, or has special ingredients. Thinning instructions will be given and so too will advice on brush cleaning. What you won't find on the side of a tin of paint is advice on storage, straining and how to get rid of a hard skin, which may have formed if the paint has been left to stand.

Use a small can-opener for prising open your tins of paint – they're cheap and most effective. Place it on the edge of the can with the point upwards and under the rim of the lid; simply press down and up comes the lid.

The reason for reading and memorising the instructions on the side of the tin is in fact a very simple one. There must be thousands of half-used tins of paint in cupboards up and down the country with their instructions obliterated by the inevitable dripping of paint down the outside of the can. A painter's 'kettle' is the answer. This is a small can (you can get them in plastic, with a handle) into which you pour just enough paint for your use that day. Keep a plastic carrier bag and some kitchen roll handy. Any spillage or drops of paint can be wiped off immediately with the kitchen roll, which can be disposed of into the plastic bag. If you use a rag for wiping paint off the side of a tin, it's inevitable that the next time you pick up the rag you'll transfer paint to your hands and then to the brush handle!

Unless you're using thixotropic (jelly) paint you'll need to stir the paint thoroughly before you pour the required amount of paint into your painter's kettle. It is important to mix your paint thoroughly, as paint is made up of various constituents, some of which will settle into a stiff sediment which you can feel at the bottom of the tin when you first try to stir it. Liquid paints have fine particles in suspension in the fluid, and it is these particles which tend to coagulate at the bottom of the tin. Standing the tin of paint upside down for a day or so before use sometimes helps to redistribute the particles, although you must make sure, of course, that the lid is firmly secured. If you have an electric drill with a stirring accessory, do be sure to use it at a slow speed. Otherwise, stir the paint with a broad-ladle stirrer, using a circular, lifting motion. Thixotropic paints must not be stirred; they do not settle as liquid paints do.

It's a mistake to store tins of paint upside down. A skin will form half-way down inside the tin and when the tin is righted for stirring, the skin gets broken and you're left with lumpy bits in the paint, which you then have to strain through a nylon. It's very difficult to avoid a skin forming on the top of paint if you've had it stored for any length of time. It's very easy, however, to carefully cut the skin close to the edges of the tin and remove the piece in one. You'll still find you need to stir the paint thoroughly, because the sediment will have settled to the bottom of the tin and any paint that has been stored will always need to be strained.

After you've rubbed down and prepared the

new woodwork, dust it off with a clean brush. Then lightly clean the surface with a rag dipped in turps. Any small defects and knots would have to be treated first. A small bottle of 'knotting' and a ½-inch (12-mm) brush are all that you'll need to ensure that the resinous areas will not 'weep' through the finished work and discolour the surface. Simply paint on the liquid to cover the knots completely. It dries fairly quickly, but will then need a light rubbing down with fine sandpaper.

If you wet your finger and apply it to new wood you'll find that the moisture from your finger is absorbed very readily into the wood. The next step in the preparation work, therefore, is to seal the wood. A priming coat of paint provides this essential seal base, so that the undercoat (and gloss or top coat) is not sucked into the wood. The primer must be well worked into the grainy surface and the wood totally covered with the priming paint. This priming coat also acts as an inhibitor to damp and moisture. It is advisable to paint new skirting boards and architraves (the moulding on the door frame) all round with priming paint before fixing in place. Don't be tempted under any circumstance to use the lazy person's method for priming – that is, with emulsion paint! Emulsion paint is water based and does dry quickly but does not offer the protection of a priming coat.

Use plenty of newspapers on the floor and on work surfaces, where you might be transferring paint from the tin into a smaller paint kettle. You'll find that a piece of string tied across the paint kettle is very useful for wiping off the excess paint from the brush. Only load the bristles to about a third of their length: dip any deeper and you'll find it running back down the handle as you paint.

When you think about it, what we're really doing when we're painting is providing an enhanced overall surface effect on a chosen area *and* protecting that surface. We are forming a continuous surface film on the wood. Only by following the correct procedures is it possible to build up a good, hard-wearing and easy-to-clean surface.

After the priming coat comes the next layer – the undercoat. This is sometimes called the 'obliterating coat' because it gives very good 'cover'. This coat has 'body' and helps build up the paint film.

In general terms, think of what happens when a brush takes the paint from the tin onto the wood. It has to end up evenly spread, with no runs and no apparent join. To achieve this, spread the paint in the direction of the grain and then lightly cross the paint at right angles. Finally, working from the adjacent (unpainted) area, stroke back into the painted area very lightly (in the original direction), lifting the brush off after each even stroke. This is called 'laying off'. Try to remember that the brush goes from dry, as it were, to wet in the laying off process. Never put the brush into wet paint to draw it along to the area where fresh paint is to be applied. Let the undercoat dry, thoroughly!

The next part of the preparation work can be done by any member of the family with the energy to spare. It's simply a matter of rubbing very lightly over the whole of the painted surface with a fine abrasive paper. Both glasspaper and garnet paper are specially prepared papers used for smoothing surfaces to a fine finish. 'Wet and Dry' refers to a silicon-carbide paper, which when used wet gives an extremely fine, smooth finish. (It also produces a residue which has to be washed off.) The paper should be kept just damp (as used on the resprayed metal of cars). An inexpensive cork sanding block should be used with the abrasive paper.

The top coat of paint must be applied in the same way as the undercoat, always working in the direction of the grain to start. Cross it at right angles and then 'lay off' in the original direction. After your final brush strokes have laid off the finished coat, make certain that there are no residual brush marks. Slight variations in the paint application should flow out as the paint dries. Don't ever be tempted to go back onto the work after it has become tacky: the most awful mess will result. Don't despair if you're not too happy with your first attempts. Remember that you can always go back to the work when it's dry. If that is the case, give it a good rub down and start again. Of course, this time you won't need to apply the priming coat, all you need to do is give it another coat of gloss.

Sometimes new wood will have been prepared with a preservative. If you know or suspect this to be true and you still want to paint the wood, then you have no option but to use an aluminium wood primer. Don't, however, use aluminium paint. If the new wood to be painted is a hard wood such as teak, degrease it with white spirit and allow it to dry completely before you begin the priming coat.

The manufacturer's recommendations concerning primer (or undercoat) and top coat must be adhered to. The chemical constituents of different paints might give you a lot of problems if you try to mix them, so stick to the same brand.

PAINT BRUSHES

For a professional finish to your painting you need a brush as good as the professionals use. If the same person painted two similar surfaces with the same paint but with two different brushes, using for the first one a professional's brush and for the second a cheap, short-bristle brush, only the surface painted with the professional's brush would be acceptable. It proves a most important point. A good paint brush will help ensure that you get a really professional finish to your work. The quality of the brush depends mainly on its bristles. A natural taper of bristles gives a good brush its shape.

If you have to paint in awkward places (behind a radiator for example) then you'll need a long-handled brush or a crevice brush. Never buy a short-bristle brush: get a better quality brush for better quality work. The main differences between good and bad brushes are in the length of the bristles and the bulky springy nature of the pure hog's bristle brush with its natural taper. This is the secret which enables the professional to apply a smooth, even coat of paint. If the brushes are not boxed or packeted on the counter in your local paint shop, pick them up and try them for flexibility. Look at a cheap brush and notice when you flex it that it has a 'mouth' through the centre of the bristles. On this type of brush, the metal housing to the bristles is loose and allows paint or water to collect in the void. See how many hairs the brush sheds as you flex it and see how much dust it holds. Make a note of the most expensive brushes: makers' names will begin to mean something to you. Most painting jobs on woodwork can be done with a 2-inch (50-mm) and a 1-inch (25-mm) brush, but a small, ½-inch (12-mm) brush is excellent for narrow areas, glazing bars and 'cutting-in'.

A cutting-in brush is used for the difficult job of painting up to the edge of glass on window frames. It doesn't take much expertise to paint without getting smudges on the glass using the angled tip to paint firm, straight lines. Synthetic fibre brushes are not as good as pure bristle and can only be used as general-purpose brushes as they tend to leave brush marks on the painted surface.

Paint pads have been the subject of extensive advertising in the past, but traditional brushes are still the best method of applying paint to a surface. However, you might find that you acquire the technique of using a pad quite easily and quickly, although they are more widely used on large surfaces or walls than on woodwork.

Looking After Paint Brushes

Promise yourself you'll always keep tools and brushes in proper order – and keep that promise! Discovering a blunt tool or a hard brush when you're ready to start work is frustrating and time-wasting. To clean a brush, press out as much of the residual paint as you can onto a newspaper with the back of a knife. Then wash it out thoroughly in whatever solvent the makers recommend. Follow this by a good washing in warm, soapy water and swill out. Don't stand the brushes up to dry: let them hang. (Wrap them in cling film if you're only stopping for a tea break.) When you've finished your painting job and need to store them, clean your brushes out in a proprietary brand of brush cleaner/restorer. A hole drilled into the wooden handle and a thin dowel will support a brush in a jar of solvent, but wash out thoroughly before using again.

STAINS

Wood has its own beauty inherent in the growing lines of the timber called the grain. If you've chosen to make the most of this pleasing natural effect by using a dye or a stain, you'll need to prepare the wood with as much if not more care than for paint. If it's new wood then it's more easily prepared, because again, you just have to make absolutely sure that the surface is clean and smooth. You'll probably need a nail punch and filler; use fine sawdust from the same wood and a transparent wood adhesive to mix together your own matching filler. Put in slightly more than you need and rub it down when it's dry using a sanding block and fine sandpaper.

There are some beautiful wood dyes available on the market in a range of natural wood colours; used properly they'll enrich the colour of the wood without raising the grain. They're not finishes in their own right but are intended to be sealed with a compatible varnish. These wood dyes are only absorbed by clean, untreated, dry timber. Read the instructions on the tin and leave for the required number of hours after treatment for complete evaporation of the solvent from the wood. Then take a rough cloth and rub vigorously over the entire surface. This will remove any excess dye still remaining on the surface. You then need to seal with a hard glaze varnish. It will take hours of hard work to achieve the same effect on old wood that has perhaps been painted, lacquered or varnished. Total removal of all previous coverings must be achieved. Any covering material left in the grain of the wood will prevent the wood dye from being absorbed evenly and an inferior finish will result. A word of warning: always wash wood thoroughly with white spirit after the use of paint and varnish removers.

Exterior Wood Stain

For the long-term protection and enhancement of all exterior woodwork, there is on the market a wood stain which provides a water-repellent, richly coloured finish. Wood stains penetrate and are absorbed into the surface of timber, eliminating problems such as cracking, blistering or flaking which can occur with film-forming products. Some wood stains contain specially selected wood preservatives and resins, which penetrate into the wood and stop fungal attack. The best wood stains for exterior timber are formulated to repel water penetration but will allow water vapour to escape in a controlled way. It is what is termed 'microporous'. Ask for it, because it works, but do take time to read the instructions carefully.

It's a pity that most instructions on tins, packets and leaflets are printed so small. It's a good idea to keep an inexpensive flat magnifier as part of your kit. These come in a plastic case and look like a small television screen. Get one and you'll never need to feel exasperated at having to check back over instructions. All specifications are based on expert technical knowledge and practical experience – so should be read and understood!

PAINTS

Think of paint as a sort of film covering a hard surface, which will provide protection as well as decoration. That film of paint, covering a wall or a door, provides protection against general wear and tear and should be durable enough to last years (or until your creativity demands a different colour!). Painting and decorating is a rewarding experience so don't be afraid to express yourself in your home; that is what it's all about. Choosing paint for interior decoration is fairly easy, mostly we choose emulsion for ceilings and walls and gloss paint for woodwork. Emulsion paint is water based, which means you can thin it with water if necessary and also wash out

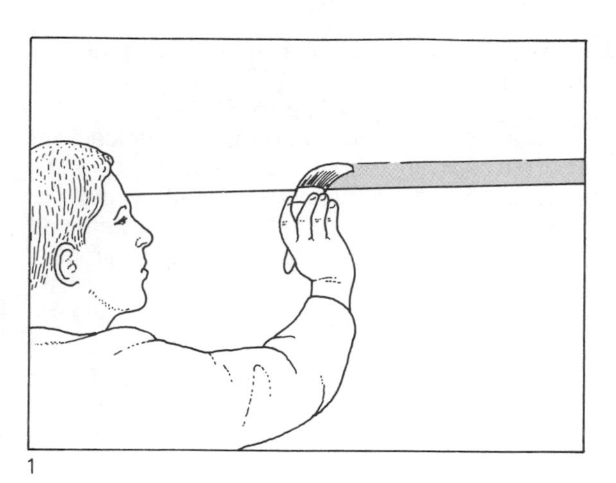

1

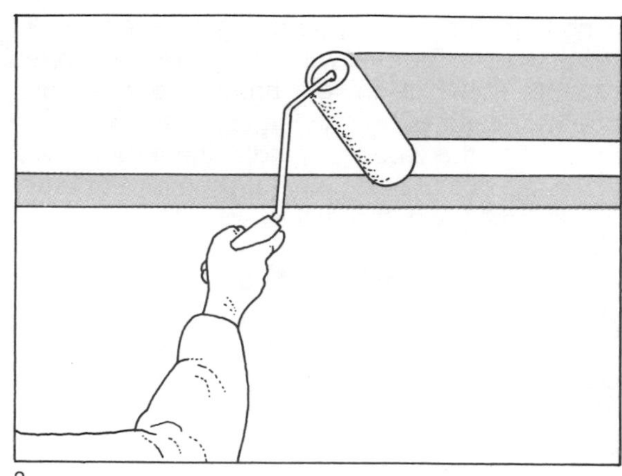

2

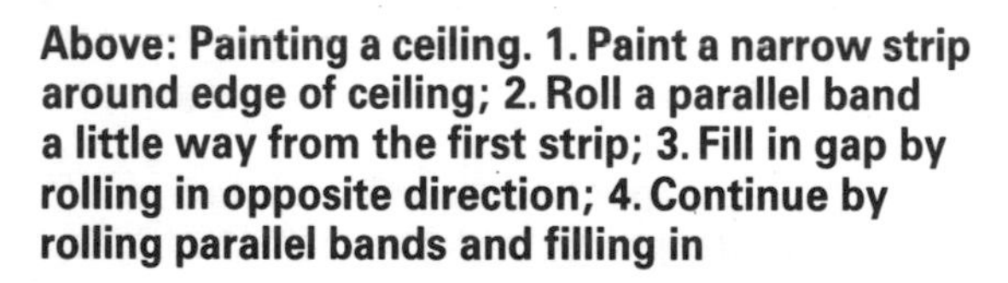

Above: Painting a ceiling. 1. Paint a narrow strip around edge of ceiling; 2. Roll a parallel band a little way from the first strip; 3. Fill in gap by rolling in opposite direction; 4. Continue by rolling parallel bands and filling in

the brushes with water. Emulsion paint does have a constituent, however, a vinyl or acrylic resin, which makes it tougher when dry. The choice of 'finish' is yours, and can be either matt (which is a dull finish), eggshell, silk finish, satin or full gloss. Again, do follow the instructions carefully.

What they do not tell you on the paint tin is what you need to do to paint over old 'distemper' (the old-fashioned whitewash used up until the 1950s). Remember that something like 60% of the owner-occupied houses in the UK were built more than forty years ago, which means it is possible that distemper still remains on walls and on ceilings. If you want to redecorate a distempered surface you really do have to wash away every trace of that distemper before redecorating. Use plenty of cloths, hot water and sugar soap and apply in a circular motion until you get a tacky mess, which is not difficult to wash down. Then use a primer sealer before applying the emulsion paint.

Emulsion is easily applied with a brush or roller (the latter will cause splashes if not used properly). When painting a ceiling with emulsion, use a 2-inch (50-mm) brush to paint a strip around the outer edge of the ceiling first. Mix the paint before pouring into the roller tray. (You'll learn from experience not to put in too much at a time: too little in the tray and you'll have dry patches on the walls. About half-way along the tray is just about the right amount so that you can roll the paint back into the shallow end with the roller.) There is no need to press too hard on the roller as you roll a band close to the edging strip that you've already painted. Next, join the two together by rolling in the reverse direction. You'll find that you get an even effect overall by working your way around the ceiling consistently in bands. Because emulsion paint is water based it evaporates as it dries. To speed up the drying open a window and a door; this will also help disperse the heady smell.

Primer Paint

Whatever surface you're painting, make certain that you use the priming coat that is compatible with the undercoat and finished coat of paint (it may be oil or water based). All that priming paint does is seal unpainted surfaces to stop the next coat of paint soaking in. Should you have only a very short time in which to complete a painting job (and I'm talking about less than a day)

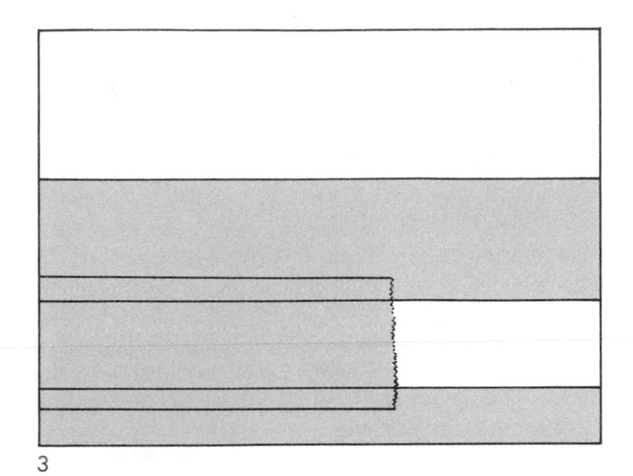

3

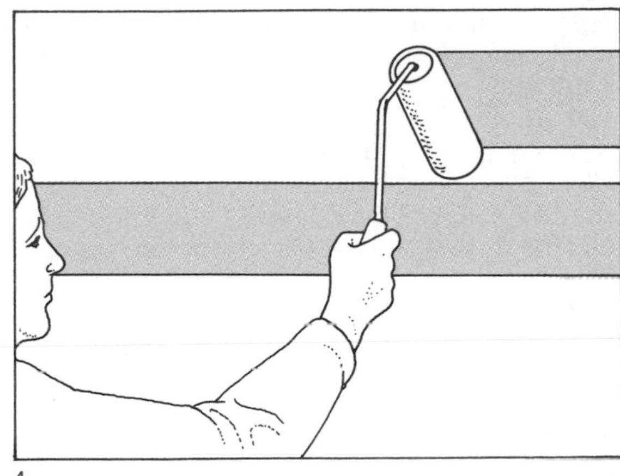

4

then an acrylic, water-based primer/undercoat is available. It offers all the protection of a conventional priming coat but dries in less than two hours, when the gloss coat can be applied. At the end of the day you can put the furniture back and admire your handiwork!

Wood, as you may know, expands and contracts, which is why many oil-based paints on the outside of a house crack and peel after one year's wear. The new acrylic resin-based paints are much more flexible and will move with the wood, preventing cracking and peeling. Two other positive factors are that they are easily used and you can simply wash your brushes and your hands under the tap.

Nowadays there are many different paints on the market, to meet every known painting problem. In kitchens and bathrooms where condensation is a problem, you must, of course, tackle the cause of that problem and go to its source. An anti-condensation paint is available, however, which prevents the surface of walls and ceilings becoming cold to the touch. It is specially formulated to be less conducive to condensation, but it's not a cure.

Did you know that there are paints known to the trade as anti-burglar paints? One of these paints stays slippery when dry. The other anti-burglar paint dries on the surface but sticks to the skin. The paint can be cleaned off the skin with white spirit but a dye is released which cannot then be removed!

Bituminous Paint

Two or three coats of this black compound paint will build up a water-resistant membrane. It will resist water pressure (provided that the bituminous paint is applied in a continuous film) and can stop damp getting past it. Again, it does not cure the source of the damp. If, after using bituminous paint (on, say, a metal tank or cast-iron gutters), you want to use ordinary gloss paint, you'll need to use an aluminium sealer first of all. If you've ever experienced a streaky brown stain creeping through your fresh paint you can be certain that a bituminous paint has been used on that surface at some time in the past. To stop it, let it dry, and then use an aluminium sealer.

Government warnings preach the hazards and dangers of fires in our homes. We can, of course, provide escapes, fire-extinguishers and buy furniture that has a fire resistant certificate, but we can also do more, and very easily. If you've any combustible surface in your kitchen, bathroom or living-room, be it polystyrene tiles, 'tongue and grooved' timber walling or hardboard (or chipboard) laminated surfaces, then you need to know about a fire-retardant paint which contains an additive to provide a fire-resistant quality. It has a far greater resistance to fire than ordinary paint and although it will not resist flames completely, it will substantially reduce the spread of fire.

Gloss Paint

Gloss paint is the 'finish' paint, the last coat to be painted. You will have thought about the colour and the quality of the paint long before the application, because the choice of the gloss paint will have dictated the undercoat and primer. Choose a hard-wearing paint for doors and skirting boards, a heat-resistant enamel for radiators, a polyurethane gloss for really hard-wearing surfaces and metal, and a water-based finish for surfaces that do not need as hard and durable a surface as, say, a front door.

STRIPPING PAINTWORK

Should you think, or have been told, to strip off all the paint from a surface that you need to redecorate, you could be wasting a lot of time! Yes, you do have to make sure the surface is properly prepared, but if paint is sound, tough and smooth (with no flaking or cracking), then all you need is a piece of sandpaper. What you must do is 'key' the surface. Often, a sticking door or window is the result of a build-up of layers of paint on the edge of the door or window. A tip before you start painting: make certain that you can get a two pence piece into the gap between the window (or door) and the frame. If there is a build-up of paint just take it off with a scraper. Then you'll have to start as for new wood. If paint is chipped, flaking or cracked, get rid of it.

When a thin film of paint has to be removed you'll need to use a drum sander, which is an attachment for an electric drill. Keep the belt action along the grain, as you do when you're rubbing with sandpaper wrapped around a block. (It's a dusty job so wear a mask.) Make sure that you brush away all the dust before rubbing down with a rag dipped in white spirit.

Chemical Paint Strippers

Don't use a liquid paint stripper: the thick jelly type is the best, especially for vertical surfaces. Also, chemical stripper is not cheap. Use it only where necessary, take careful note of the instructions, use gloves and protect your eyes and nose. Don't forget the floor – cover it with old newspapers. When you see the paint shrivelling, remove it with a flat paint scraper. You'll soon get the hang of it, but do allow the stripper time to work. You'll need to finish off by rubbing over the surface with medium steel wool. Because chemical stripper is a liquid, wood will suck it in beneath the surface. This must be neutralised before you can apply fresh paint. The way to do it is to wipe down the surface thoroughly with white spirit or a solvent which is sometimes recommended by the manufacturer of the stripper. When stripping paint from door mouldings, you'll need to use a shave hook. These are inexpensive flat pieces of metal with a wooden handle. A heart-shaped scraper will deal with all mouldings that you might find on doors and windows. It's always best to apply two or three layers of paint stripper before the wood is revealed. Use a metal container, pouring in a little of the stripper. Brush on as much as you can without it running down the surface. It will shrivel very quickly – then apply another coat. Start scraping and use plenty of old newspapers to contain the paint and to protect the floor.

Blow-Torches

A blow-torch for heat stripping paint comes in two parts: the gas cartridge and the burner head which screws on to it. There are two sizes of gas cartridge so be certain that you buy the one that fits your hand.

A word of warning: these are easier to use than you think – but also far more dangerous than you think! Make a list of procedures and follow it methodically. Remove all curtains from the area where you are working and all other inflammable materials. Put all tools and materials onto a work-bench or table. Have no trailing flexes or cables nearby and if you stop for any reason, turn the torch off and put it down.

Try out the blow-torch on an old scrap of

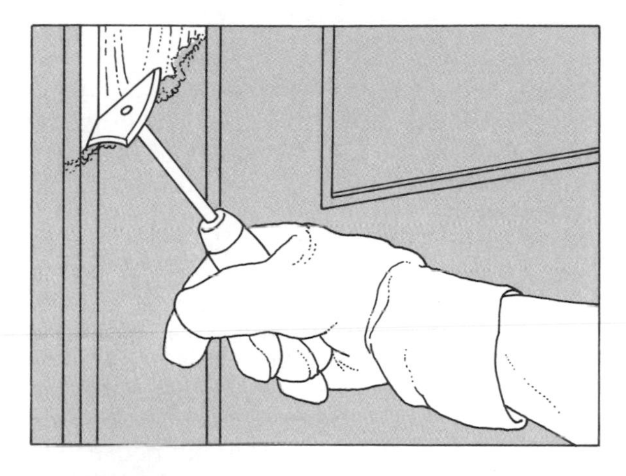

Stripping paintwork; Left: A shave-hook and chemical paint stripper; Below left, centre: Blow-torch; Below left, bottom: Drum-sander

painted wood: you'll be amazed how easy it is. After application of the heat, you'll see the paint start to melt; it's then ready for scraping and lifting off. The paint will go cold very quickly and as it goes cold it goes hard, but you have the means of softening it in your hand, so you control the action carefully.

Obviously you shouldn't use the blow-torch around a window. There, it does make sense to use the more expensive jelly-type chemical stripper. I must emphasise how important it is, once again, to read and to follow instructions. You must have protection from fumes, and you must protect your eyes and skin. Hands are particularly vulnerable when burning and scraping off hot molten paint. Don't scrape up into the hot paint allowing it to fall down on your bare hand. Always keep the scraper at an angle, so that your hand is not directly under the hot paint as it drops to the floor. Don't use newspapers on the floor because the hot paint could cause a fire – use a sheet of non-combustible material to protect the floor. One of the irritating aspects of burning-off paint is clogging. There is, however, something that you can do before you start to make life a little easier. Buy a little bag of garden lime and mix it with water into a strong solution. Simply brush it onto the paint sometime before using the blow-torch.

EMULSIONING & GLOSSING A ROOM

If, like the majority of people, your repair and maintenance activities are confined to evenings and weekends, schedule your painting work for the weekend. The reason is very simple: working by artificial light is much more difficult. You'll be amazed at how many small areas can be missed when not working by daylight.

Redecorating a room without using wallpaper is as simple as it sounds and you really can make it an easy operation. Draw up a plan and stick to it. The first stage in the plan is preparation: this starts by clearing the room of as much furniture as possible; large pieces can be covered over in the centre of the room.

Remember that all paints stay fresh-looking if applied to a properly prepared surface. Buy the best materials and tools that you can afford and make sure that everything you need is in the room to start. (This also means a safe and adequate way of reaching into every corner.) Give yourself twice as much time as you think it's going to take, although painting really doesn't take that much time; a ceiling can be given two or three coats of emulsion paint in less than a day. This is especially true if you learn the simple technique of using a roller. A point worth remembering is that cracks, blemishes and bumps show up much more when freshly painted, so the answer once again is good sound preparation. Most walls and ceilings are plaster-based – ideal for taking emulsion.

Always start by painting the ceiling. The easiest paint to apply on the ceiling is also the one that is most commonly used, that is, vinyl emulsion. As always, however, before you start painting you'll need to prepare the ceiling. A tedious but essential part of the preparation is to fill all hairline cracks, but don't try to squeeze filler into a narrow crack. You'll get a far better bond if you scratch away at the crack to widen it. Then press into the crack or hole tiny pieces of filler, building up until you fill the hole or crack. If you try to fill in one go you'll trap an air bubble and then the filler won't have anything to grip. You'll find it sagging and wonder why.

A roller is certainly better for painting a ceiling than a brush, but because the roller won't get into the corners or up against the walls, you'll have to paint around the edges with a brush first. When you begin to use the roller, roll the first stroke away from you and don't press too hard. You'll soon get the hang of rolling back and forth to even up the paint. The secret is not to have too much paint on the roller – then you won't get splatter. Any excess paint can be pressed out in the shallow end of the tray.

If this is the first time that you've used emulsion paint and a roller you might be alarmed by the patchiness of the paint as it dries. Don't worry: within an hour or so the surface will be flat and even.

A tip before using a roller. New rollers (and brushes for that matter) need loosening up before you can use them. A new fibre roller should be soaked in warm, soapy water for half a day, swilled in clean water and then rolled out on a clean, dry, brick wall. You'll then be rid of all the loose bits of fibre. Long-handled extensions are available for use with the roller, but because of the energy expended on the leverage alone I think you're probably better off without one.

You'll need to take special care if the ceiling that you're painting has previously been papered. A bubbling or loosening of the paper when you clean the ceiling indicates that it won't take paint as it is and you'll have to strip it.

If you own a large paint pad, you'll know that you can cover walls and ceilings quite quickly. A small paint pad will get you into corners and around light-fittings and switches.

Work safely and comfortably, at the right height and without too much stretching. Don't try to balance on wobbly furniture. If you do have access to a plank, use it with a step-ladder supporting one end and a sturdy chair the other.

The next part of the job, painting the walls, is far easier. Paint a neat line about 3 feet (1 m) long at the top of the wall where it meets the ceiling, using a small brush or a pad. Paint vertically in the corner and then horizontally just above the skirting board. The filling in is fun because you get immediate results. Unless you have a cove or cornice between the wall and the ceiling you'll find that most plaster joins are uneven. The best way to avoid painting an uneven line is to keep the wall colour marginally lower than the join. Never let the wall colour creep onto the ceiling and never try to paint a straight line actually in the join; it never works. Work right round the walls in

Painting frames using masking tape; Right: an 1⁄8-inch (3-mm) gap between tape and frame will seal the frame with paint right up to the glass

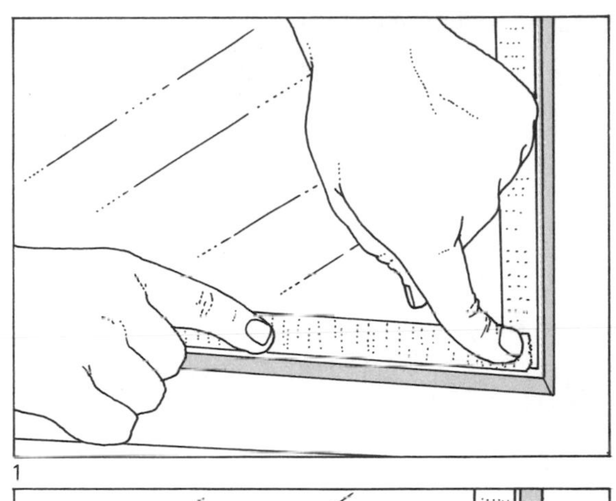
1

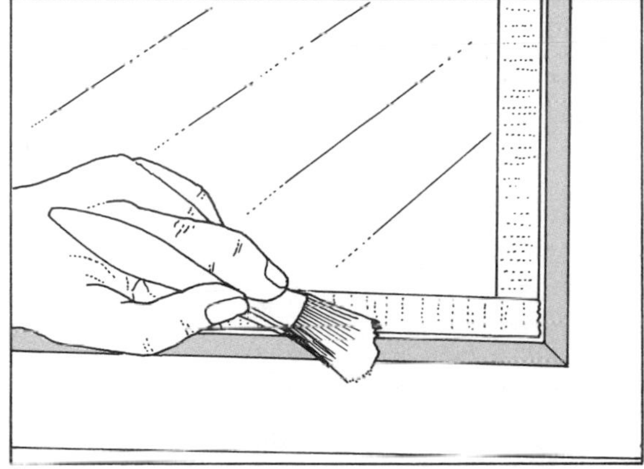
2

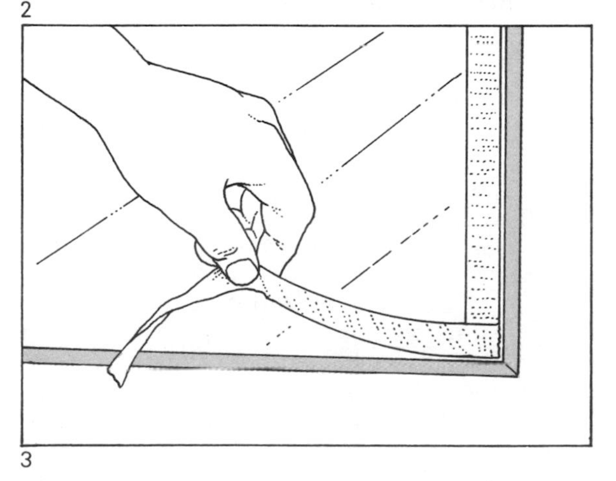
3

bands about 3 feet (1 m) wide, starting at the top. When it's dry you'll have to judge whether you need a second coat or not, although a cheap paint will always require a second coat. (It will also depend on the previous colour.)

Lastly, all the woodwork will have to be painted. See 'Starting From Scratch On Woodwork' (page 13). Preparation work should already have been done but you must still be sure to go through the work in the correct order.

If you're painting the whole room, all woodwork, including doors and windows, should be painted last. If you are using wallpaper, however, the woodwork needs to be painted before the wallpaper is hung. You can then allow the paint to stray onto the wall before it's papered and trim the wallpaper with a neat, clean edge, giving a very professional finish.

PAINTING WINDOWS & DOORS

Masking tape is a cheap, effective remedy for an unsteady hand in painting windows. Use a small brush (an angled, 'cutting-in' brush or a small sash paint pad) for painting up to and over the masking tape. Don't make the mistake of allowing the paint to dry before you take off the masking tape. You'll get a crisp, clean edge if you remove the tape before the paint is fully dry.

Casement Windows

These are windows that have hinges and open out. Start first by painting the glazing bars (the thin wooden bars separating the glass). Then paint the rest of the opening casement window, but remember – only the hinge edge matches the indoor paint! The other three edges of a window (the top, bottom and 'leading' edges) match the outdoor paint. Lastly, paint the frame.

Sash Windows

When painting sash windows, to start with, push the lower half up as high as you can. Then, with

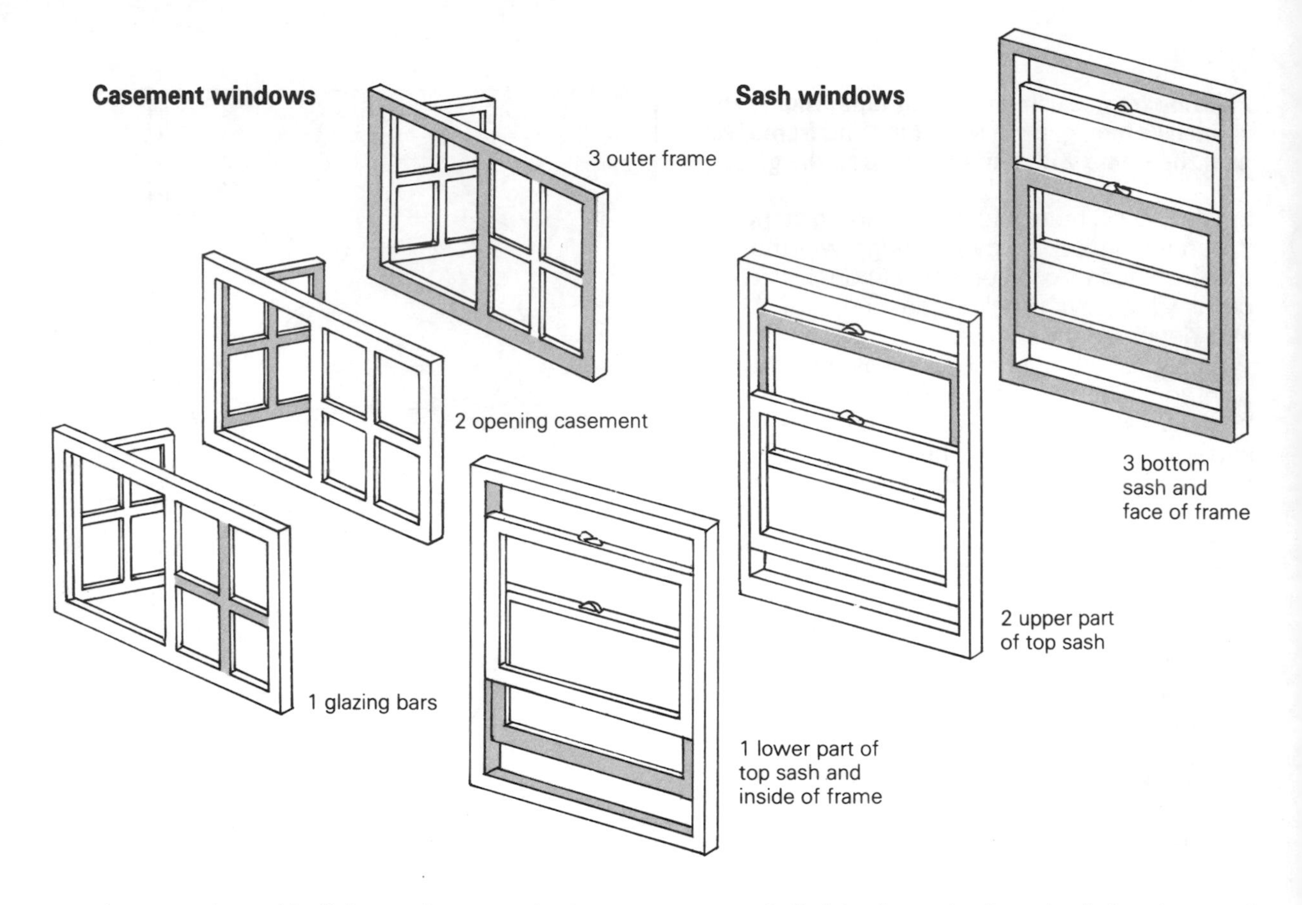

the upper (outer) half down almost to the bottom of the frame, paint as much of that as you can. Next paint the inside top and bottom of the main frame and as far as you can up and down the sides of the frame. When dry, change the positions of the sashes and complete the upper (outer) sash from the top: you can then paint the whole of the lower (inner) sash and the rest of the main frame. Remember to leave the windows open slightly, going back every couple of hours to move them a little, to prevent sticking.

Panel Doors

Remove the door furniture and begin by painting the panels and mouldings. Next, when you paint the horizontal pieces (or members), allow paint to stray slightly onto the vertical ones (stiles), which you paint last of all. This will ensure a smooth finish along the length of the door and will hide brushmarks effectively.

RECOGNISING PROBLEMS

There is one reason, and one reason only, why problems such as blistering, flaking and bleeding occur and that is bad or insufficient preparation! Dust and damp are the enemies to beware. If any surface that you're going to paint has even a suspicion of damp, don't paint it until it's dry. If damp gets behind a painted surface, 'lifting' will occur, and if paint has been applied onto a damp surface then you'll certainly get flaking. If you paint over a previous coat which isn't absolutely dry you'll get the 'old master' look: crazing. The outside of the house traditionally gets a new coat of paint in spring. A few months later, surfaces could be spoiled by blistering, which is caused by

Panel doors

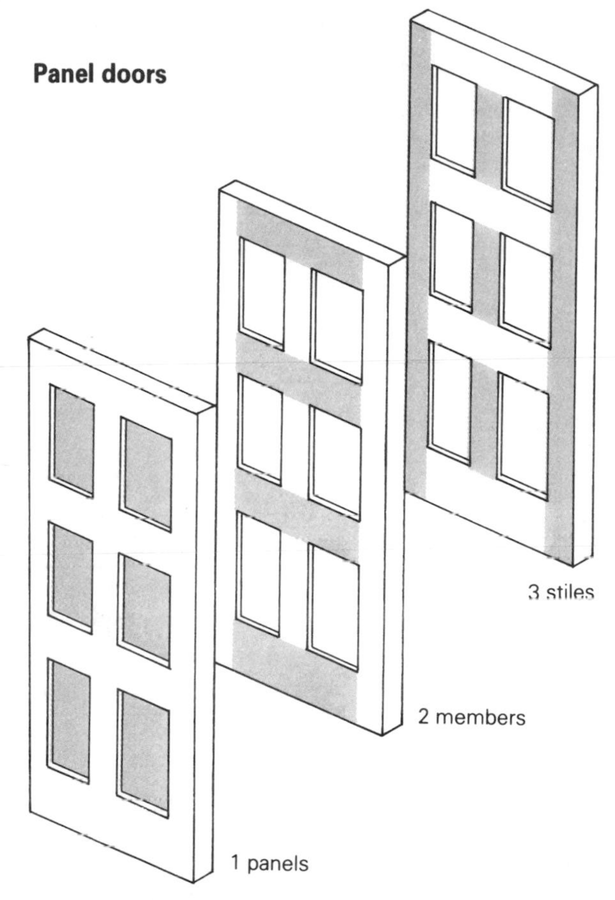

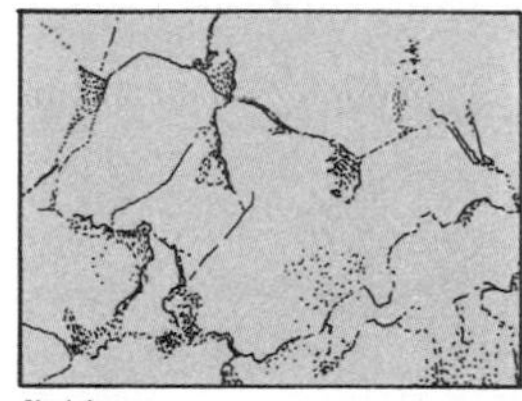
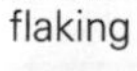
flaking

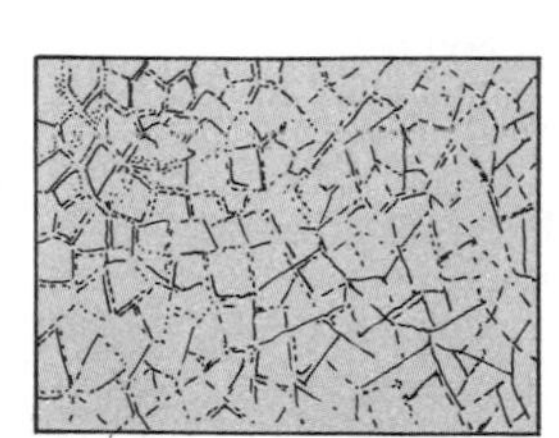
crazing

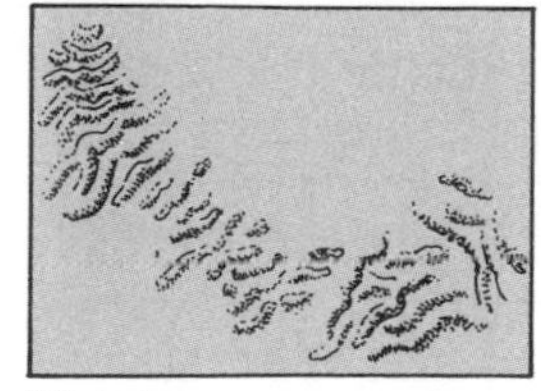
blistering

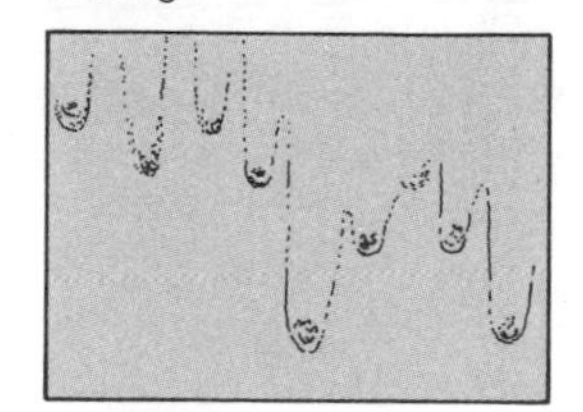
curtaining

the heat of the sun drawing out damp or resin.

When too much paint has been applied to a vertical surface and no attempt has been made to 'lay off' the paint, rivers (drips) will show. An unattractive 'curtaining' effect will result.

STRIPPING WALLPAPER

The easiest and most effective way to strip any wallpaper is to hire a steam stripper. By following the instructions carefully, you will learn the technique quickly and you'll be amazed at how swiftly the job can be done.

The traditional way to strip wallpaper is more laborious but just as effective and, of course, cheaper. Use a serrated scraper or wire brush to score the paper before soaking the paper in small patches with warm water. A few drops of washing-up liquid in the water will help it 'creep' and penetrate. Keep dousing with water until the old paste has broken down and be sure to use a flat scraper and not a filling knife, otherwise you run the risk of digging into the plaster. Do protect the floor and don't splash sockets and switches.

Papers that have been painted over are more difficult to remove. You go through the same procedure, it just takes a little bit longer and you have to make cuts or holes in the paper, through which the water can penetrate to the paste.

Certain types of vinyl paper are the easiest to strip off. It is manufactured as two layers, a top plastic film and lining paper. If you can get your fingernail behind the corner of the top layer it should peel off in one long length. You're then left with the lining paper. If it's sound you can leave it and get on with your decorating.

Patterned and 'anaglypta' wallpapers have been used extensively since Edwardian times. If you have to remove an old anaglypta, you'll probably find it's brittle. These wallpapers also come in two layers, so again you have to remove the top one first. A scraper is the best tool to use. The bottom layer will then have to be removed in the traditional manner – soaking and scraping. You'll have to remove the backing paper too: there'll be a raised pattern on it.

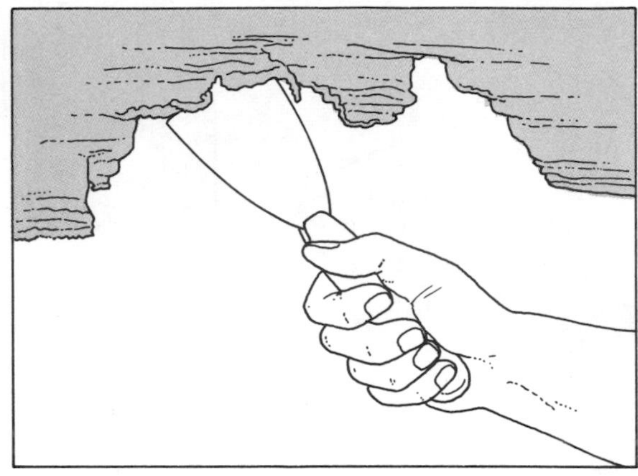

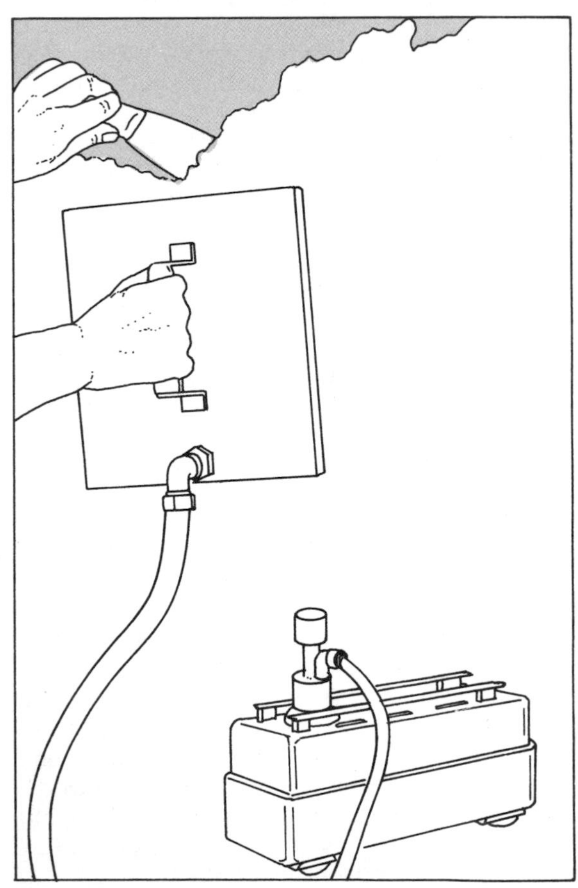

Stripping wall coverings; Above left: Wire brush; Above: Stripping knife; Left: The invaluable steam stripper

HANGING WALLPAPER

Should you be hanging a very bold patterned paper, you'll need to start in the centre of the chimney breast and work your way around the room to the door, stopping at the door frame. Then work your way around the room from the other side of the chimney breast to stop again at the door. Otherwise, the general rule is to start at the corner diagonally across the room from the door and go around the room from there, first in one direction and then the other, stopping each time at the door.

The Starting Point

First you need to mark a vertical line on the wall, against which your first piece of paper will be positioned. The best idea to obtain that vertical line is to use a struck chalk mark. Don't use a pencil: when wet, pencil marks can creep through to the surface of the paper. Chalk the string of your plumb bob, pin it at the top, hold your foot against the weight at the bottom and strike the chalked string against the wall. The position of the plumb line will govern the first piece of paper, which should be hung in the corner of the room, with the first ½ inch (1 cm) pasted onto the adjacent wall. The first piece of

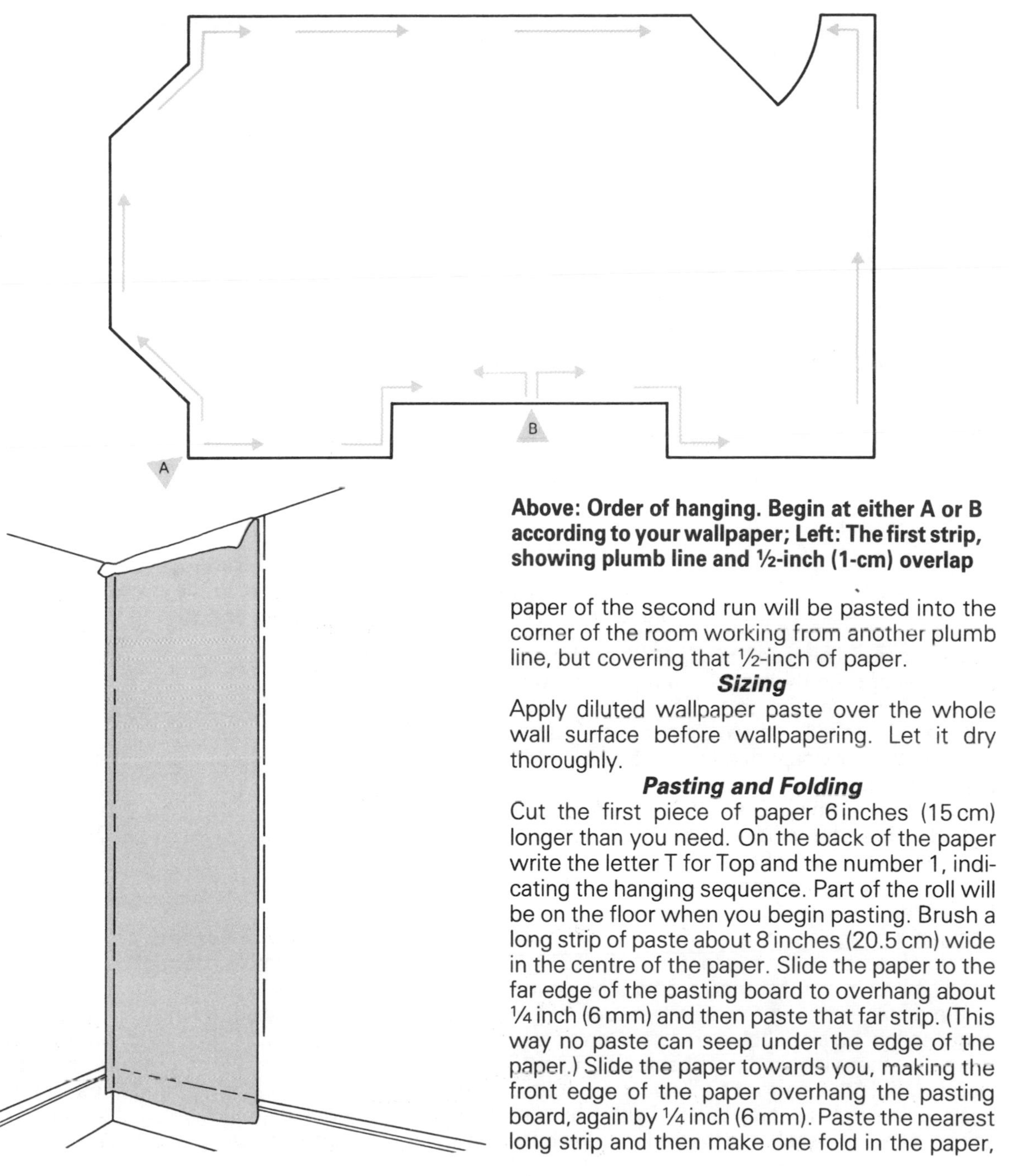

Above: Order of hanging. Begin at either A or B according to your wallpaper; Left: The first strip, showing plumb line and ½-inch (1-cm) overlap

paper of the second run will be pasted into the corner of the room working from another plumb line, but covering that ½-inch of paper.

Sizing

Apply diluted wallpaper paste over the whole wall surface before wallpapering. Let it dry thoroughly.

Pasting and Folding

Cut the first piece of paper 6 inches (15 cm) longer than you need. On the back of the paper write the letter T for Top and the number 1, indicating the hanging sequence. Part of the roll will be on the floor when you begin pasting. Brush a long strip of paste about 8 inches (20.5 cm) wide in the centre of the paper. Slide the paper to the far edge of the pasting board to overhang about ¼ inch (6 mm) and then paste that far strip. (This way no paste can seep under the edge of the paper.) Slide the paper towards you, making the front edge of the paper overhang the pasting board, again by ¼ inch (6 mm). Paste the nearest long strip and then make one fold in the paper,

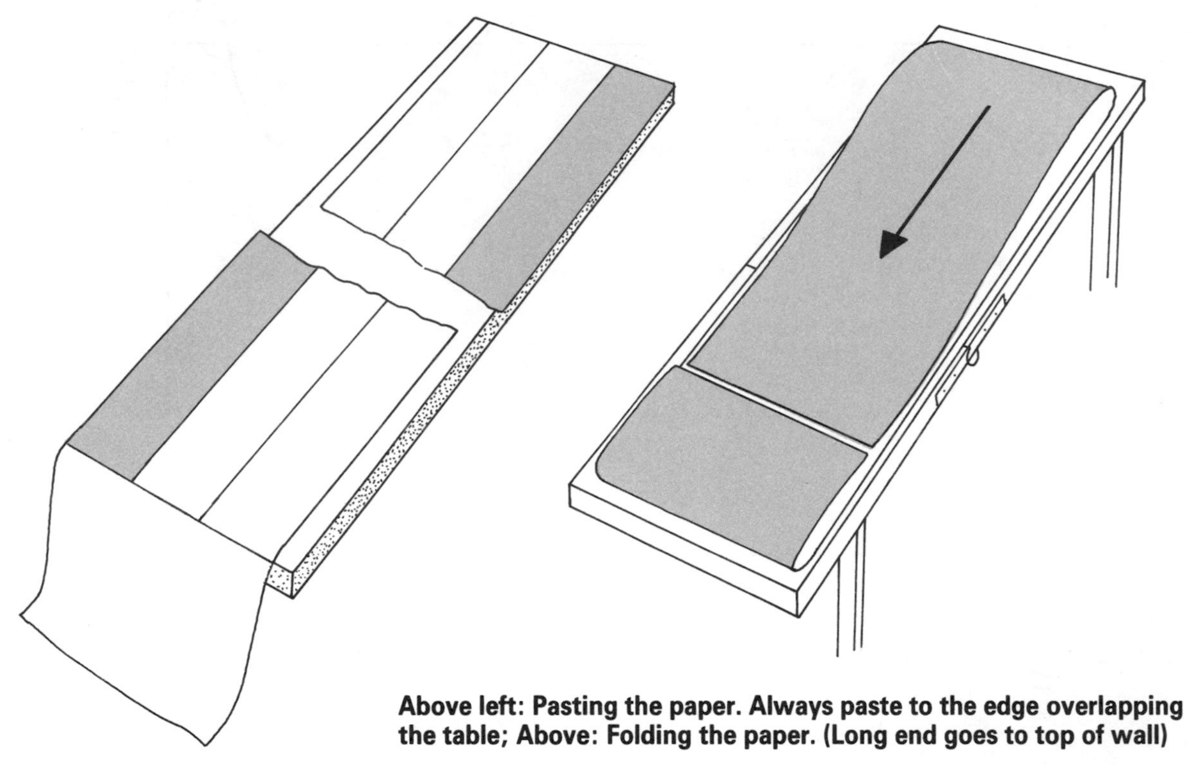

Above left: Pasting the paper. Always paste to the edge overlapping the table; Above: Folding the paper. (Long end goes to top of wall)

paste to paste, lining up the edges. Slide the rest of the paper onto the board and repeat the process. Thin papers can go straight onto the wall and don't have to be left in order for the glue to soak in, but thick papers do and the heavier the paper the longer the time needed to soak (usually five to ten minutes). Wet papers stretch so make absolutely certain that each piece soaks for the same length of time.

Hanging and Trimming

Unfold the top half of the paper and slide it into position up against the plumb line. Allow a couple of inches at the top for trimming. Using a hanging brush, gently smooth down the centre of the paper, working towards the edge of the paper so that no air bubbles are left. (Don't press too hard otherwise you'll get paste oozing out.) Gently unfold the bottom and repeat the action, again using the hanging brush. With a pair of scissors held almost flat to the wall, run the back of the blade first along the edges of the ceiling and then along the edge of the skirting board (and later on around the fittings, window frames and door frames). Without stretching the paper, peel it back and cut carefully along the crease at the ceiling. Brush the paper back into place. After making a good straight cut your expertise will amaze you! Each subsequent piece of paper will be slid up to butt against the last one. Repeat the process of creasing and trimming, always at the ceiling first.

Internal Corners

Don't try to hang a whole sheet of paper around an internal (inward) corner. Cut it, along its length, so that it goes around the corner by about ¼ inch (6 mm). Draw a vertical line on the next wall (using a plumb bob), so that the off-cut is positioned against this vertical and goes into the corner covering that small overlap. A seam roller is useful to flatten down the seams after you have pasted two or three strips of wallpaper, but don't try to use a seam roller on embossed wallpapers. If any surplus paste appears anywhere on the surface of the wallpaper, wipe it off quickly but gently with a damp sponge using a lifting – not rubbing – motion.

External Corners

Again, as for internal corners, the secret is to take the paper over by about ½ inch (1 cm) onto the next wall. However, you will invariably find that the paper is no longer vertical when it has 'turned the corner'. You must then overlap that ½ inch (1 cm) of paper with a new piece placed vertically on the wall (again using a plumb bob).

Don't try to cut the length of paper with the scissors – it never works. Use a straight edge and a trimming knife. If you find you can hang the remaining piece with an imperceptible butt-join, do so; otherwise slightly overlap it.

Chimney Breasts

Crease and cut the paper along the mantelpiece shelf first; the paper will then fall down the side of the mantelpiece, but take its weight, otherwise it will tear. Never ever tug at wet wallpaper. Having experienced trimming at ceilings and skirtings, you'll now find it fairly easy to trim around the ends of the mantelpiece. Little nicks in the paper will help you turn round small mouldings.

Patterned Paper

If your paper has what is called a drop pattern (i.e. with horizontals), match that pattern on the pasting table as you cut each piece. (You are bound to waste a little paper each time you match and cut.) Remember two points: order sufficient paper and still allow 2 or 3 inches (5 or 7.5 cm) top and bottom for trimming.

Doorways

First of all, be ready and prepared to wipe off paste from the door frame! As before, hang the

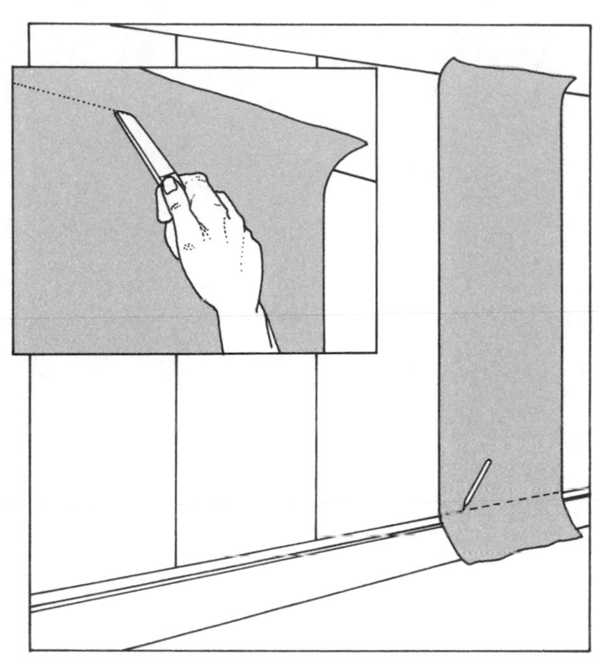

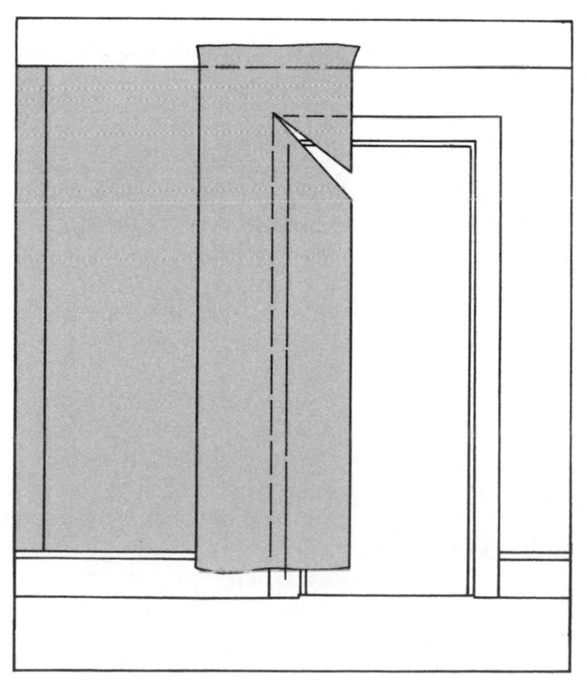

Above right: Using closed scissors to crease the wallpaper before trimming; Right: Hanging paper around a doorway, using frame as guide. Remove surplus paper before trimming

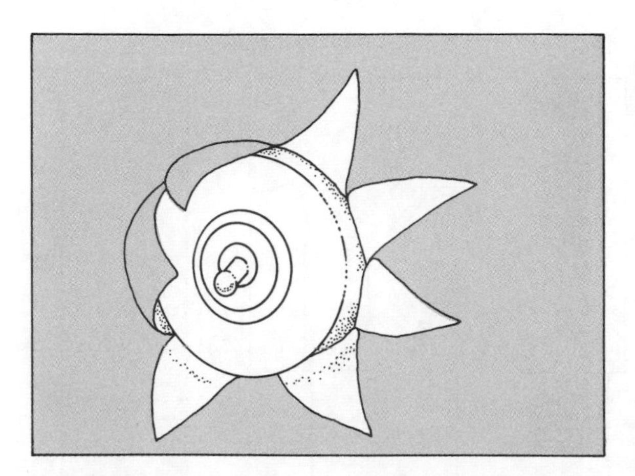

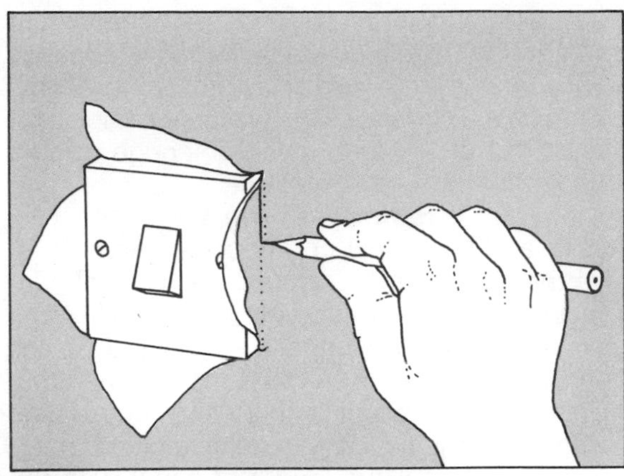

Above left and above: Papering around light switches. Cut out from centre, crease with pencil and either trim wide of pencil mark and tuck in or trim exactly on mark and butt to edge of switch

paper butted to the previous piece and overlapping the door. Using the centre line of the architrave (or moulded door frame) as a guide, cut off most of the surplus paper. At the top of the frame, cut an angle into the wallpaper following the mitre of the architrave. Crease the paper into the top and side of the frame and trim as before. Carefully brush the paper into position. Go to the other side of the frame and repeat the process. Then you'll have a small piece to fit in above the centre of the door.

Electrics

You'll either have round switches or square ones depending on the age of the house. The round ones are fixed; the square ones you can unscrew and lift off. You'll obviously get a much neater job if you can tuck the cut ends of the paper underneath the switch. It's simply a matter of turning off the electricity, lifting the socket or switch a little (by undoing the screws) and making the cut so that at least ¼ inch (6 mm) of the paper tucks underneath the switch plate. In both instances, hang the paper down over the switch and cut out from the centre to the corners or edges, before trimming and brushing the paper back into place.

Window Openings

The easiest method for this is to paper the 'reveals' and the 'soffit' first. These are the recessed parts of the wall nearest and adjacent to the window frame. Paper these, overlapping onto the main wall about ½ inch (1 cm). Continue to paper the main walls covering that small overlap. The alternative, and more professional way, is to paper the wall and reveals in one, in which case start above the window at the centre.

Paper right into the window frame from the ceiling and continue either side until you come to the top corners of the window frame. When you hang ceiling-to-floor lengths either side of the window, cut the paper at the top of the opening and at the window sill with straight cuts, so that you have a hinge. You then brush it onto the reveal. Crease and cut against the window frame in the usual way. (The short bits that are left to be hung underneath the window sill should come as light relief!)

EXTERIOR WORK

Brushing Down Walls

Never ever paint a wall before preparing it, although brick and stone should not really need painting. A 'rendered' wall, being rough cast, tends to hold dirt, mould and algae, so use a good stiff hand brush to brush it down, starting at

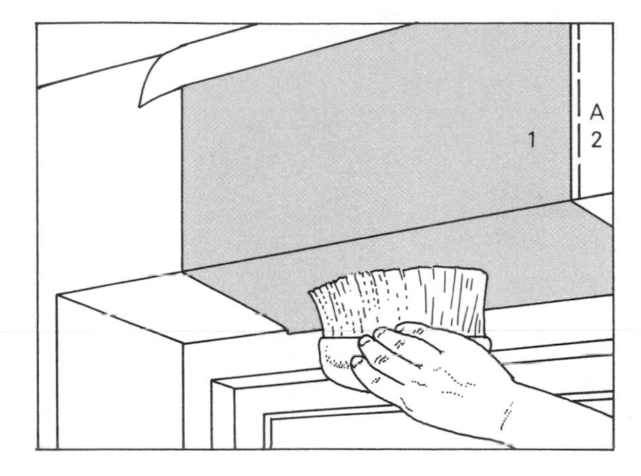

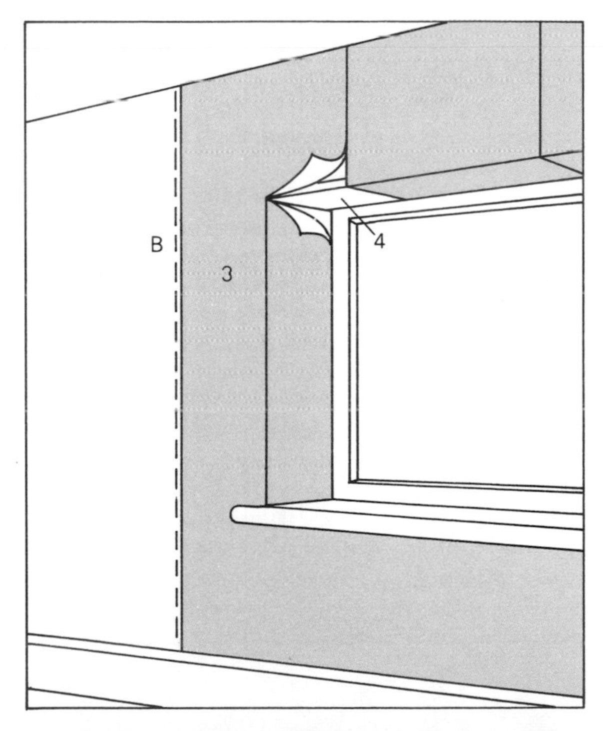

Top: Papering under soffit. Butt first and second pieces against plumb line (A) and brush under; Above: Butt third piece against plumb line (B) and cut 'hinge' (at soffit and at sill) and brush back. Fourth piece should tuck under third

the top. (Don't use a wire brush: bits of wire can become lodged in the render and show through as rust, after repainting.) If you have any mould or algae of any sort, paint with a fungicide or mix your own, one part bleach to four parts water. Hose it off after a day.

Be certain that there is no build-up of damp behind holes or cracks before you fill them. Most rendered surfaces need a stabilising solution before repainting (which can be easily purchased).

Most putties that need replacing are on the lower edge of the window. Often a tiny black line will indicate a crack in the putty, although more often than not it's more than a crack and the putty flies out when you prise it with a knife. Remember that rainwater will creep into the tiniest of cracks. Water resting on the inside ledge of the window is often caused by condensation, but just as often by putty shrinkage. After you've reputtied, a light touch with a wet brush will seal the putty to the glass, but do allow the putty time to form a skin before repainting.

One of the most neglected areas where water penetration occurs is between the exterior window frame and the brickwork of the reveal. Use a mastic gun to form a watertight seal by squeezing the mastic into the gap.

If a pipe is close to the wall and you want to paint the back of it, use a piece of thin card to protect the wall. When working from a ladder on the outside of a house, never lean out or try to stretch. Use an 'S' hook to hang the paint kettle or tin on a rung of the ladder, but not a butcher's meat hook, which is dangerous because of the sharp points. Paint splashes on windows are easily cleaned off, either immediately with a rag and a lifting (not rubbing) motion or when dry with fine wire-wool. A screw-eye (see page 111) into a facia board can be used to secure the top of a ladder by tying a rung to it, and the bottom of a ladder can be secured by tying it to a peg driven into soft ground. If the bottom of the ladder is on hard ground, find a suitable joint to drive in a steel peg and tie off with a longer piece of rope.

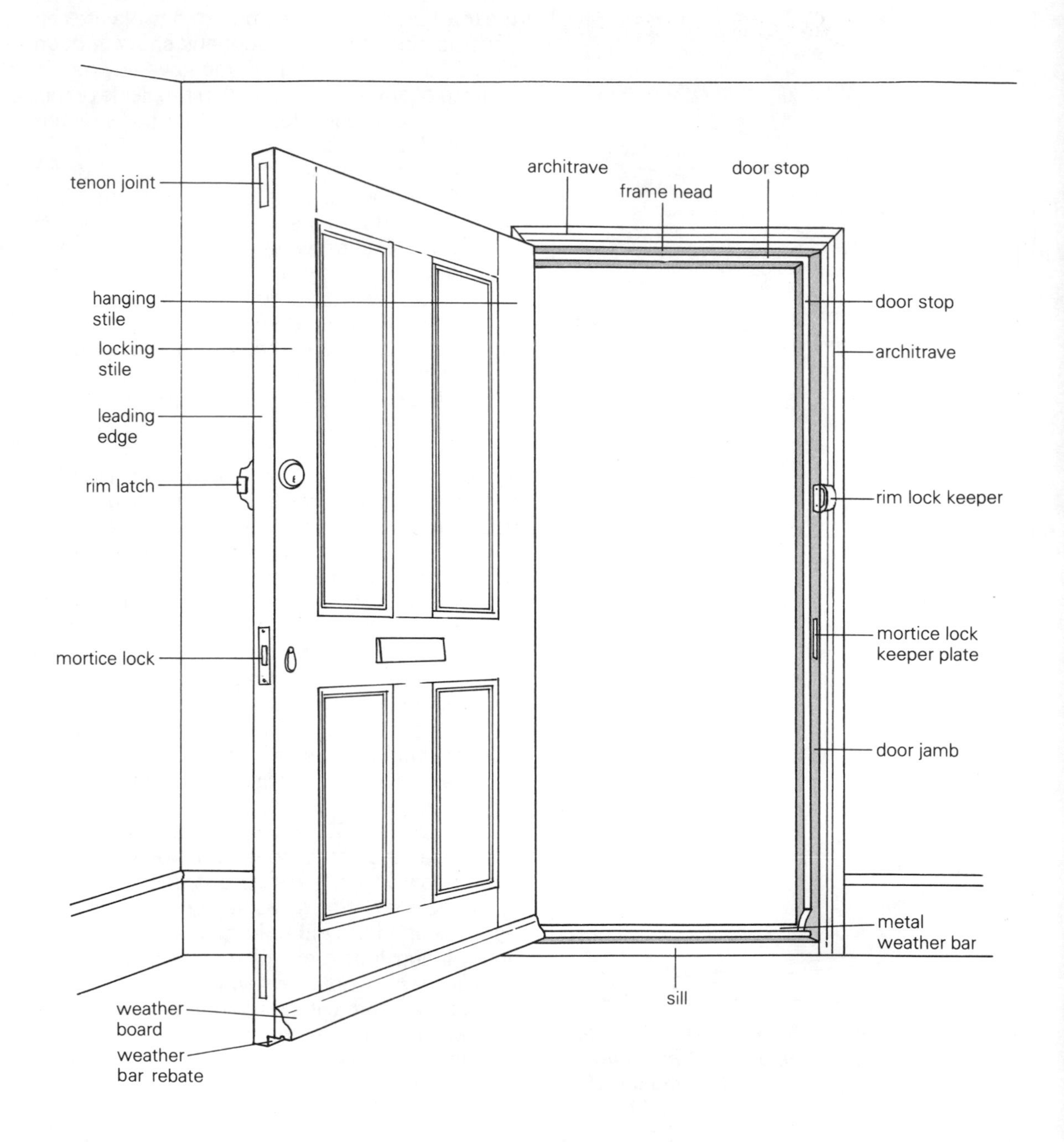
tenon joint
hanging stile
locking stile
leading edge
rim latch
mortice lock
weather board
weather bar rebate
architrave
frame head
door stop
door stop
architrave
rim lock keeper
mortice lock keeper plate
door jamb
metal weather bar
sill

DOORS & WINDOWS 2

DOORS

Both doors and windows are subject to a great deal of wear and tear, whether it's from the elements outdoors or temperature and moisture changes indoors, however slight. We rely on them completely but take them for granted just as much! Don't put up with minor problems: they won't stay 'minor' for long.

Doors which Stick

If your doors stick, the first check that you should make is around the door itself, the gap between the door and the frame. You should be able to slide a two pence piece right around this gap. You'll probably find that you have one or two tight spots: if they're on the leading edge of the door, you can plane these off without removing the door.

A second check is looseness of hinges. If the hinges are loose you can either refix them with longer screws or plug the holes. Whittle down pieces of soft wood and glue them into the holes. If the gap around either hinge is excessive and the door is tight up against the door jamb immediately opposite that hinge, you need to reset the door by cutting the hinge recess slightly deeper. Take care that you don't cut too much. If the contrary is true and the hinge is set too deeply in the recess, you can bring the door back into position by inserting a 'shim' into the hinge recess. This can be as thin as a piece of card or as thick as folded sandpaper.

If the latch or lock is hitting the striking plate below its squared hole, it's probable that the door has dropped. If the hinge screws are still tight, the easiest way to overcome this problem is to take off the striking plate first. Extend the morticed recess (that is, the squared hole cut in the door frame), plug the screw holes and re-position the striking plate.

The next check is the door itself at the joints. If it's a panel door, the outer frame of a door is made up of four pieces (see illustration). Squared holes are cut into the top and bottom of the upright pieces (called the 'stiles') and the top and bottom 'members' or rails have squared pieces at either end called 'tenons' which fit into the mortice holes. Then wedges are glued and hammered in to tighten and strengthen the door. If any of these joints on your door have worked loose, all you have to do is force glue into the joint and cut and fit new wedges. If the wood is generally sound you can do something else: drill a hole right through the door so that it goes through the tenon and then glue in a peg or dowel to make a tight fit. Saw it almost flush with the door and smooth down with sandpaper.

When paint is wrongly applied to the edges of doors and windows, a build-up can occur which can then stop the door or window closing. This often happens on the back edge of a door. Use a scraper to pull off the bubbles of hardened paint.

If a door sticks when it's about to close, often it's simply a case of tightening either the screws that hold the face plate on the edge of the door or the screws that hold the striker plate on the door frame. It could also be that the door is distorted or twisted. In this case the door is not flat and tight against the door stops. (The door stops are the pieces of wood against which the door bangs when you close it.) If the door is not touching the door stop around the area of the lock, then the door is warped and needs to be sprung back.

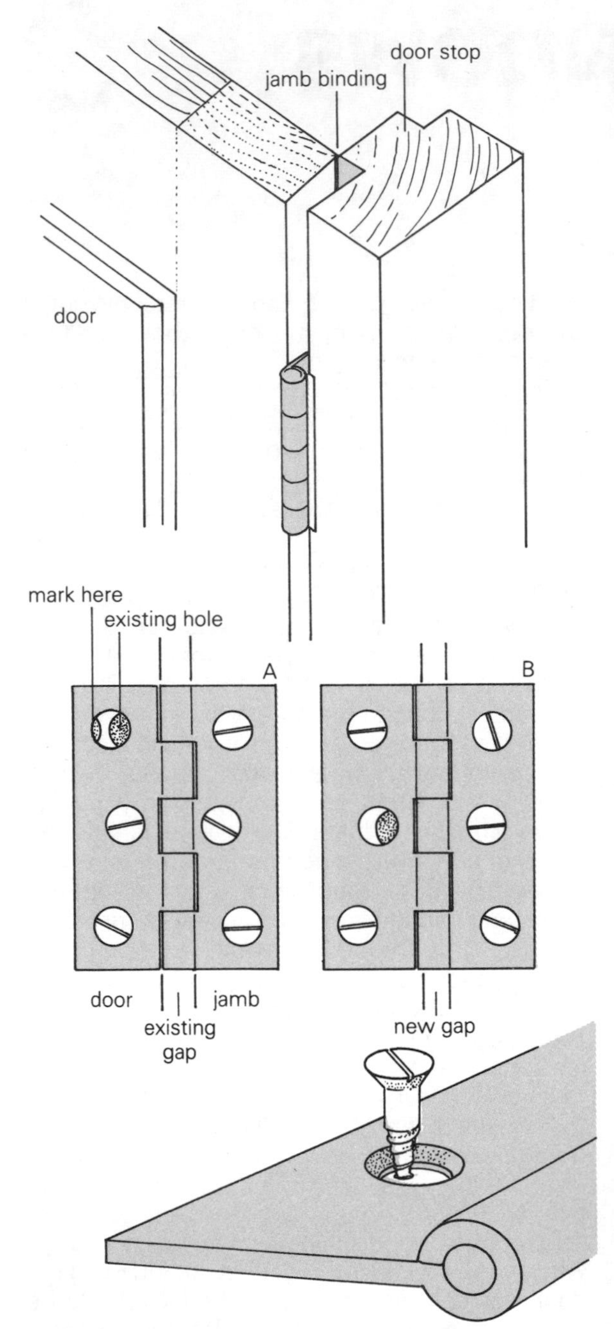

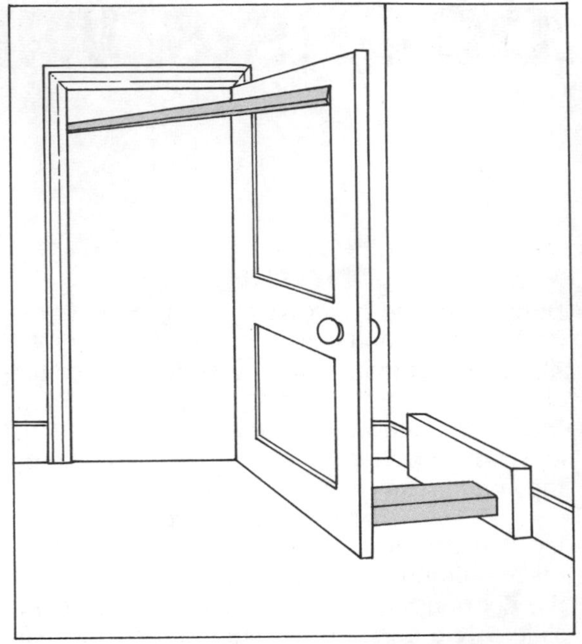

Above left: Jamb binding; Left: Shift hinges slightly by moving screws. This narrows gap between door and jamb; Below left: Place screw off-centre in hole. As screw is tightened, hinge will shift; Above: If a closed door only touches at the top or the bottom it needs to be twisted. Two pieces of wood pushing in opposite directions will correct it; Right: A 'G' clamp and two wooden battens will correct a bowed door

Take the door off and lay it flat on battens either end; then place a heavy weight on the centre of the door. (This could take days to rectify!) Alternatively, use a 'G' clamp and battens of wood to distort it in the opposite direction. Strain the door a little at intervals until you put it into 'purgatory'. This means distorting it slightly past the straight line. When released, the door should be flat.

Frame Out of True

Over the years it's possible for a door frame to distort and for the top member to slope. In this case people often trim the top of the door to fit the frame. A better looking job is accomplished

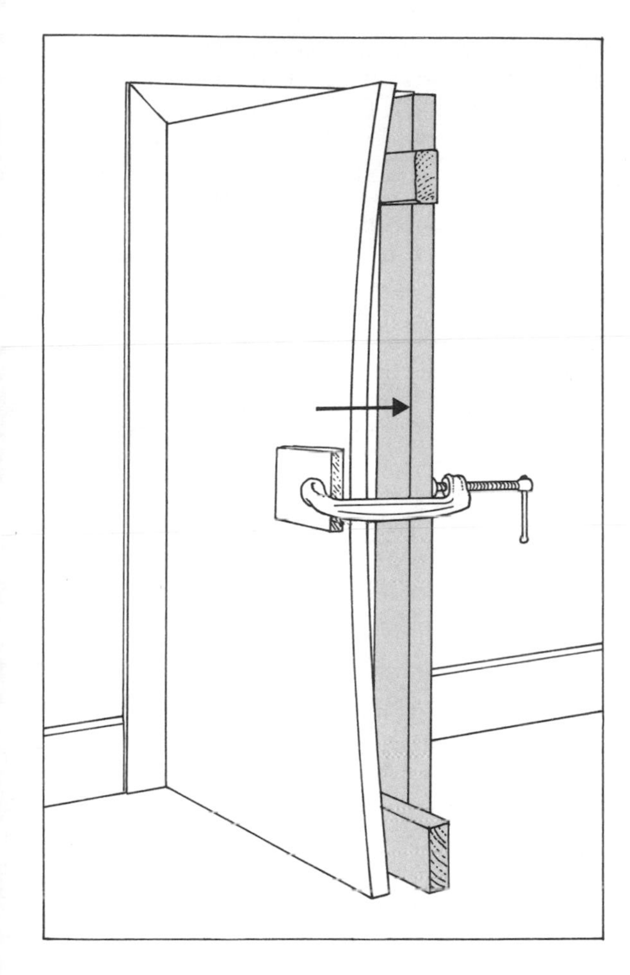

by first of all taking off the door stops. Cut and fix a wedge-shaped piece of wood underneath the head of the frame to level it. Trim the door to fit. Then prise off the architraves and adjust them to the horizontal.

The other way in which a frame 'moves' is by either door jamb moving in a little at the foot. Sometimes a simple remedy is effective. Two bits of timber, placed vertically each side of the painted door frame to protect it, are wedged apart with a sturdy horizontal prop. Cut the prop so that you force the door jamb just back to the vertical. Then you need to refix it to the wall. A couple of Fischer fixings, where the plug stays in the frame and in the wall, will successfully hold any frame to a brick wall. If the frame is up against a stud wall, a couple of 4- or 5-inch (100- or 125-mm) screws should do. Countersink, so that the head of the screw is slightly below the surface of the wood, and use a wood filler.

Rehanging a Door

There are a few checks that you have to make first of all. Firstly, check whether the door stops are 'planted', that is, nailed on, or are an integral part of the frame (rebated by being cut into the frame). Checking the measurement of that rebate gives you the required thickness of door. If you are rehanging an interior door, check that you've bought an interior and not an exterior door. Check that the height and width of the door will fit the opening. Whether it's a secondhand or new door, check that it has no warping or twisting. Check for damp; ask where it has been stored and whether or not it was stored lying flat.

When you buy a new door, don't be disconcerted by finding protruding bits of wood at the top and bottom. These are protective 'horns' which you have to cut off. Check the door frame with pinch rods and make sure that it is square. (This is a simple method to test measurements which should be equal. Take two rods and slide them together to fit exactly into the diagonal of the door opening. Hold them tightly so as not to alter the measurement, then slide them into the other diagonal. If the frame is square they should fit exactly.) When buildings 'settle', it is frames in openings that tend to move first, however imperceptibly!

If you do have a slight bow in the centre of the frame, this is easily remedied. Carefully prise off the door stop and plane the frame to a straight line. (It is always better to take off the door stops, if you can, before rehanging a door.) You have very little fitting to do if the door that you are replacing is a standard height and width, providing the frame is true. Carefully saw off the protective protruding pieces at either end of the door and then lay the door on its lock edge so that you can check the butt (or hinge) edge first (which must be straight). Now check and write down the door frame measurements, top and bottom widths and heights both sides. Allowing ¼ inch (6 mm) on each measurement, transfer those measurements to the door. Measure, from the hinge edge, the width and the height from the top. Make sure you draw straight lines. If you are going to fit a carpet you need ½ inch (1 cm) clearance. Now, before cutting, prop the door up against the opening to make your first check of measurements. (Make it your rule that you'll always double check measurements.) You must guard against too loose a fit. If the hinge edge of the door is not true to the frame, mark it and plane it. Work on the width of the door first. You have to get a reasonably loose fit, about ⅛ inch (3 mm) either side of the door. When planing the lock edge (or stile) to fit, it should be slightly bevelled. This ensures that the leading edge of the stile does not hit against the frame.

Top and Bottom Clearance Use a spirit level to check the floor at the open and closed position of the door. If the floor is not level at the open door position, then you might have to make an adjustment to the bottom of the door. If the floor drops under the frame you can always fit 'rising' butts (hinges). This means that you'll have a

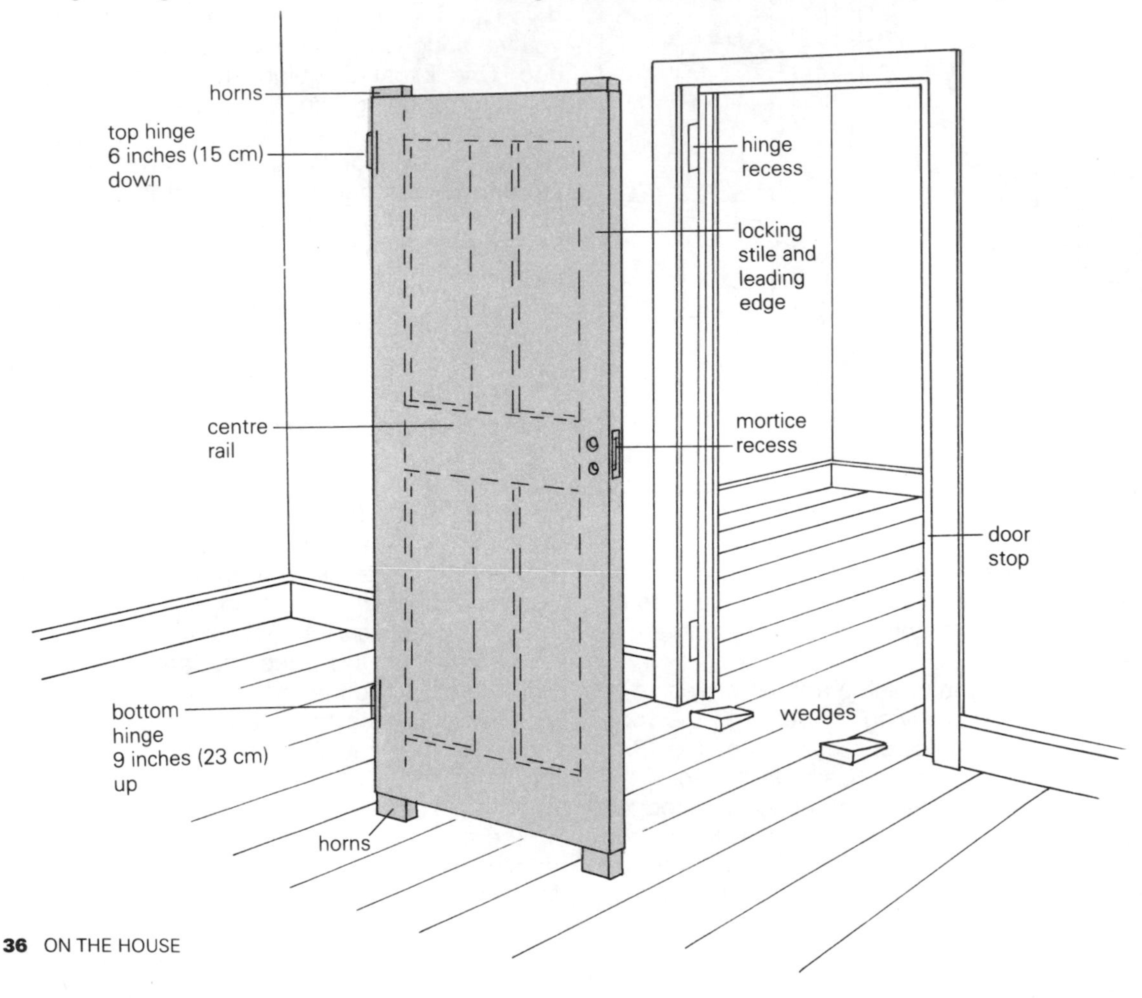

good fit when the door is closed but the door will also rise over the higher floor in its open position. Always work from the edges to the centre when planing the top and bottom rails, otherwise you'll split the corners of the end grain.

Once you've got acceptable clearances all round the door, support the door in the frame on wedges. Pop little wedges into the gaps each side of the door to give the correct clearance and to hold it steady. If the original hinge recess in the frame is to be used again, use it as a guide for marking the hinge positions on your new door.

Fitting the Hinges Lay the door on its locking stile, supporting the door in a portable bench or

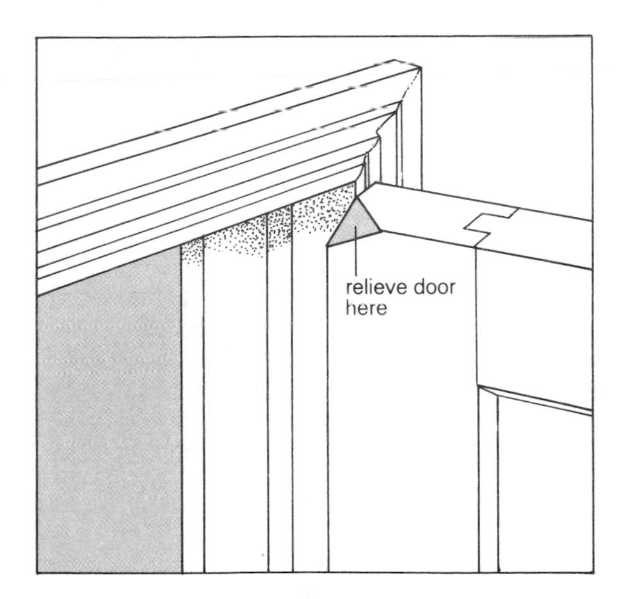

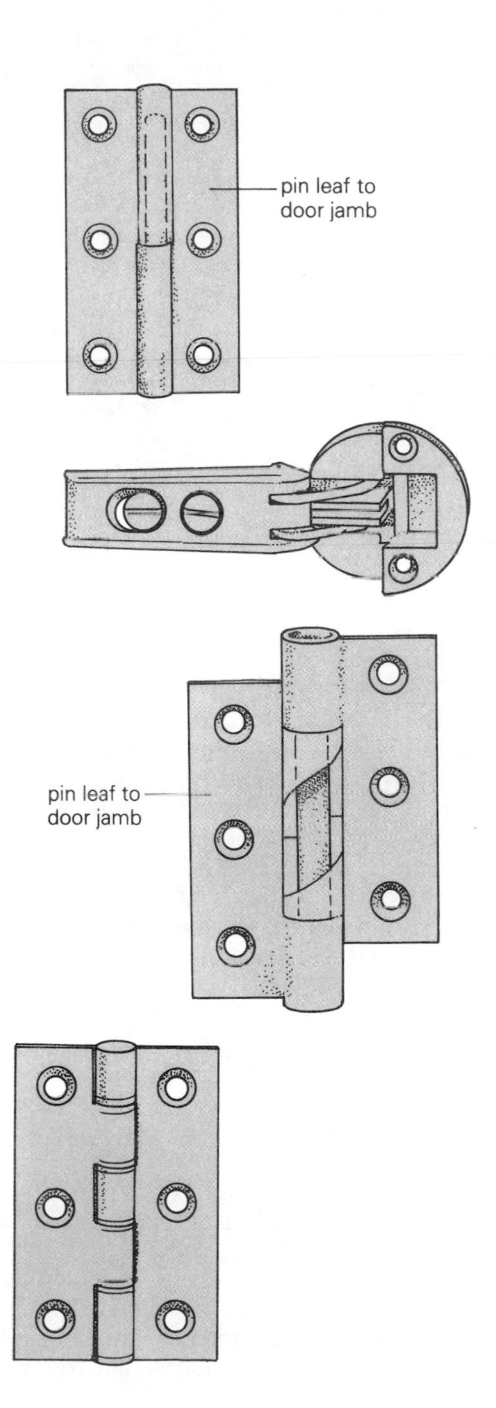

Left: Hanging an interior door. If the door stop is not rebated into the frame (i.e. if it is not part of the same piece of wood as the frame) but is nailed on, take the door stop off and fix the door in position first. Then put door stop back on against closed door; Above: If rising butts are used to clear carpet, it may be necessary to taper off the corner of the door at the top; Right, top to bottom: A selection of useful hinges. Lift-off hinge; concealed hinge; rising butt; brass butt

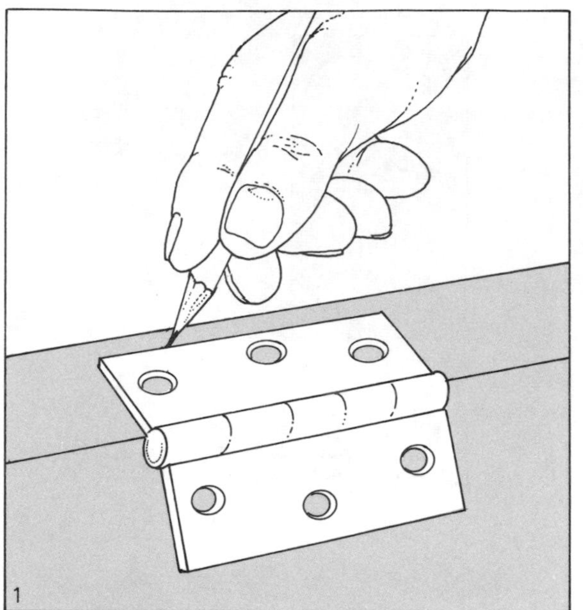

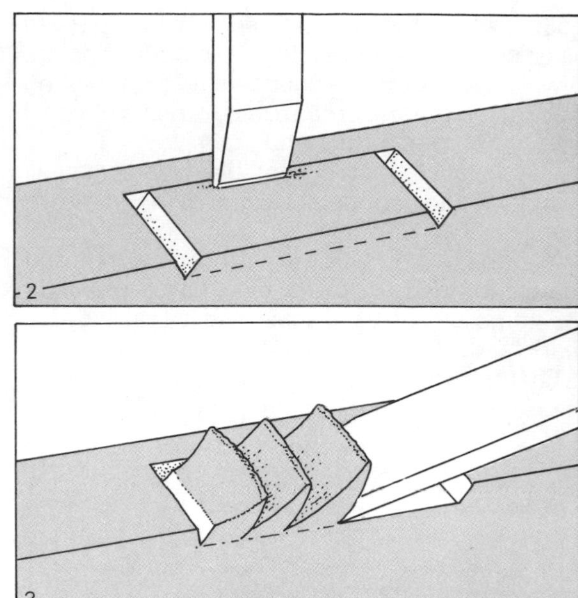

Above: Cutting a recess to fit a hinge. 1. Pencil around outline; 2. Chisel edge; 3. Make initial cuts lengthways; 4. Clean out recess to depth of hinge; 5. Mark holes and insert screws

by straddling it with your legs. Lay the new hinge against the old hinge marks on the door, with the knuckle or pin hanging slightly over the inner face of the door. Mark around the hinge flap with a pencil and mark the hinge thickness on the inside door face. Score just inside the pencil marks with a trimming knife. Then tap a chisel into the cut to the hinge depth. Always work with the bevelled edge of the chisel towards the wood that you're cutting away. Next, make several cuts across the width of the recess, again to the depth of the thickness of the hinge. With the chisel slightly higher than the depth line and the bevelled edge facing up, tap out the feather cuts and chisel the recess level. Now you can screw the hinge into that recess. With both hinges screwed to the door, prop the door in the open position on the wedges already mentioned. The flap of the hinge should sit comfortably into the recesses on the door frame.

Should you need to cut new recesses in the frame, prop the door in the open position resting on the wedges and mark around the hinge flaps. Check that the knuckle of the hinge is equidistant between the door and the frame and follow the same procedure for chopping out the hinge recess as before. There are two things, however, that you must try to do. Make the bottom cut of each recess slightly higher than the pencil mark; this allows for any drop in the door. Make the facing edge of the cut slightly higher than the pencil mark and the rear of the recess slightly deeper. All this allows for adjustment later on. Use a bradawl or an ⅛-inch (3-mm) drill bit to start the screw holes to a depth of about ½ inch (1 cm). One screw in the centre of each hinge will support the door sufficiently for you to test it. The door should now close gently against the door stops, with no binding or springing back. Should the back edge 'bind' against the frame, it means that one of the hinge

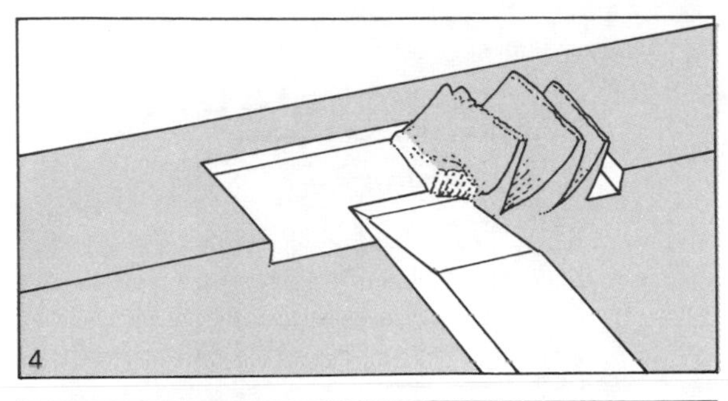

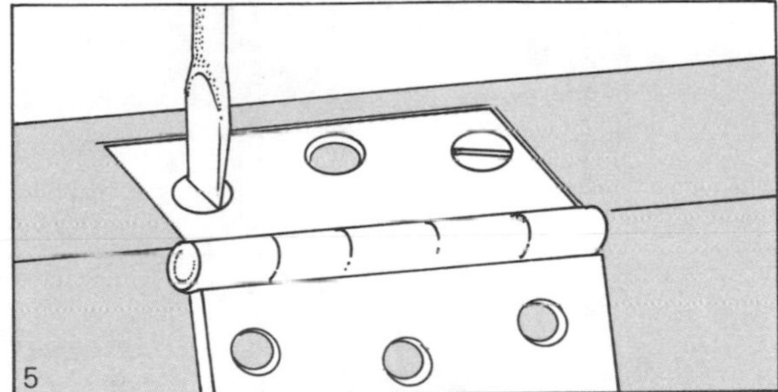

recesses is too deep. You'll need a little piece of cardboard as packing. If, on the other hand, the door leans away from the frame, the hinge recesses will need extra cutting.

Locks

To fit a mortice lock onto a panel door, first position it against the centre rail. (On a flush door you have to find the inside rail provided for that purpose.) Then mark the area of the lock by holding it against the door edge. Press a bradawl through the spindle (or handlebar) and keyhole openings. Now take into account the thickness of the face plate and move those marks accordingly. Drill holes through the door for the spindle and keyhole. Mark a centre line along the edge of the door and cut out the hole on that line (into which you will push the body of the lock). Start by using a brace and bit to bore mortice holes along the centre line. You'll get the same depth each time by sticking a piece of tape onto the drill bit to mark the right depth. With most of the wood

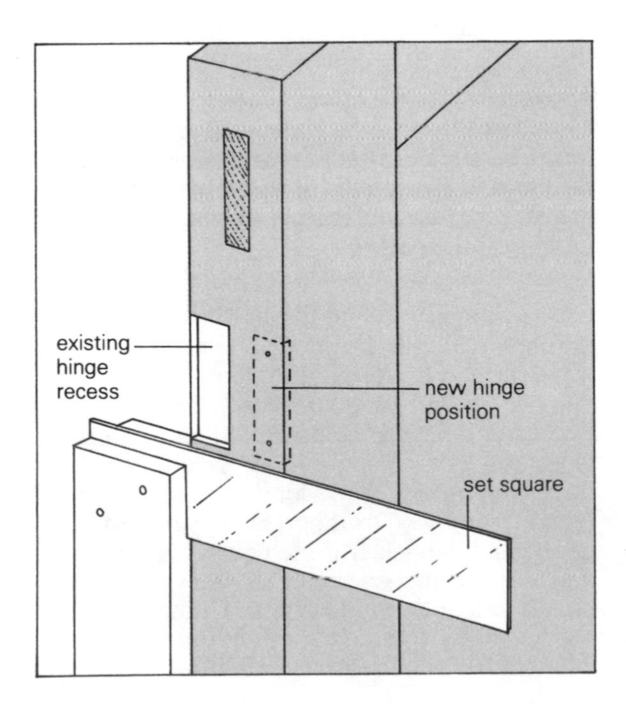

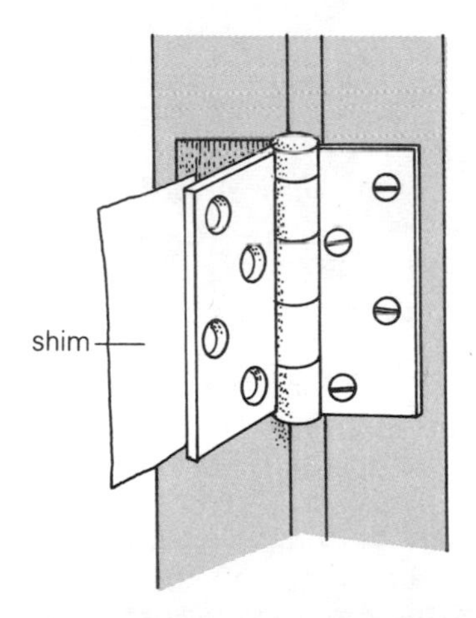

Left: Changing a hinge recess. Using a set square to mark correct horizontals, mark around hinge flaps in new position and then chisel out as shown; Above: If a recess is too deep, bring the hinge out by inserting a paper or cardboard shim into the recess before replacing screws

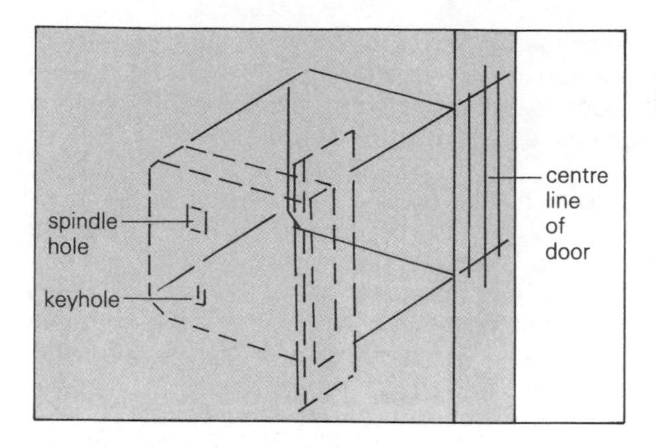

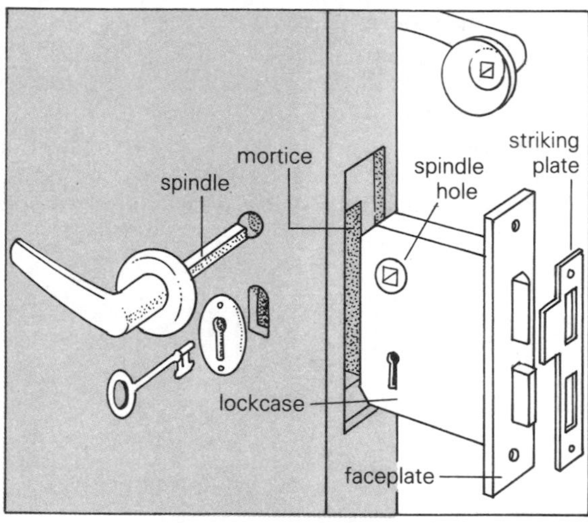

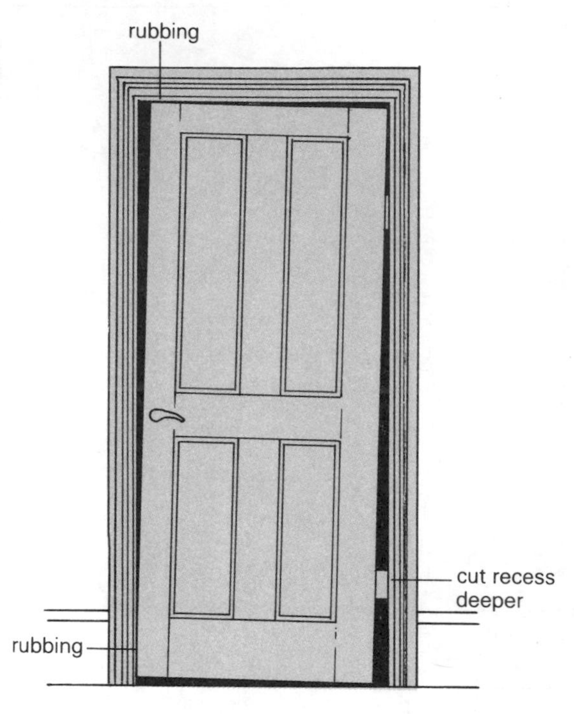

Above left: Use the mortice lock to mark out the correct position on the leading edge of the door (make sure it's centred) and a bradawl to mark positions of the spindle and keyhole; Left: Parts of a mortice lock and recess; Above: Examples of rubbing and wedging

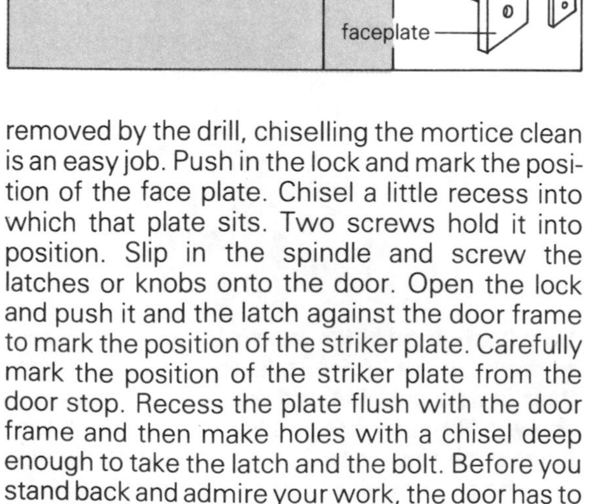

removed by the drill, chiselling the mortice clean is an easy job. Push in the lock and mark the position of the face plate. Chisel a little recess into which that plate sits. Two screws hold it into position. Slip in the spindle and screw the latches or knobs onto the door. Open the lock and push it and the latch against the door frame to mark the position of the striker plate. Carefully mark the position of the striker plate from the door stop. Recess the plate flush with the door frame and then make holes with a chisel deep enough to take the latch and the bolt. Before you stand back and admire your work, the door has to come off again so that the bottom edge can be primed! This is in order to prevent damp attacking the bottom of the door.

Rubbing and Wedging

Should you have problems with a door rubbing along the locking edge you will normally chisel out the hinge recesses slightly deeper. To do this without removing the door is very simple and is a good idea, especially if the door is big or heavy. You cut each recess separately but with the door supported on wedges and the alternate hinge still screwed to the door and frame.

Should you need to use rising butts because of

a carpet or a sloping floor (see page 37), always screw the pivot side to the frame. You'll probably find that you'll need to chamfer the top of the door slightly, in order that the top of the door clears the frame as it opens and rises. This also makes it easy to take off and put on.

If, when closing a door, you have to force it in order to click the latch, it's probable that the door is binding on the jamb. Check that the back edge is not rubbing against the door stop before the door is fully closed. If it is, you need to bring the door slightly away from the door stop, which means moving the hinge slightly into the door. Another reason could be that the hinge leaf has been cut too deeply into the recess. Pack a shim behind the hinge to bring the door forward.

Should a door need to be hung to open in the opposite direction, you will have to cut new hinge recesses. This means, of course, that you're left with the old recesses to fill in. Cut a piece of soft wood which fits the recess but is slightly thicker and glue it into place. Then use tiny nails, punching the heads well in and filling with plastic wood. Plane down the face and the edge, fill any cracks and then paint.

If you are changing the door opening to the other side of the frame, follow the same procedure for marking out the hinge positions on the door and the frame. The same applies to the lock, latch and handles. If it's a spring-loaded door-catch that you're using, the chamfer will be facing the wrong way round, but they are reversible. To find the striker plate position, close the door and mark the position of the catch against the door frame. Alternatively, a little paint of a different colour on the catch will mark the door frame in the exact position for tracing the outline of the striking plate.

Whether you are cutting recesses, changing positions with door stops or narrowing the door, the methods of procedure are all very similar. If you are changing the position of a door but the stops are an integral part of the frame, the door needs to be narrower. Remove hinges and all the fittings before trimming each side of the door.

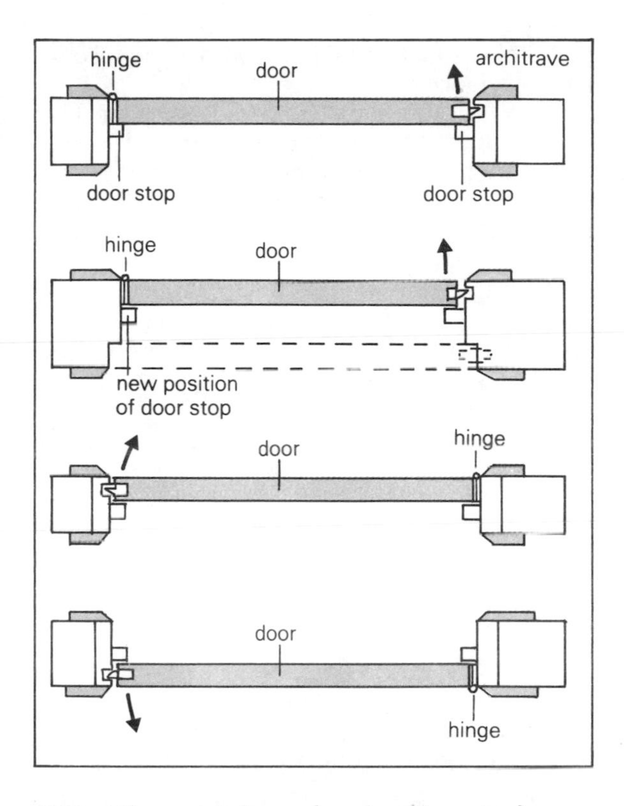

Above: Door openings, showing (from top): Usual position; New recesses cut for change of direction; Hinge transferred for opposite side opening; Hinge transferred and direction of door opening changed

Plane the sides of the door to fit the new position in the frame. You'll then have to fix new door stops, after you've fixed the door and it closes against its latch. Prime and paint as before and replace fittings, to complete the job.

Fitting a Letter Plate

Whether you are fitting a vertical or a horizontal letter plate, whether it has a knocker attached or an internal draught-proof plate, the method is always the same. Obviously if you're fitting a new letter plate and it's the same size as the old one, the job is very easy! However, cutting a larger hole for a new letter plate, or just cutting a new hole, is fairly straightforward if you follow a set of guidelines.

Think first about the choice of letter plate. Find one that matches the style of the door. If you live in a terrace or there are houses similar to yours close by, it's worth making a mental note of other letter plates which match the doors on which they are fixed.

Once again the adage is true, you get what you pay for. Buy a letter plate that is going to last, not one that is going to rust. Brass or chromed steel is the best – this ensures that the elements are not going to damage it.

The other consideration is to match the existing door 'furniture', which refers to the screwed-on fittings on the door. You might consider replacing an old-type latch with a more sophisticated, up-to-date one. Making the front door as burglar-proof as possible will obviously make you feel more secure. Make certain, for example, that the letter plate is not too large and not too near the door latch. Whilst fitting the letter plate, fit a sprung letter flap on the inside of the door. The finished job will look far more professional and, of course, it will stop a lot of draughts.

Planning and Preparation First of all, say to yourself that the job is going to take a couple of hours. Then make a note of tools and materials that you'll need and plan each stage. For marking the position of the letter plate on the door you'll need the letter plate itself, a pencil, a tape measure, a paper template and some sticky-tape. Four holes are to be drilled, so you'll need a hand brace and bit or an electric drill. Jig saws are relatively inexpensive, but if you don't have one you'll need a pad saw. Next on your list is a drill bit slightly larger than the holding bolts and a flat bit (to countersink the nuts).

Fitting Most front doors in the UK are the panel type. This means that you either fit your letter plate vertically or on the horizontal rail between the panels. If you have three panels across, you have no alternative but to fit it on the centre rail. If you have a flush door, then you have to make certain that you fit the letter plate onto the block fixed inside the door which is always provided by the manufacturers for this purpose. They also make provision for locks and latches.

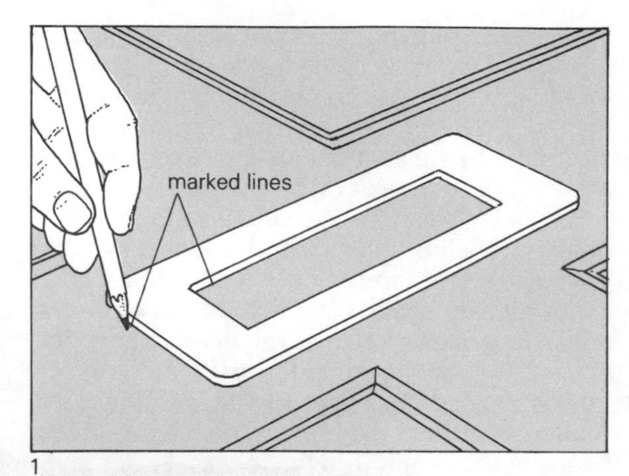

1

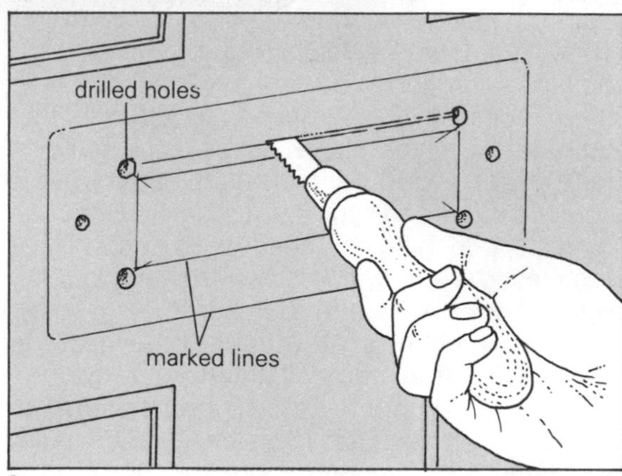

2

Top and above: Fitting a letter plate. Use plate to mark position and then a jig saw or pad saw to cut opening from drilled holes at each corner

Doors which have been in place for a number of years can cause trouble when you try to remove them. They can also be heavy and cumbersome, so, unless you feel very strongly about it, there is just no need to take a door off its frame in order to fit a letter plate. Having measured your door, find the centre point and mark a horizontal or vertical line. Hold the letter plate centrally in position, and draw a line around the inside opening. Mark a point diagonally in from each corner ⅜ inch (10 mm). These marks are to be the centre of your drilled holes, for which you'll need a ¾-inch (20-mm) drill bit. These holes now give you the means of getting your pad saw or jig saw into position to start cutting. You'll need to cut on the outside of the line so that the inner edge of the letter plate opening will not have wood showing inside it. (In effect, the hole in the door will be marginally larger than the hole of the letter plate.) Once you've started to cut on the long edges, switch to a panel saw to speed up the process. The lower edge should have a slight 'chamfer', or slope, so that letters slide more easily through the opening. Smooth the cuts with sandpaper ready for painting.

Now you need to find the positions for the holding bolts. Most new letter plates come supplied with a template, a paper cut-out. This matches exactly the size of the letter plate and indicates the correct positions for the fixing bolts. Sticky-tape will hold a template in position whilst you mark the two positions for the bolts. A flat ½-inch (12-mm) bit is useful to drill just deep enough so that the holding nuts can be recessed. Then drill through these holes with a drill bit which measures ¹⁄₁₆ inch (1.5 mm) larger than the diameter of the holding bolts. An electric drill with a spirit level attachment will ensure that your holes are drilled horizontally, although a slight tolerance is acceptable if you use a hand brace. When drilling through to the front face of a painted or polished door, it is possible to shatter the wood. To prevent this happening, support a piece of scrap timber against the face of the wood and use the drill gently. The bolts should now slide into the holes. If you have to use any pressure, protect the face of the letter plate first. As you tighten the nuts, the back of the letter plate will be drawn tightly to the face of the door, giving a good seal.

The internal letter flap will come with instructions. Usually it's a simple matter of fixing it on with two screws. It couldn't be easier and you'll find that an internal letter flap makes sense both aesthetically and practically.

Door Insulation

If you haven't fitted any draught excluders around your front door you might just as well have one brick missing from the front wall of your house. Think of it this way: on average, the gap between a door and a frame is about ⅛ inch (3 mm) and you have about 20 feet (6 m) of this gap around the door. It doesn't take long to calculate that if the length of a brick is 9 inches (23 cm), you can turn the draughty 20-foot-long (6-m) gap of ⅛ inch (3 mm) into 9 inches by about 3 inches (23 cm × 7.5 cm) – the size of a brick. What a thought that is! It certainly does make sense to insulate. Statistics which show just how much wind whistles in through that gap making the house cold are frightening. It could be that one is paying a hundred times more than the cost of a roll of foam-strip to heat the outside every winter! To prevent all this, you only need to spend ten minutes and little money on one of the easiest of DIY jobs.

There are a couple of points to remember about fixing. The adhesive backing will not stick to a damp, sooty or dirty surface so, once again, preparation is vitally important. The other point is that you need to stick it on to the *side* of the door frame on the hinge edge, but the *face* of the door frame on the top and the other side. (If the gap is very wide two strips can be used.)

Sprung Strips Another type of draught excluder is the sprung metal or plastic strip which is not stuck to the frame but nailed. (Small tacks are provided by the manufacturers.) This method is only effective if the door and frame are straight and smooth. An old door or frame with undulations or chips would still allow air to pass the excluder.

If you have metal windows you can buy an aluminium excluder strip which has a groove to fit the frame. It is essential for this method that the frame is smooth and straight. If the metal is

Right: Metal strips need 1/16-inch (1.5-mm) gap (use a coin to test); Below right, centre: Foam-strip; Below right, bottom: Brush strip

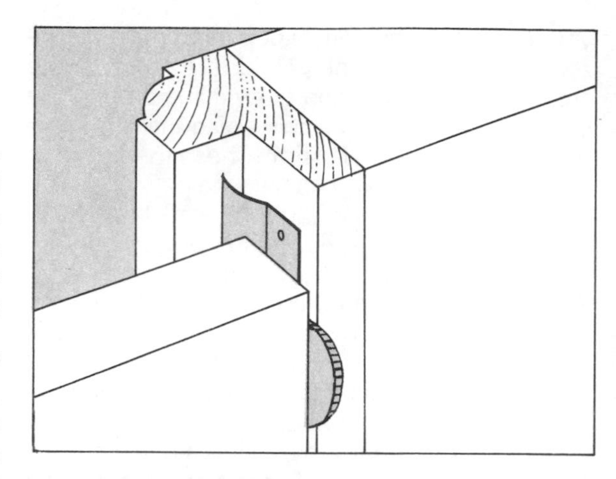

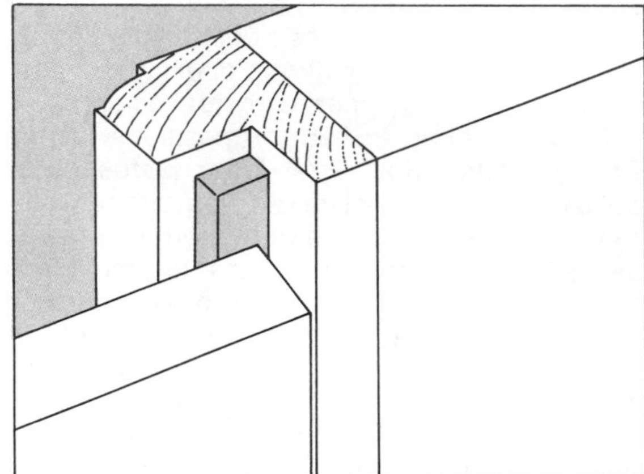

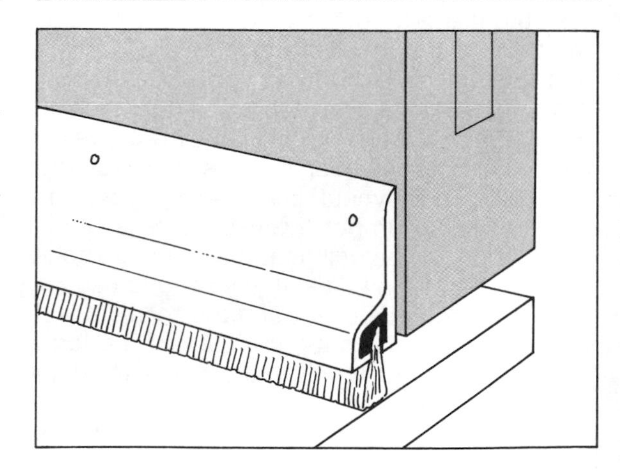

pitted, you'll need to prepare the surface by cleaning it off thoroughly before using a metal primer. Then straighten out the surface with a two-part plastic filler. Instructions are given with the strip which has to be cut to the size of the frame. Clips are supplied to hold the aluminium strip in position.

Threshold Seals There is a wide range of underdoor draught excluders, threshold strips, brush excluders and flexible strips on the market. Some you fix to the floor, but most to the door itself. Don't buy one that needs the door taking off and cutting. The easiest and most simple to fit are the rubber or plastic strips and the brush strip. These are simply screwed to the inside bottom edge of the door. The plastic strip or the brush strip touches the floor or carpet and is an effective seal against draughts.

A more effective exterior fitting combines a weather bar and a draught excluder: the two parts combine to keep out the rain and the wind. Careful measuring and fitting is required, but the results justify the extra work involved. The weather bar is screwed to the exterior of the door whilst the draught excluder is screwed to the floor. This aluminium strip has a rubber insert against which the door closes, so it seals out rain and draughts.

A Knocker or a Bell

Statistics show that the old-fashioned door-knocker is now superseded in popularity by the electric bell or buzzer. If your choice is still the knocker, you could have one fitted with the letter plate. (They often come as an integral part of the plate.) If, however, you prefer a hanging knocker, then it simply means two holes need to be drilled into the door. One bolt attaches the knocker to the door while the other holds the striking plate in position; nothing could be simpler and it certainly enhances the look of a front door. Instructions will tell you what size drill to use and what distance apart the holes need to be. Sometimes you'll find it necessary to shorten the bolts, but this obviously depends on the thickness of the door.

If your choice is a bell or a buzzer, go to your local DIY store where you'll find one in kit form. There are dozens to choose from, some of which are highly sophisticated, although the principle on which they work is very simple. The simplest type of bell runs off dry batteries. Alternatively a kit is available with a small safety transformer, which has to be connected to the mains supply: as the bell needs only 8 or 12 volts, the transformer safely reduces the 240-volt electricity supply. If you're keen to have your bell-push lit up at night, you'll need to buy a system with a transformer. The important thing is to shop around and to read up the relevant pamphlets.

There is no magic to the principle of how a door-bell works, nor to the installation of one. When pressed, the bell-push outside the door causes two contacts to meet. The contacts are connected to the electrical circuit so electricity flows around the circuit through an electromagnet, which promotes a vibration in the form of a ringing bell or buzzer. As for fixing one up, all bells and buzzers come with explicit instructions. You will be advised on the required distance between the bell-push and sounding-box or bell; how to fix the bell-push and how to connect up the wires. Batteries are relatively inexpensive and need to be renewed about once every six months.

For the more advanced DIY'er, it is possible to fix bell-pushes at both front and back doors. If you want further sophistication, you can also fit a second sounding-box or bell elsewhere in the house. There is one check that you ought to make before purchasing your kit: check the manufacturers' installation instructions as to the recommended maximum distance between the bell-push and the bell (usually about ten yards, including up or down walls). Because of its thickness, the wire supplied with the kit will only work effectively under a certain maximum distance. If it is really necessary for you to have a bell much further away from the push you can ask your supplier to either give you a higher-voltage battery or a slightly thicker wire. Suppliers are usually happy to discuss an installation with you and give you any advice you need.

WINDOWS

Exterior Repairs

The most common problem on the exterior of any window is perished putty. It's also the most troublesome because it allows water to seep behind the putty and into the wood. To put it right, however, is one of the simplest of DIY jobs. The first indication that something is wrong is minute cracks running across the putty. You will be amazed at how easily little squares of putty can be prised out of the frame. To help the new putty adhere to the glass, clean off with methylated spirits.

Putty is never ready to use straight from the container. If it's a new tub you'll probably find oil on top of the putty. The putty has to be thoroughly 'worked' with your hands so that it has no lumps and is not too oily. Glaziers like to knead their putty, just like dough, on a plank of wood. If yours is too oily and sticks to your fingers then try rolling it out on a newspaper. To apply, press the putty firmly between the wooden frame and the glass. (If you keep moistening your fingers you'll find that the putty will not stick to them.) Then, using a putty knife or a very clean scraper, smooth the putty out to match the old. To help you get the glaziers' professional finish, dip a soft, clean brush into water and run it in even strokes over the putty. You'll be amazed at how this smooths out irregularities and seals the putty to the glass and the wood.

Replacing a Pane of Glass

If the pane of glass that you have to replace is not in a window on the ground floor, you're faced with either working up a ladder or unscrewing the window and working inside the house. If you've hired a scaffold tower to work on gutters or are redecorating the outside of the house, this is the perfect time to repair broken windows. In the past, glazing hasn't come into the DIY'ers category of repair jobs around the home. Replacing a pane involves handling broken glass, cutting a new sheet of glass and the 'art' of puttying. It's not difficult, however, if you approach it carefully and professionally.

Your first reglazing job should really be on an easily accessible ground-floor window. As well as the tools illustrated you'll need: a pair of gloves; a container for the broken glass; a small brush and some water. If you're going to cut the new piece of glass yourself you'll also need a glass cutter, a straight edge and a little oil for the cutting wheel.

As in all DIY jobs, think in stages and jot them down on a notepad before you start the work. The stages for reglazing are simple: remove the old putty; tap out or pull out the broken glass and the sprigs; prepare the rebate for the new glass; put putty right round the ledge to gently cushion the new glass, and then bevel the 'holding' or 'facing' putty to match the rest of the window.

A hacking knife or an old chisel can be used to remove the old putty. If it's a small pane of glass in an old house, it's likely that the glazing bars (the strips of wood between the panes) are fairly lightweight. Hacking out on the heavier edge of the frame is fairly safe but against a lightweight glazing bar you have to use extra caution. Do wear gloves when tapping out the broken glass. As you're clearing the ledge of old putty and little chips of glass, you'll come across tiny nails with no heads. These are the glazing sprigs put in by the glazier to hold the glass in position. Gently pull them out with a pair of pliers and keep them – you can probably use them later. Next use a quick-drying primer to prepare the wood for the putty, but do let it dry first.

Your new pane of glass should be cut ⅛ inch (3 mm) smaller (on each measurement) than the opening. If you're cutting the glass yourself, place it on a couple of sheets of newspaper laid out on a flat surface. Mark the glass accurately with a thin felt-tip pen and lay your straight edge

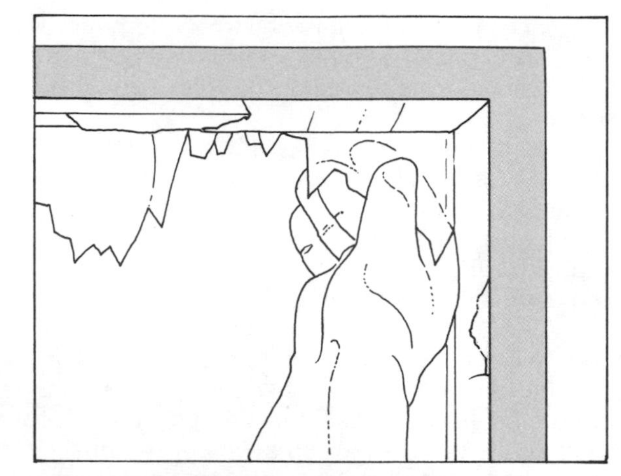

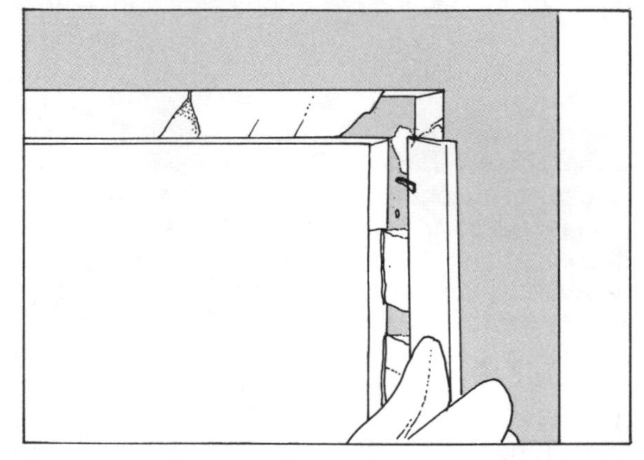

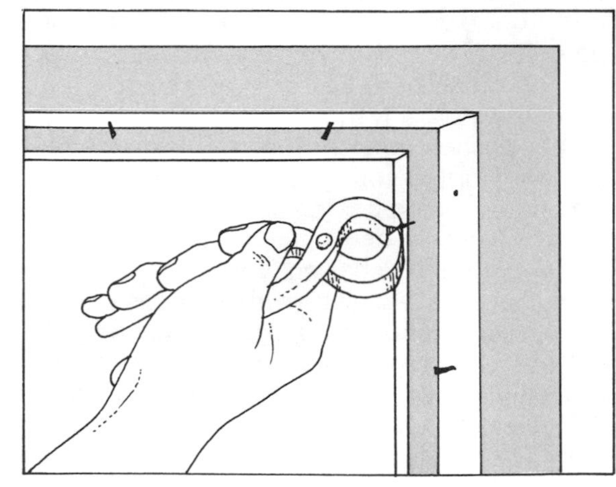

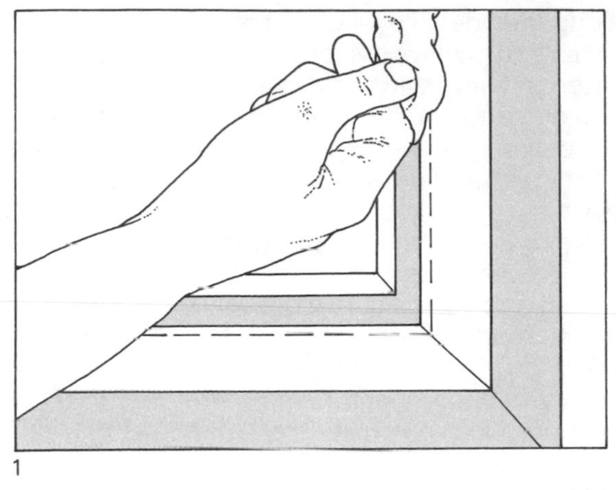

1

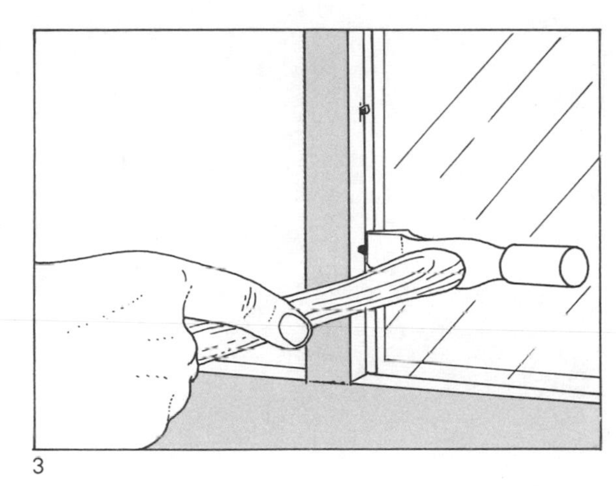

3

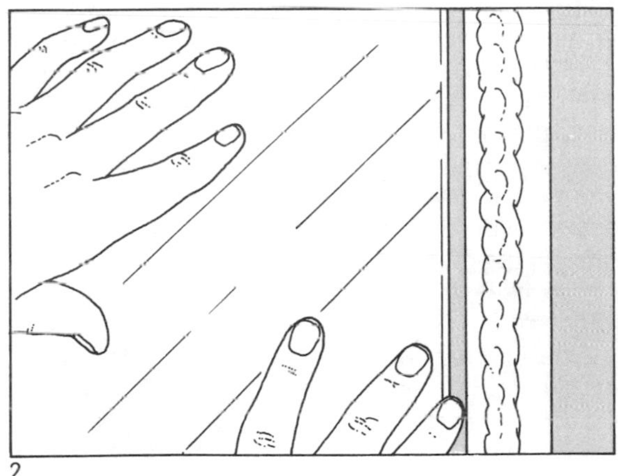

2

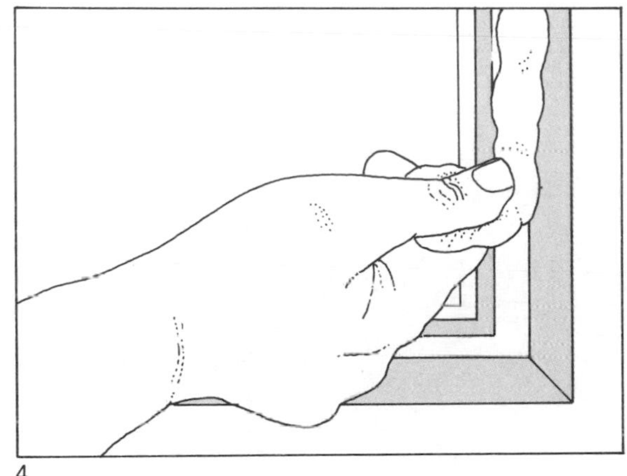

4

Opposite page: Preparing a wooden frame for glazing. Top left: After tapping broken pane out with hammer (onto newspaper), remove shards, wearing gloves; Centre left: Chip out all the old putty; Left: Remove sprigs from frame

This page, above: Putting in new glass. 1. Push enough putty into rebate to cushion pane of glass; 2. Press glass into place; 3. Tap in glazing sprigs to hold glass to frame; 4. Squeeze putty onto glass, making fillet, before smoothing with knife (see pages 48 and 49); Right: Cross-section of corner of window showing position of glass in putty bed and mitred fillet of putty

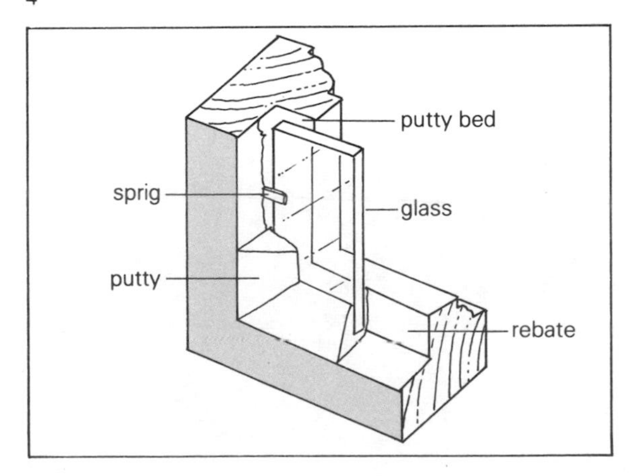

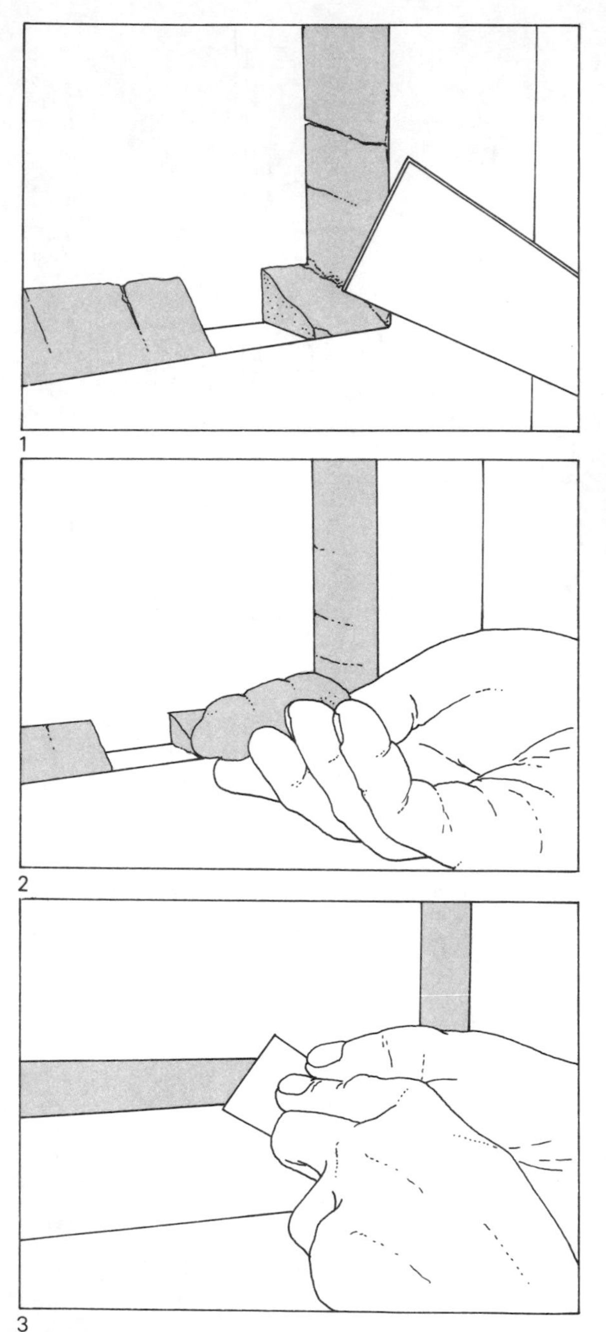

along the line (allowing for the thickness of the cutter, so that you score directly on the line). After scoring with the glass cutter, lay the straight edge underneath the glass with one edge directly underneath the score mark. Press gently either side and you should have a nice clean cut.

Next, take a piece of putty about the size of a golf ball and make sure it's pliable. With your thumb and forefinger, work the putty into the rebate (appearance doesn't matter here at all). What you have to end up with is a cushion of putty of about ⅛ inch (3 mm) after the glass is squeezed into position. Press the glass only on the edges, not in the centre. You saw the little sprigs in position when you cleared out the old putty; now you have to replace them to hold the glass securely. Tapping the sprigs into the outside, thicker part of the frame is both safe and easy, but a word of warning if you don't want another broken pane of glass: take extra care when dealing with the glazing bars. If a sprig is tapped even a minute amount too far it will go through the glazing bar, hit the next pane of glass and break it. A maximum of two sprigs a side is sufficient.

When squeezing in the facing putty, try to get just the right amount to form a triangular fillet, as it were, which slopes away from the glass. In this way you won't have a lot of excess putty to contend with when you use the putty knife to form the bevel. You'll soon get the knack of joining the corners together into what is called a 'mitre'. To form a good mitre, start with your putty knife in the corner at an angle and work away from it. Again, a brush dipped in water and run gently over the putty will give it a smoother and neater look, as well as sealing the putty to the glass. The excess putty on the inside of the window is cut away with the edge of the putty knife; a wet brush will smooth it out. You'll have

Left: Replace perished or cracked putty as soon as cracks appear, to avoid water penetrating and rotting the frame

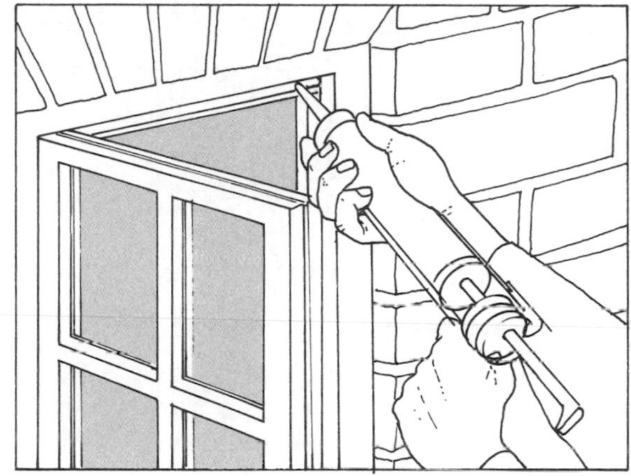

Left: Use putty knife at an angle to create bevel; Above: A cartridge gun makes applying silicone sealant to windows easy and quick

to wait some time for a skin to form on the putty before painting.

Metal Windows There are two differences in the procedure for reglazing metal windows. Special metal casement putty must always be used and glazing clips instead of sprigs are used to hold the glass in position. As you remove the old putty you'll find the 'S' shaped clips clamped into a hole in the frame and sprung around the pane of glass.

Sash Cords

Sash windows are less common these days but still need maintenance, mainly in the form of sash-cord replacement. Never just replace the one that's broken; it's always worth doing both. The box frame which houses the sliding sashes is not the mysterious assembly of pulleys, ropes, pocket pieces and hidden weights that it seems. Once you've taken one apart you'll find it simpler to understand and easy to repair. The staff beads prise off very easily. As they're mitred at the top and bottom, you need to spring them out from the centre first. (Normally it's only necessary to release one staff bead to ease the sash out.) The cord is secured in a groove by clout nails which are easily pulled out. To get at the weight and the rest of the cord, gently ease out the pocket piece. Work from the bottom, because the top of it is chamfered (sloped) to wedge it into position. Try threading a new cord over the pulley at the top and down the box to the pocket opening. If it's difficult, drop down a 'mouse' on a piece of string (this can be any small weight). The string can be used to pull through the cord, which is knotted to the weight and fixed at the right length to the groove in the sash. This deals with the upper window.

If the cord is broken on the lower sash you'll have to remove the parting bead which separates the two sashes. Both sashes will have to come out in this instance, but then proceed as before.

Silicone Sealant

If metal or wooden casement windows have become distorted or warped, a lot of cold air will blow in through the gaps. An ideal solution to this problem is silicone sealant. Not to seal up the window but used to make your own draught excluder. Apply the sealant with a cartridge gun to the three faces of the rebate but to the back of the rebate facing the hinges. Now comes the strange part: petroleum jelly or liquid detergent

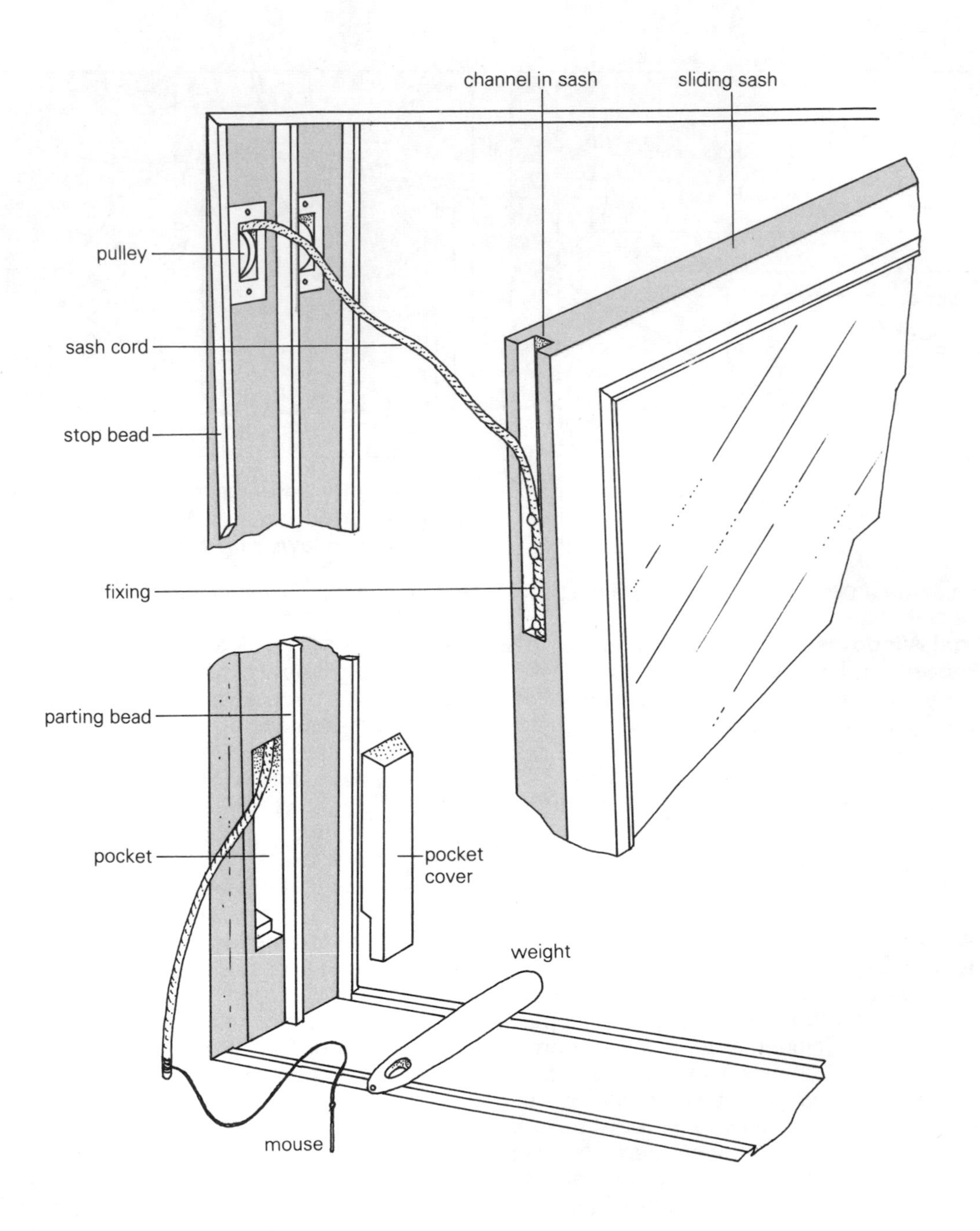

Replacing a sash cord

must be spread on the parts of the window that are going to touch the silicone sealant. This stops the silicone sticking to the window when you close it to mould the seal. The silicone forms a skin over a period of twelve hours, after which you can cut off any excess with a trimming knife.

Replacing an Internal Sill

Condensation is the prime cause of rotting wooden sills. The wood sucks in moisture and retains it for long periods, often remaining there when painted over. Rot is then inevitable. To remove the old sill is fairly easy if you know how the sill was fixed in the first place. They are usually nailed into timber pieces set into the wall below the sill and plaster is then applied to the reveals to cover and secure the ends of the sill. All you do is reverse the process: hack off a little of the plaster from either end of the sill and then lever it up to release the nails. To make the job easier you could first of all cut the edge of the sill with a panel saw.

Clean out the space for the new sill, which must fit snugly against the window frame. Prime and treat the hidden parts of the new sill before securing it, but also nail through the back edge of the sill into the window frame.

Replacing Leaded Lights

The more aware one is of the principles of construction in the home, the easier it is to understand how to put things right when repairs are needed. This is certainly true of leaded-light windows. These are made up of H sections of lead soldered together within an outer frame. The separate panes of glass are held in the H sections with gold-size putty. The strips of lead, called 'cames', can easily be prised apart to replace a broken pane. Cut the lead diagonally at each corner so that the lead can be levered back from the glass, then carefully take out the broken glass and clean out the groove. Nowadays grey

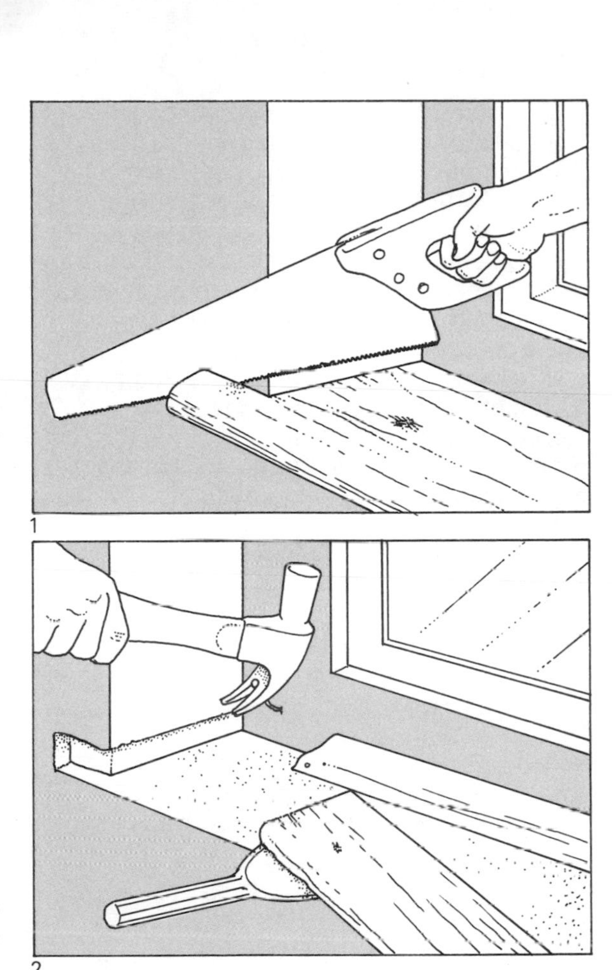

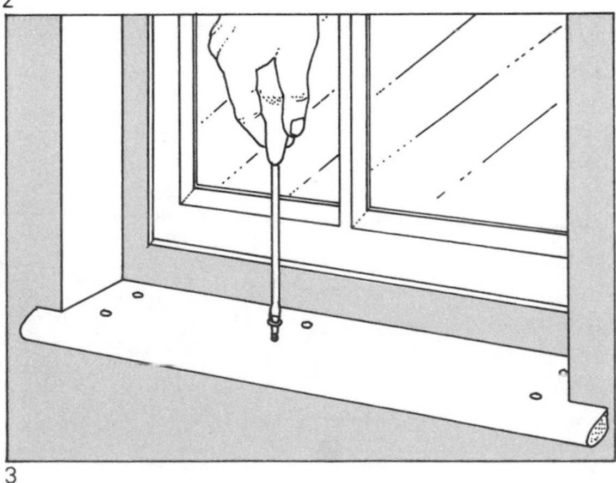

Right: Replacing internal window sill. 1. Cut 'nosing' off old sill; 2. Hack away plaster at either end and lever off sill; 3. Measure new sill to fit and fix with screws and plugs

mastic compound is used to bed glass into leaded-light windows. Slide the glass first into the top groove and push it against the mastic on the other three sides (very gently). Add more mastic before easing back the lead flanges from the corners. Clean them up with glass paper before resoldering. An inexpensive electric soldering-iron will have full instructions, but do use a soft, resin cored solder.

If leaded-light windows are old, it's possible that some of the putty may have perished. You can carry out an excellent repair using the same method as above. The mastic will seal the glass to the lead, stopping penetration of rainwater.

Most households at one time or another experience a rot problem in some exterior woodwork. The most common are rotten window frames (usually at the lowest joint) and decayed wooden sills which have suffered water penetration. It is impossible to put this right with a coat of paint! The remedy, however, is very simple and you can effectively repair wet rot in exterior wood provided it has not gone too far and the frame is not falling apart. First of all, clear the rotted wood back to a sound surface. Then you'll know, by the depth of the hole, whether you need to replace the whole frame or whether a repair will be effective. A system is available whereby you first of all paint on a wood hardener, which strengthens the decayed wood and forms an effective seal against any further water penetration.

You should then mix together and smooth in a two-part wood-filler, leaving it a little bit higher than the original surface of the timber so that it can be sanded to make a perfect join. Little holes can be drilled around the previously affected area and wood preservative tablets inserted to prevent the wet-rot recurring. A special one-coat paint is available to complete the treatment.

FIXTURES & FITTINGS 3

When we talk about fixing something to a wall we usually think in terms of a nail or a screw. Indeed, these are still the most widely used methods of fixing. In this technological age, however, there is now available a range of products to fix pretty well anything to any construction. The designers have had to cater for the professional, the DIY enthusiast and the householder who has little or no practical experience.

Becoming aware of the available fixings and methods of application on the market increases one's understanding of how a job should be done. You might, for example, want to fix a shelf bracket to a wall. Your DIY store will give you a chart showing various fixings for different walls, but if it's a plastered wall you can't be sure what's behind the plaster. So you need to find out. To do this, drill a hole with a masonry bit. Powder will emerge. If it's pale grey powder the wall must be lightweight or aerated concrete; dark grey and it will be standard concrete; blackish means breeze blocks and reddish powder indicates brickwork. If the wall is a stud partition wall you'll either hit nothing or wood.

There are easy-to-use, safe fixings specifically designed for many different types of walls, but it isn't only the fixings that need to be safe. You need to know whether or not it is safe to drill into a wall; never ever drill, for instance, directly above or below light switches or socket outlets (power points). There is on the market an inexpensive metal detector that is simply slid over the wall which indicates by a neon light whether there are any conduits, electric cables or pipes buried in the wall. A more expensive and sophisticated version will also indicate whether an electric cable concealed behind the wall is live.

Manufacturers of fixings and fastenings produce pamphlets which you can pick up in any DIY store. Most manufacturers want us to be aware of the wide range of fixings available to carry out any holding job around the house. Two qualities that you need to look for in a fixing are strength and reliability. Any fixing that you need to make in concrete; bricks; breeze block; aerated concrete; hollow cement blocks; plasterboard; insulating board; solid timber; ply or chipboard; hollow doors and solid or hollow ceilings can be made with an inexpensive holding device. Once you've decided on the fixing appropriate to the job being undertaken and the construction of the wall, you'll find full instructions on the package.

Remember, though, that there are right ways and wrong ways to tackle anything. Do not use a drill bit that is just a tiny bit larger than the recommended size, thinking 'Oh, it will do, I'll just pack the hole out a little.' This is an attitude that can ruin many a job around the house. Be certain that when you fix a job, it stays fixed because you've tackled it properly.

NAILS & SCREWS

For fixing to wood, there are certain types of nails and screws that you ought to know about.

Nails

Wire Nail. This is a general-purpose nail with a large unattractive head. It can split wood if too large a size is used. Available up to 6 inches (150 mm) in length.

Oval Nail. Again a general-purpose nail, but mostly used in joinery work. Unlikely to split wood providing that the oval head runs in the

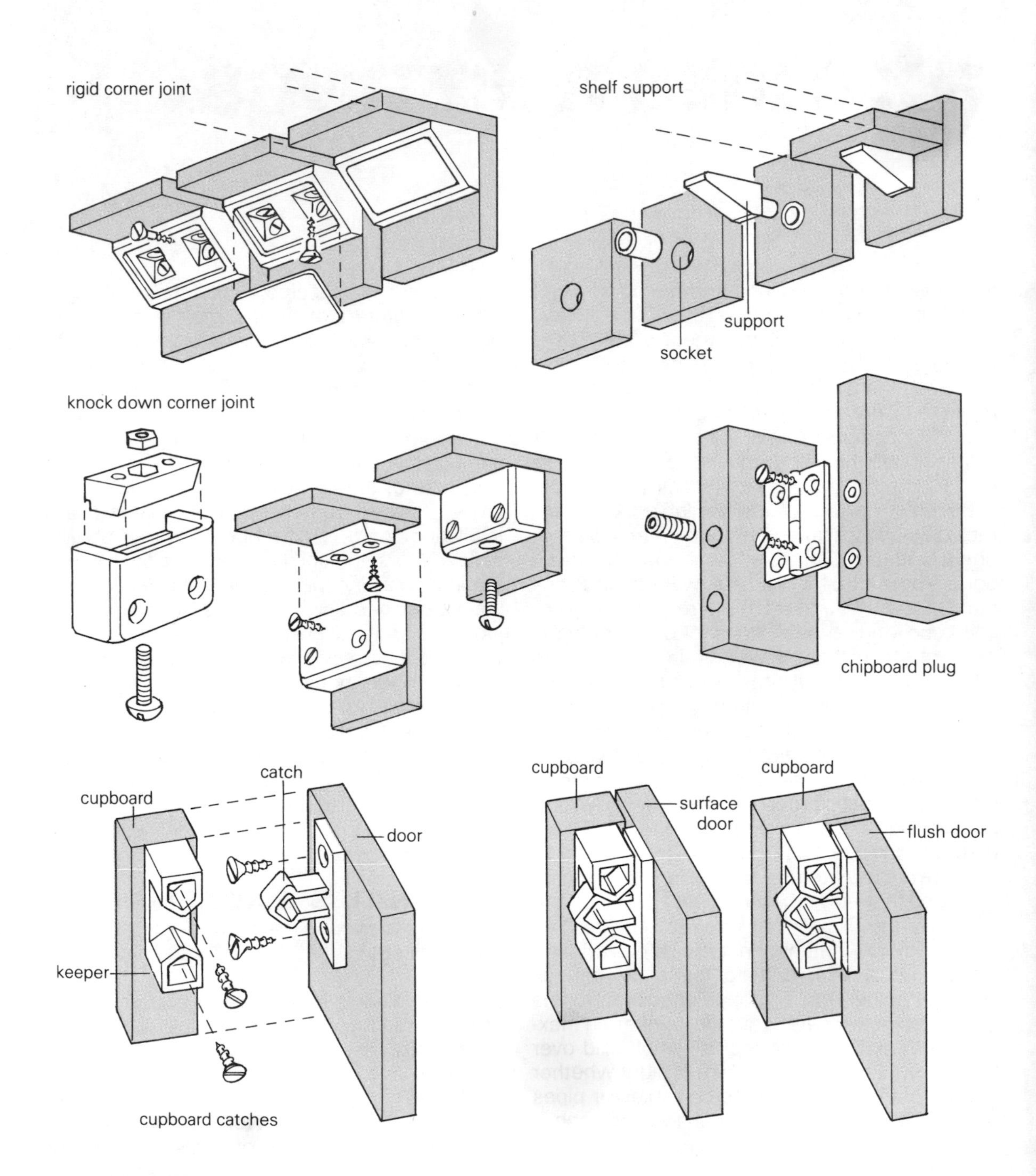
rigid corner joint
shelf support
support
socket
knock down corner joint
chipboard plug
catch
cupboard
door
keeper
cupboard catches
cupboard
surface
door
cupboard
flush door

direction of the grain. Again up to 6 inches (150 mm) in length available.
Floor Brad. This is a square type nail with a small head to one side, and is used to fix floorboards.
Lost Head Nail. As the name indicates, a 'lost head' nail can be punched below the surface of the wood and the hole filled. Used in general carpentry and comes in lengths up to 6 inches (150 mm).
Cut Nail. Also called a clasp. Indicates that it has a strong grip in wood and masonry, so used for holding skirting boards. Available up to 8 inches (205 mm) in length.
Clout Nail. Comes galvanised for outdoor work. Smaller type used for roofing felt. Holds window sash cords. Available in ½ inch (12 mm) to 2 inches (50 mm).
Panel Pin. Used for all types of fine work. Has a small head so can easily be punched in and hole filled. Available in ½ inch (12 mm) to 2 inches (50 mm).
Masonry Nail. Used in walls where it provides a strong grip in mortar; soft brick; breeze block. Available up to 4 inches (100 mm) in length.
Hardboard Pin. Should only be used for fixing hardboard. The chamfered head holds the board securely but is hidden beneath the surface. Available up to 1½ inches (38 mm) in length.
Staples. Galvanised for exterior work such as wire fencing.
Cable Staple. Has plastic protective piece for holding electric cables and one fixing nail. Use correct size to suit cable.

Screws

There are two sizes that you must know of before buying screws. One size is the gauge, which is the diameter of its 'shank' (the thick part of the screw). The other size is the actual length of the screw, measured from the rim of the head to the tip of the thread.

Opposite page: Five aids to fixing. Becoming familiar with the various products on the market means you can select the one which is exactly right for the job in hand

Screws are manufactured in various metals, the most common being mild steel. This type of screw is used in general-purpose carpentry and being steel it can be attacked by moisture, so it's unwise to use it out of doors. Screws are also made of brass, copper, gunmetal and aluminium; they can be galvanised for exterior use; black japanned for decorative use; or plated with nickel, tin, zinc, and chrome.

Always make a pilot hole smaller than the screw gauge before driving in a screw. If you're repeating holes of the same size and the same depth, stick a piece of adhesive tape around the drill bit to mark the correct length of hole: this will act as a depth gauge. One would normally drill only a small hole for a screw used in soft wood; hard woods need more clearance, otherwise the screw will bite too hard and you'll damage the head of the screw. For heavier gauge screws, use a little candle grease to ease the penetration. (A pump screwdriver with interchangeable bits is recommended for every household.) The depth of a pilot hole for small screws should be half the screw length but for heavier gauge screws the holes can be the same diameter as the screw shank.

After marking and drilling the piece to be fixed, use a countersink bit. Then hold the piece in position and push a bradawl through the drilled holes to mark the screw positions.
Countersunk Screw. Used in general woodwork. Holds wood to wood and fittings to wood. Screw head finishes flush with the work or slightly below the surface. Available from ¼ inch (6 mm) to 6 inches (150 mm). Slotted type for use with conventional screwdriver.
Cross-head Screw. Similar to the countersunk but has cross slots in the middle of the head. Needs special screwdriver.
Raised Head. Screw used for door handle plates and decorative wall lights. Is designed to be countersunk to the rim of the head. Up to 2 inches (50 mm) in length.
Round Head. Similar to raised head but is not countersunk.

Dome Head. Screw is used for fixing bath panels and mirrors, when only the dome is seen and screw is hidden. Up to 2 inches (50 mm) in length.
Self-Tapping Screw. Various types of head. Cuts its own thread as it's driven in, usually in metal, plastic panelling and car bodies.

NAILING WOOD TO WOOD

As a general rule, use a nail two to three times longer than the thickness of the timber it is to hold. If you can, try to nail light work to heavier timber. If you're fixing a lighter piece of wood at right angles to a heavier piece and nailing is the only method of fixing, 'skew-nail' the joint. Drive the nails in about ½ inch (1 cm) from the joint at 45°, so that you have an X inside the joint.

Two pieces of wood that have to be joined lengthways (and overlap at one end) should have nails 'clenched' for strength. Drive in longer nails than necessary at each end of the overlap and then bend them over, so that the points go back into the wood.

If you're fixing a piece of wood to the end grain of another piece, use glue and 'dove-tail' the nails by driving the nails in at opposing angles.

If you have to fix a piece of timber with several nails along the grain, stagger the nails so that they're not in a straight line. This prevents splitting. Before nailing in, tap the points with a hammer to flatten them.

When using hard wood, drill holes slightly smaller than the nail shank to avoid splitting the wood.

To avoid hitting your fingers when using tiny nails or tacks, push the tacks through a strip of thin cardboard and use it as a guide.

It is not necessary, when using masonry nails, for the nail to penetrate the brickwork more than an inch (2.5 cm).

It is also useful to remember to always drive nails a short distance into the timber (against a hard surface) before applying it for fixing. Try to do as much of the work as you can on a workbench – it's more accurate and much safer than trying to hold the piece you're fixing in position while you drive in the nails.

MAKING FURNITURE THE SIMPLE WAY

You can design, construct and assemble simple pieces of furniture, no matter how unskilled you believe yourself to be. Often the designing is the hardest part of the job! It is possible to buy prepared and polished timber in most sizes and lengths. The secret, however, is in the simplified assembly methods. This is due to the wonderful choice of metal and plastic fittings with which to hold the parts together.

Most people should find making a coffee table simplicity itself. Buy a piece of laminated blockboard cut to size and four 'turned' legs and plates. The plates are screwed underneath each corner of the table top and the legs – with their threaded bolts – are screwed into the plates.

It is also possible to design and construct a larger kitchen table without having to do much carpentry. To make a table top of parallel boards, use 'knock-down plates'. Round-head screws are positioned close to the edges of the parallel boards. The plates are then dropped over the heads and tapped home to tighten the joints. Boards that hold the legs apart (and to which the top is screwed) are called 'stretchers'. These can be fixed together at the corners by using metal 'corner plates'. Round-head screws are positioned so that the corner plate can be slotted on to them. The plate is then tapped against the screws and this draws the timbers together at right angles, holding them very firmly. Similar metal plates are available for fixing square section legs into the corners. 'Shrinkage plates' are then used underneath the table top to fix it to the inside of the stretchers. These are right-angled metal plates with round and slotted holes.

Other useful fittings include keyhole plates; flush-mount-fitting; and a self-locking fitting. These allow for easy dismantling. The keyhole plate is a slotted plate screwed to the back of a wall unit. A round-head screw protrudes slightly from a wall-plug, enabling the keyhole plate to be firmly slotted over it.

Kitchen units bought as flat packs have full instructions for easy assembling. There is usually little carpentry or cutting involved, and the success of the self-assembly units is due mainly to the well-designed fastening methods.

SOLID WALL FIXINGS

The three points which you must consider before you start are the type of wall, the plug to be used and the load to which that fixing is going to be subjected. If you're fixing a shelf bracket to a wooden wall or to an upright stud in a stud partition wall then you simply use the appropriate screw; you will not need a plug. For going in to most solid building materials you will find that a nylon plug with deep teeth bites into the wall when the screw is driven home, and holds very firmly.

If you have drilled a hole too large or have to go in to an existing hole which is oversized, there are plugs that fit inside other plugs to overcome this difficulty. You'll find that plugs have two splits along their length, called expansion splits. If you have to insert one into another, make certain that these splits are not lined up but are at 90° to each other.

Drilling the Hole

For many reasons it's not always possible to keep a drill bit in a straight line. You might find that, as you're drilling, the bit begins to wander; this can be caused by either hard or soft material not consistent with the wall itself. If it happens, tilt the drill towards the 'wander' to bring the bit back into line. You must try to do this before you get to half the depth of the plug. Should the hole become too big to start, you might have to drill deeper and use a longer plug and screw. Use the size of drill bit recommended by the plug manufacturers (all packaging of plugs gives this advice). Drill the hole to the recommended depth

Below: Tilting drill to correct off-centred hole; Right, from top: Standard plug; Ribbed barrel plug with wings; Nylon plug with helical wings

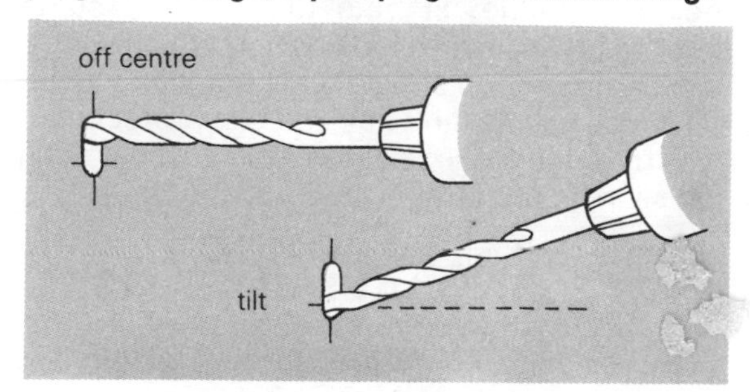

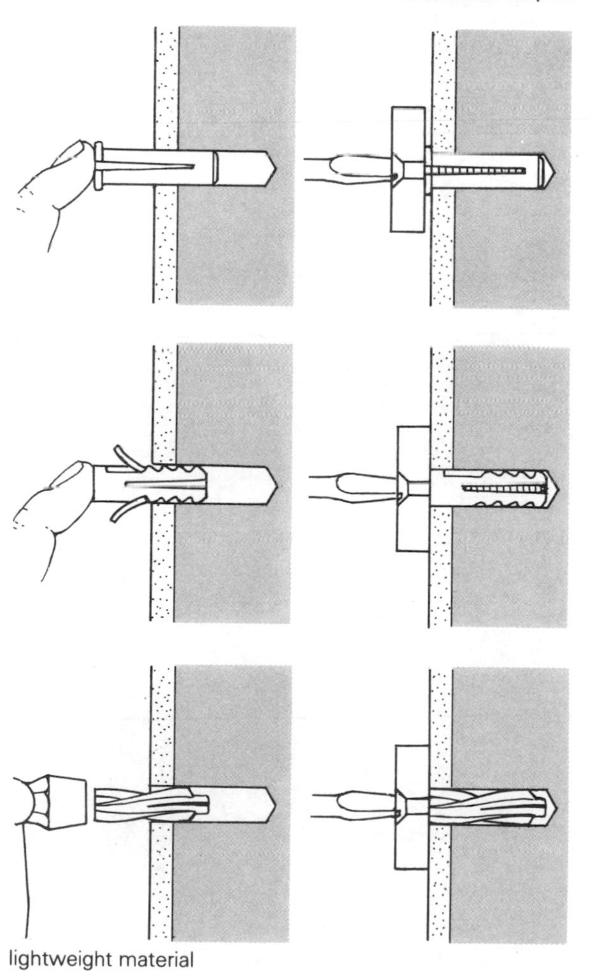

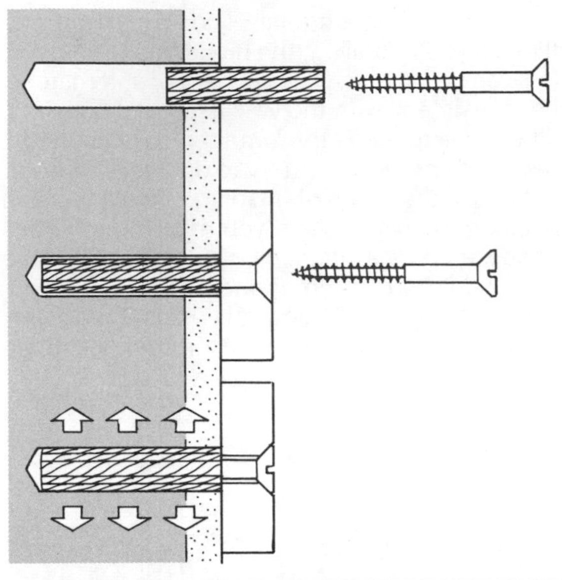

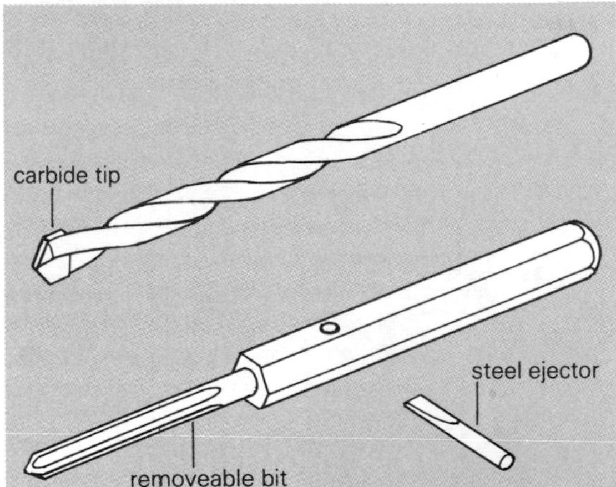

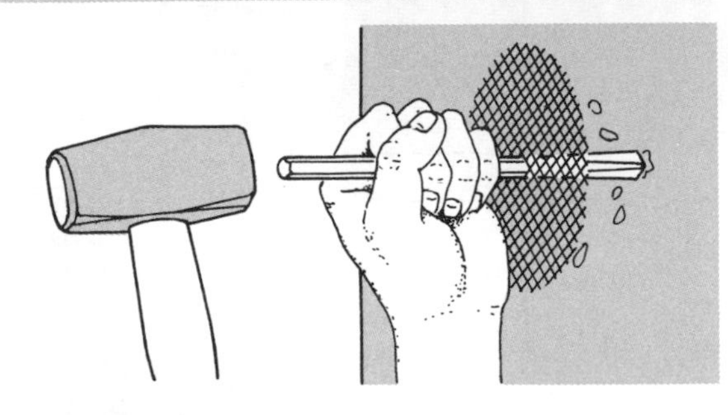

Left: How a fibre plug works; Below left, centre: Carbide-tipped bit and hand jumper; Below left, bottom: Jumping bit with mesh; Opposite page: A selection of plugs, anchors and toggles

and insert the wall-plug. The best general-purpose plug is made of tough, 100% nylon, has no lip or 'flange' at the neck and is non-expanding. Sprung 'ears' flex out from the sides of the plug to stop turning or pulling-out when the screw is driven home. This is the plug that can be pushed right through your facing work to sit snugly inside the drilled hole in the wall.

For internal walls made of breeze block (or if you suspect that the wall underneath the plaster is soft or crumbling, or is aerated concrete block) a special type of plug is needed for fixing. Use a nylon wall-plug with helical wings. The wings grip the sides of the drilled hole before the screw is even driven home. Drill the hole the same size as the plug body. The wings are wider and you must therefore hammer the plug into the wall first. When tightened in the plug, the screw will hold the fitting securely.

Where you have a high temperature area, for example round a fireplace or cooker, you must use a fibre, not plastic, wall-plug. After you've drilled the hole, pop the plug in to just below the wall surface. You'll then need to turn the screw into the plug in order to expand the fibre wall-plug which then fits tightly into the hole. Withdraw the screw, offer up your fitment and then screw it into place.

Should you come up against a particularly hard wall, try using a hammer drill to make the hole for the plug. If the bit gets too hot and starts smoking, try using a hand-held jumping bit and a club hammer. You should wear goggles for this job, but if you haven't any you can protect your eyes by cutting a piece of cardboard or fine mesh and slipping it on to the shank of the bit.

PLASTERBOARD & CAVITY WALL FIXINGS

If a cavity in a hollow wall is quite small, it is still possible to screw a fitment to the plasterboard

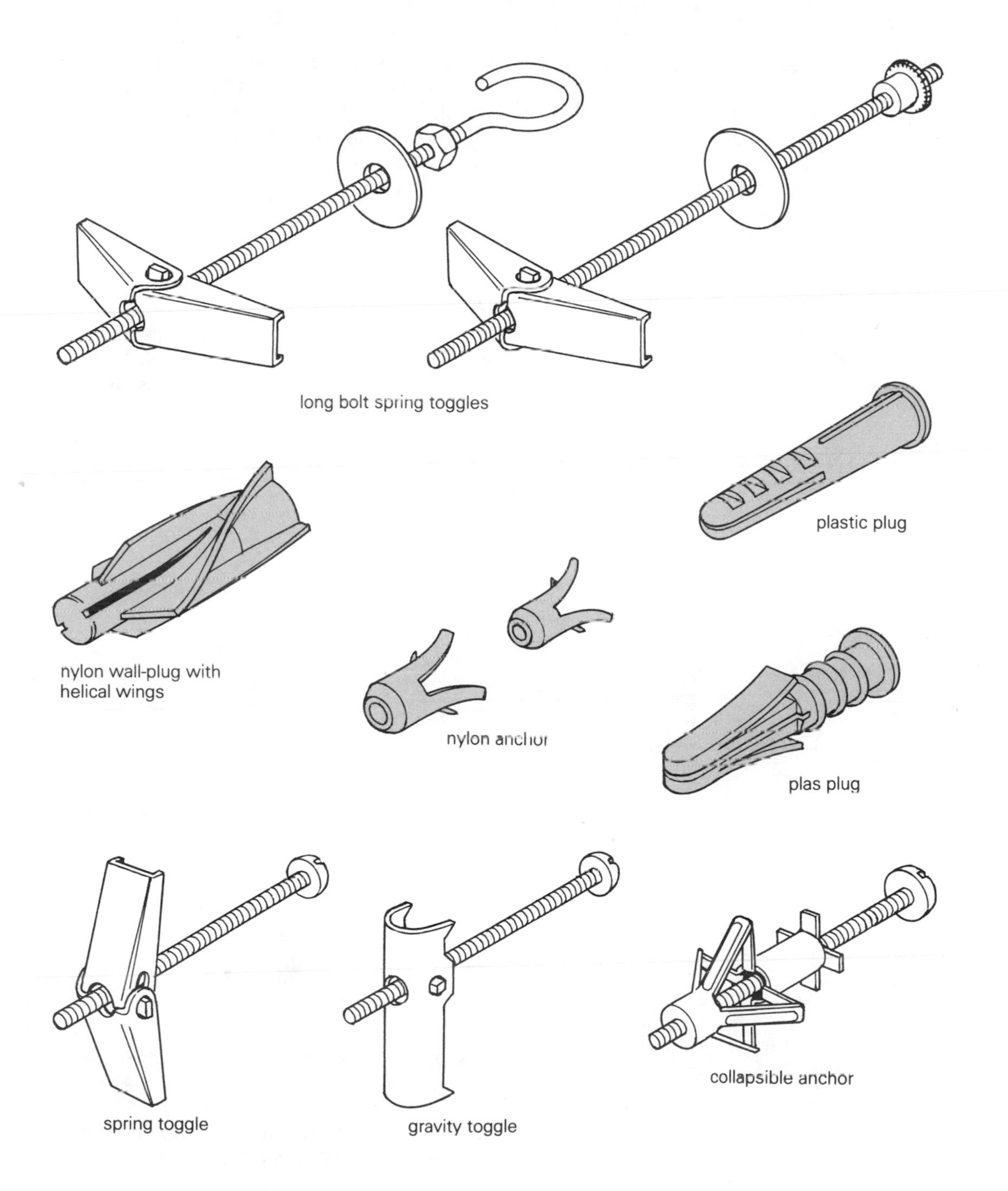
long bolt spring toggles
plastic plug
nylon wall-plug with
helical wings
nylon anchor
plas plug
spring toggle
gravity toggle
collapsible anchor

using a clever little device called a nylon anchor. Decide first of all where your fitment is going to be hung or fixed and drill the correct size hole as suggested in the instructions. (Screws and anchors come as a package.) Choose a screw that is slightly longer than the combined length of the nylon anchor, the thickness of the plasterboard and the thickness of the fitment that you're fixing. Pop the screws through the fitment and into the anchor tongue end; one or two turns is enough. Push the anchor through the hole in the plasterboard with the screw. As you tighten the screw the anchor tongues open up on the other side of the plasterboard and begin to pull the fitment to the wall. Be careful not to over-tighten the screw.

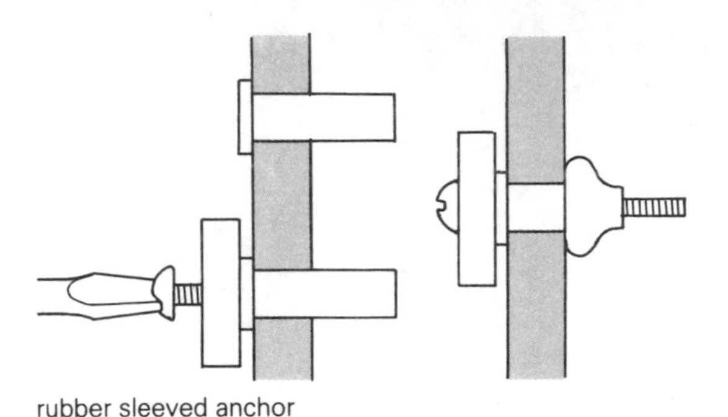
rubber sleeved anchor

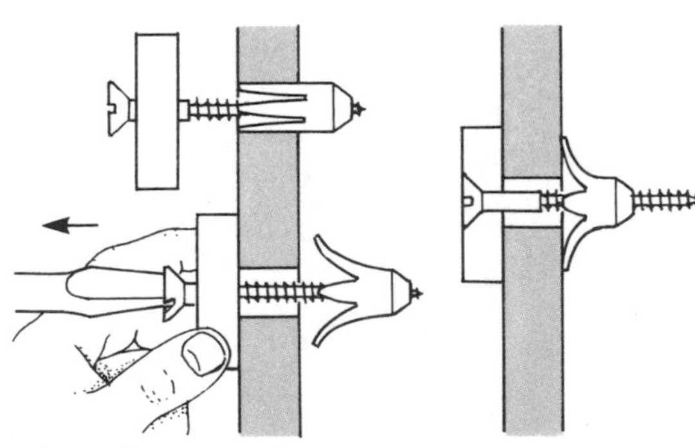
nylon anchor

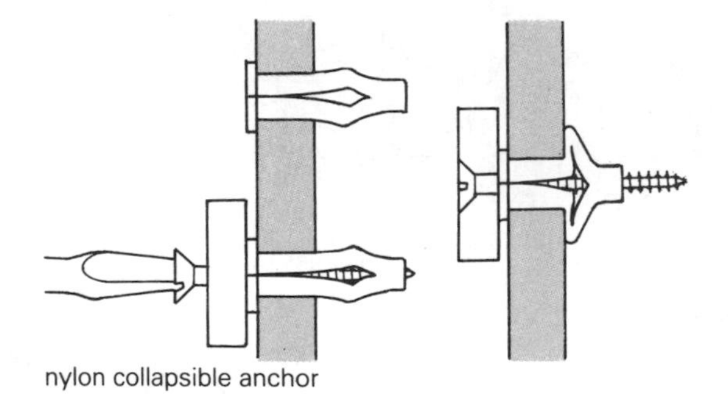
nylon collapsible anchor

Spring Toggles

These are made of metal and spread the load over a wider area, so heavier fitments can be supported, even on a plasterboard wall. The same principle is involved here as with the nylon anchor; the holding device spreads its arms on the inside wall of the cavity. A hole is drilled just big enough to allow the toggle to be passed through, with its spring-loaded arms squeezed together. When the arms are far enough into the cavity they will spring apart. By tightening the screw, the toggle arms and the fitment will close together over the hole.

For cavity wall fixings, the two most common types are the gravity toggle and the spring toggle. Each has a pivot enabling the arm to be pushed through with the screw, although the gravity toggle opens up by its own weight. Should the screws need to be removed at any time, both of these holding devices will fall into the cavity.

One that is retrievable but does the same job is the collapsible anchor. As the screw is driven home, the light metal body of the anchor opens up to form its own holding arms. It works in reverse when the screw is opened, so that the whole fixing can be withdrawn.

An excellent plasterboard fixing can be made using the plas plug. The body of the plug fits neatly into the hole drilled into the plasterboard and stays there. As the screw is driven home the body wedges more tightly in the plasterboard and the arms spread out and take the load behind the plasterboard.

Left: Small 'holdings' for lightweight loads on plasterboard, cavity walls etc.

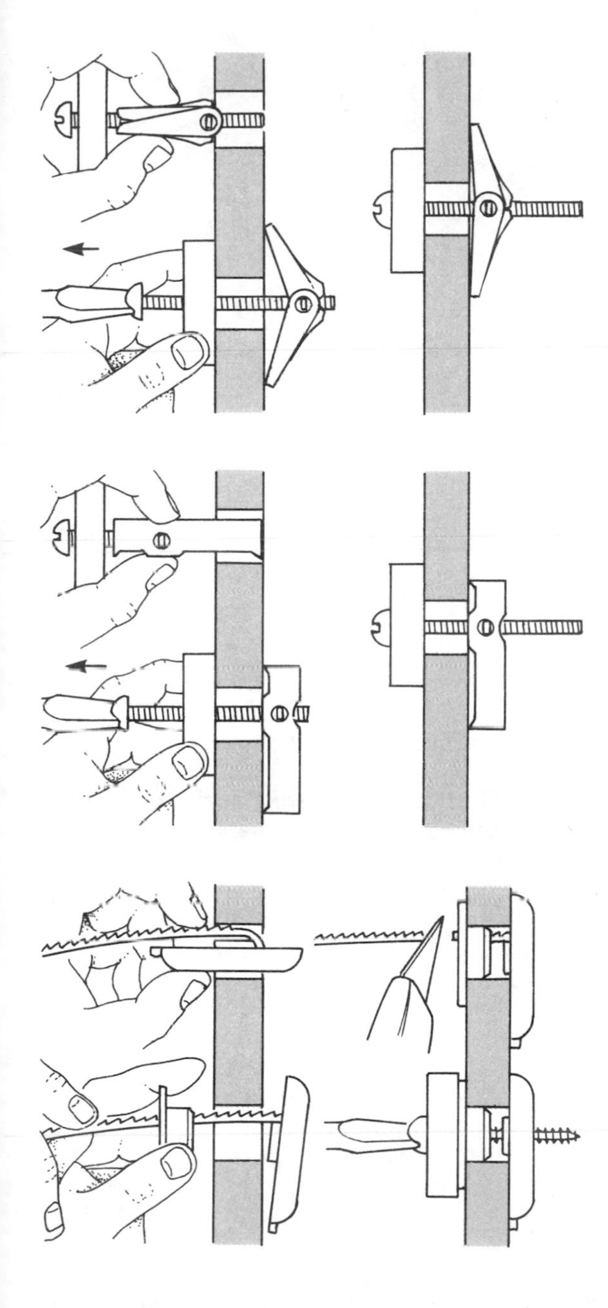

Above: Efficient and secure ways to grip pieces to panel walls of all kinds

Making the Drill Hole

To make holes in plasterboard is fairly easy, but you can weaken the plasterboard considerably if you use gorilla tactics! Pushing hard with a high-speed drill will shatter the back of the plaster-board, thus losing a great deal of strength.

Drilling into wood is easy: the secret is to be gentle. Take care though – larger bits especially can pull the drill too far forward into the wood. Drilling into masonry also calls for care and caution, but you must remember to remove the drill frequently to clear the dust from the hole. If the dust is allowed to collect it sets up a lot of friction and generates heat. Don't stop the drill as you keep removing it, it helps to stay cool that way. For drilling into masonry you'll need a tungsten carbide-tipped drill bit. The package will tell you what size drill, plug and screw to use.

If you're fixing through a window or door frame, extra long drills are available. You will then need to use a frame-fixing plug and screw, which come as a set. You drill through the frame and into the wall in one. The plug is hammered through the wooden frame and into the wall but is designed to be long enough to stay in the wooden frame. This gives a tremendously strong fixing when the screw is driven home. The more sophisticated electric drill will have a hammer blow or percussion action. This is useful when you have to get through hard brick or con-crete. (A carbide-tipped bit is essential for this.)

Fixing Wall Cupboards to Stud Partition Walls

When plumbers need to fix a wash-basin to a stud partition wall they use the principle of bridg-ing. This simply means that they fix a strong piece of timber to two of the posts that make up the stud partition wall. The cross member is bolted to the wooden uprights, so that the wash-basin is absolutely safe and secure. Cavity wall fixings such as spring toggles and collapsible anchors are meant for lightweight fittings, not basins and cupboards. If you are confronted with the problem of hanging, say, a wall cupboard to a stud partition wall, you'll discover that it is still

Right: Two faults and how to put them right; Top: If drilled hole is out of alignment, fill it before starting again; Bottom: If drill jumps, a second smaller plug will fill the hole

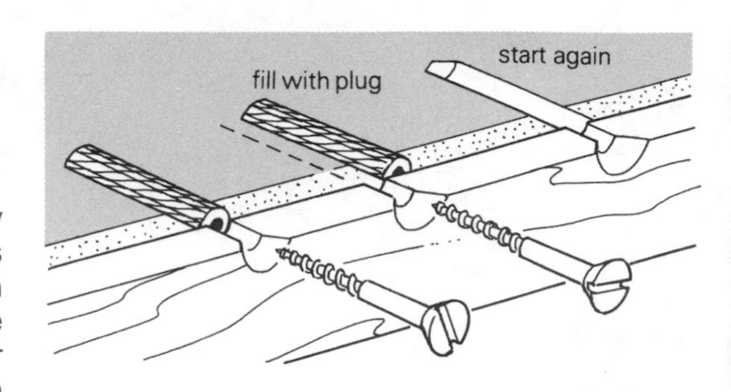

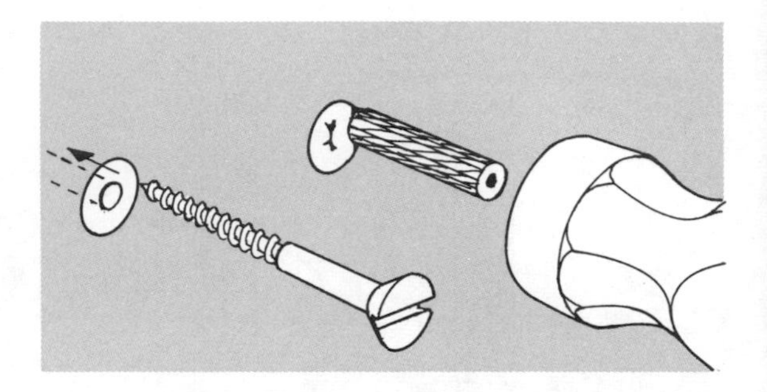

possible by 'bridging'. Locate the studs by tapping the wall, then find the centre of the studs by making a series of small drill holes. (These can be filled in with plaster later on.) Studs are usually 16 inches (40 cm) apart. Mark out your timber support and drill holes to coincide with the centres of the studs. Coach screws are the ideal fixing when strength and reliability are needed. Either fix the cross member on the face of the plasterboard or cut the plasterboard and fix directly to the studs.

If you want the face of the cross member to finish flush with the plasterboard, cut the cross member 6 to 8 inches (15 to 20.5 cm) longer than the outside measurement of the studs. Hold it in position and mark around it with a pencil, cutting out the plasterboard with a trimming knife. If the plasterboard is ½ inch (12 mm) thick and your cross member is 1 inch (25 mm) thick, make a housing joint ½ inch (1 cm) deep in the uprights. (This is simpler than it sounds!) Make horizontal cuts in the uprights ½ inch (1 cm) deep and chop out with a chisel. The cross member is then bolted into the joints, making an incredibly strong support for your wall cupboard.

STRONGER & HEAVIER FIXINGS

Outside the house there is often a need to use a stronger, heavy-duty fixing. Putting up shelves in the garage to support tins of paint; fixing hooks into a brick wall on which to store the ladder; even fixing a washing line or an aerial: all these fixings need to be extra strong and dependable. First of all they must be treated against corrosion and there are special type fixings available. There is even a non-corrosive steel anchor-type bolt, which can be used for fixing fire-escapes and for securing lean-to roofs to the side of the house. When driven home the collar on the bolt produces an airtight seal which protects the holding area from corrosion.

Fixing Curtain Tracks and Poles

If your curtains are going to hang either side of the window, allow 12 to 14 inches (30.5 to 35.5 cm) on the width of the window opening when you order the track or pole. The alternatives are either wall-to-wall curtaining or fitting the track onto the top of the window frame within the recess. Fixing to wood is easy, clean and quick.

Spanning across the tops of all windows is a lintel. These can be timber, especially in older houses, but are more often reinforced concrete. If you are faced with a concrete lintel, you have two choices with which to make the holes for the plugs. A hand-held tool is available, and it's cheap: it's a steel handle into which a hardened bit is inserted. Banging it with a club hammer does make a neat hole, although it can be a bit tiring! Keep twisting the bit to stop it jamming and to clear the dust from the hole. An electric

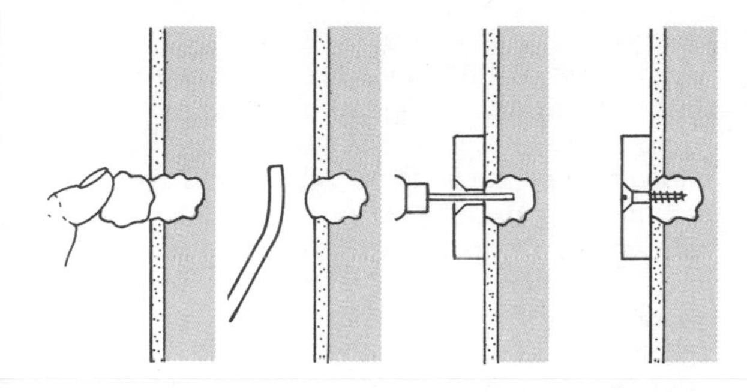

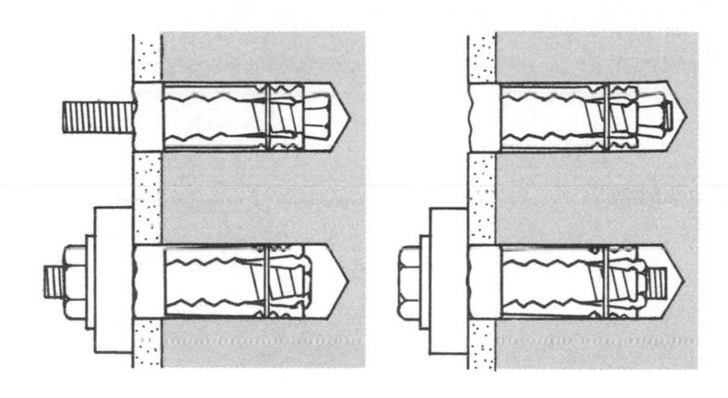

Left: An irregular or oversized hole needs to be filled with a compound filler, which can then be used as a plug; Below left: Two types of expansion bolts, for extra strength

drill with a hammer action is easier and quicker. If you don't own one, it is worth hiring one, especially if you have a number of holes to drill.

To ensure that your curtain pole is going to be level, fix a bracket at one end first and level up the other end by using a piece of string and a spirit level. Space out the intermediate brackets using the string as a level guide. To make fewer fixings in the concrete lintel, you can screw the curtain track or pole to a long batten fixed above the window. You'll need only half the amount of holes to fix the batten to the lintel. Yet another alternative is to fit a much longer curtain pole, so that the brackets either end miss the concrete lintel and are easily fixed into the brickwork.

Most curtain tracks and poles come supplied with screws and plugs. If, for some reason, you find it necessary to use longer screws, make certain that you choose the same gauge, otherwise they will not go through the holes in the brackets. Also, if you find that you are producing a grey powder as you drill and possibly going into a lightweight breeze block, you might have to change the style of plug. Usually a straightforward general-purpose plug is supplied with the kit. If you find that you're going into a lightweight porous block wall, change to the spiral type of plug with the flexible fins.

Flat Packs

Make a scaled plan of your kitchen. Check that the units you want will fit into the space by referring to the illustrated brochure. Check that your cooker and fridge will fit comfortably and check positions of lights and power points. Most self-assembly kitchen and bedroom units are based on a similar principle. They arrive at your home in a flat pack, ready to be assembled with the manufacturer's own specially-designed fixings and instructions. Each part is precision made, all holes drilled for assembling the framework, shelving and hinges. You'll also find packaged all the necessary screws, handles and connector pieces. Involve the family; it will be quicker and more fun.

There are a number of considerations which make it worthwhile to buy self-assembly units. For the budget-conscious homeowner, the thought that tailor-made units are probably twice as expensive must be the most important consideration! Most manufacturers' units are similar in design but methods of fixing vary considerably. All units come with adjustable feet, so unevenness in the floor can be accommodated, before the plinth or toe-kick is clipped on to the feet. Check the alignment of the walls, because if they are uneven you might need to use packing pieces before screwing the frames to the wall. Any gaps showing between the work-top and the wall can be hidden with beading or by decorative tiles.

All manufacturers supply wall cupboard fixings. Some manufacturers supply plugs, with hooks to simplify the job of hanging wall units. The back of the wall unit has two steel plates with slots. The wall needs to be drilled and plugged and fitted with a hooked screw. The unit is then simply lowered on to the hooks and tightened from inside the cupboard. The cupboard is drawn tightly to the wall by a special screw in the hook. This means that it is held securely and cannot be dislodged.

Shop around before you buy. Choose a make that suits your space and pocket.

Glue Gun. An excellent general-purpose adhesive is produced by heating a solid stick of compound in an electric gun. The solid stick is prodded forward to the heated element, resulting in a hot molten glue. The gun is capable of producing a very strong bonding glue, useful for fixing most materials. Manufacturers' instructions are very explicit and will tell you what you can and cannot bond with the glue. The gun is lightweight, inexpensive and very safe if handled properly. Practically every room in the house needs something repairing, sticking or bonding. The gun is suitable for general woodworking, mending furniture, repairs to ornaments; sticking handles to drawers, clasps to handbags, nameplates to doors, and has many more applications.

ELECTRICS 4

All householders should get to know a little about what electricity is, how it gets into our homes and how it works for us. By means of a button or switch, electricity can cook a meal or wash our clothes, so what we're talking about is a source of energy. That energy is available to every one of us via the national electricity grid system all over the UK. It is brought to our homes either by an overhead cable or by cables hidden underground. Somewhere in the house, usually near the front door, is the electricity company's main cable and main fuse. Adjacent to these will be a consumer unit (or fuse box) and a trip switch. A number of wires or cables from the consumer unit take the electricity supply around the house.

If something goes wrong with the electricity supply, lights go out, the kettle doesn't boil or the radio doesn't work. Most people's reaction is 'Oh, a fuse has blown', so a fuse is replaced and the power is switched back on. The lights, however, could go out again! The reason is simple: the fault is still there and it's imperative that the fault is traced.

To many people, electricity is something of a mystery and something that they fear: unless you know what you're doing, electricity can be dangerous. So it's the duty of all householders to get to know something about it. Ask yourself these questions. Do you really know how to wire a plug correctly? Do you know the correct colour coding? Do you know the correct fuse for different appliances? Are you aware that outside lights need special fittings and do you know about continuity testers? This all adds up to awareness of the fundamental principles of electricity.

Perhaps strangely, all the work that electricity does is the result of 'pressure'. Pressure, in electrical terms, is called the 'voltage', and is exerted by the supply. For example, 2 volts, which is what a torch battery gives, produces a small light, whereas the 240 volts mains supply will light up the whole house. It is also the pressure, or number of volts, in the supply that can cause problems if something goes wrong. No harm comes to you if you touch a 2-volt battery, but an accident with 240 volts can be dangerous. Treating electricity with circumspection means that you will become more aware of what you can and cannot do when dealing with wires, sockets and appliances. Think of it this way: electricity flows through wires; if something goes wrong, the very first thing that you must do is stop the flow. First at the nearest power point or socket and then at the consumer unit or fuse box. If a person accidentally touches a live wire, the electricity will flow through that person causing a shock, in which case you'd switch off the flow, or supply, immediately. The alternative is to remove the person from the electricity supply, using something that is non-conducting. You should always remember that metal and water (or wet materials) are very good conductors of electricity, so never use anything metallic or damp near live electricity.

The electricity supply to your home is the electricity company's responsibility as far as the beginning of your own installation; near to your consumer unit is their sealed main fuse. From your consumer unit, wires and cables of different thicknesses carry the supply to the various outlets in the house. The 1 mm cable

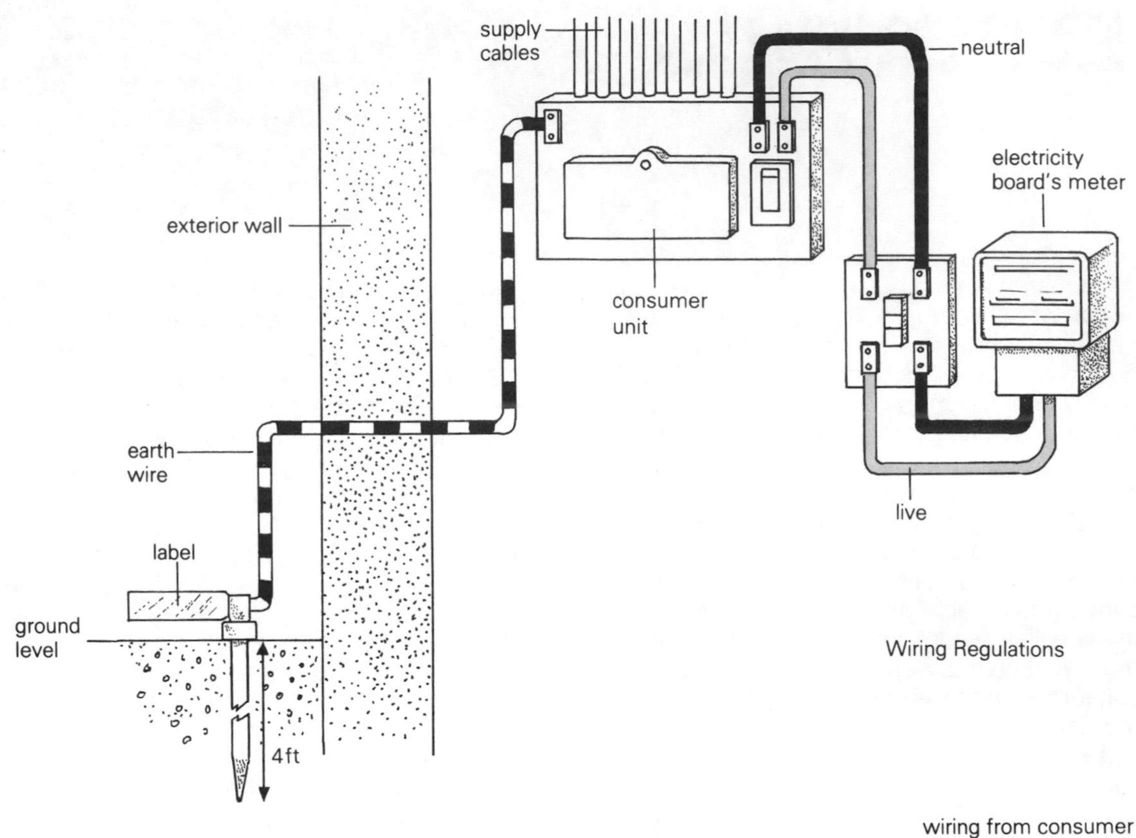

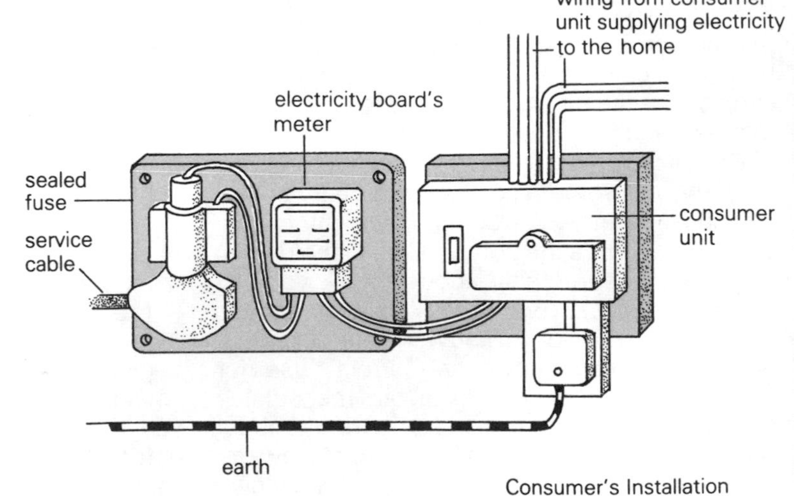

Above right: Simplified layout of meter and consumer unit. The responsibility for all installations and wiring beyond the electricity board's meter is the house owner's; Right: A detail of the consumer unit (also known as the fuse box)

supplies all the lighting points, whilst a 2.5 mm one runs to all the power sockets. Heavier cables are used for such things as cookers.

Probably the most important factor in any electrical installation is 'earthing' and this is our own responsibility. It is a safety factor. Should a fault occur in the circuit, the cause could be damage to a cable: perhaps a nail or a screw has pierced a cable through a floorboard or into a wall. First of all, check all appliances, especially plug connections; check connections in ceiling roses and connections behind wall lights and flexes. You must, of course, switch off the source of the power at the fuse box before dealing with any fault.

The Institute of Electrical Engineers has produced a book which every householder should have handy: a clearly-illustrated 'Guide to Electricity'. It's written by experts but in layman's terms. It tells you, the householder, what you can do with electricity and how to do it.

Probably the simplest electrical job that you'll have to tackle is putting a new fuse in a plug. It's simple, but it's also vitally important, for your safety and for the appliance, to fit the correctly-rated fuse. Electric blankets, tape recorders, clocks, and lighting up to 720 watts need a 3 amp fuse, whereas electric irons, fires, washing machines and fridges need a 13 amp fuse. Always follow the instructions carefully. Never ever be tempted to use anything other than the correct fuse. And if you have any doubts when dealing with electricity, consult an electrician.

FITTING A FUSE

Remove the plug cover by removing the central screw. Lever out the cartridge fuse and try not to disturb the clips. Whilst the cover is off, first of all check that all the screws holding the wires in the terminals are tight. Check that the plastic sheathing covering the wires meets the terminals. Check that all the wires are safely housed inside the terminals. Make sure that the outer covering of the wire is held securely by the cord-clip. Now push the correctly-rated cartridge fuse into the two holders and refit the cover.

WIRING A PLUG

Some older houses might still have socket outlets or power points which take round-end plugs. However, houses built in the last forty years will certainly have been wired with 'ring-main' circuits and the sockets will be single or dual 13 amp outlets with rectangular holes. These take the more common plug which has three flat pins. Whilst wiring the plug, make certain that the fuse is correctly rated. Your television set and possibly your vacuum cleaner could be rated at less than 720 watts, so you might think that a 3 amp fuse is sufficient, but appliances of this nature require a high starting current and the manufacturers recommend a 13 amp fuse. Check the recommended rating every time you wire a plug or replace a fuse.

Always go to a reputable electrical showroom or store to buy your plugs. Poor quality plugs give poor service and could cause problems. The pins can move and cause bad connections and overheating.

Get to know, and understand, the colour code first. Remove about 2 inches (5 cm) of the outer insulation without cutting into the coloured insulation covering the flex. The colour code of the flex is standard. Brown or red is live, blue or black is neutral and green or yellow and green is earth.

After you have removed the cover of the plug, the earth terminal will be at the top of the plug with the clamp at the bottom. The 'live' terminal marked 'L' is on the right near the cartridge fuse and the 'neutral' terminal marked 'N' is on the left. Pop the wires underneath the clamp so that it secures the outer insulation. Your plug may have a 'V' shaped grip, in which to force the outer insulation. You'll see that it is then clamped and cannot be pulled out. Lay each wire as far as its appropriate terminal and carefully remove the insulation with wire strippers or a sharp knife. The insulation must not be short of the terminals and there must be no straggling wires! Allow about ½ inch (1 cm) of bare wire to go into the terminal. If your plug has clamp type terminals, unscrew them to wind the wires round the terminal posts in a clockwise direction. Then replace the screw. You will have wired blue to the neutral terminal, brown to the live terminal and yellow and green to the earth. Make a second check before replacing the cover.

When you buy a new plug, you'll find a cartridge fuse inside it, probably a 13 amp. Don't automatically think that this fuse is the correctly-rated one for your fitting. If you put that onto a metal table-lamp which then goes wrong, you won't have the protection that you should. A light fitting must have a 3 amp fuse in its plug.

REPAIRING A CIRCUIT FUSE

When electricity passes through a wire it produces heat and the thinner the wire the more heat is generated. If a fault occurs in a circuit, the fuse will blow. A fuse is the safety factor in every electrical circuit. It's a thin piece of wire which heats up quickly and melts if more than the safe amount of current passes through it. There are also master fuses either in the consumer unit or in an older type of fuse box. A master fuse will blow if the fuse wire or cartridge is too low a rating, or if an appliance is faulty and is used with an unfused plug or socket. Passage of time can

SAFETY POINTS

1 When dealing with any electrical appliance or electrical connections, whether you are carrying out an investigation or just checking, remember the all-important rule of making it safe by first switching off the power.

2 If the fault is with an electrical appliance, switch off the appliance at the socket and pull out the plug. Remember this too: the fault may be in the switch itself, so don't just depend upon switching off to make it safe.

3 If an emergency occurs and the lights have gone out, make sure that your repair kit is handy. In the kit should be a couple of screwdrivers, a torch, a pair of pliers, a trimming knife and spare fuses.

4 Never load an adaptor with another adaptor and try to run four or five appliances from it.

5 If you can't get the pins of a plug into a socket, don't try to open up the socket with something like a steel knitting needle!

6 Always keep a chemical fire-extinguisher handy in the house. Never use water to put out a fire in an electrical appliance.

7 Extension cords and flexes should never be trailed over radiators or heating pipes. The insulation could dry out, crack and cause a short-circuit.

8 The lighting circuit must only be used for lights. Never change the plug fitting of an appliance to use it in the lighting circuit.

9 Lightning has to go to earth somewhere. Being high up, television aerials are especially vulnerable. Switch off your set during a thunderstorm.

10 If you want to change the shade on a table lamp, wait until it's completely cool: a lot of heat is generated around the fitting. It can become difficult to unscrew, but take out the plug (as *always* when dealing with light fittings) and take your time.

11 If you have a test screwdriver that is activated by holding your finger onto a metal button, treat it with caution. Should it be faulty in any way at all, *you* will be the conductor of electricity.

12 Wire-strippers will do their job efficiently virtually unaided, so don't pull at the insulation. Always measure carefully the amount of insulation you need to remove: none of the wire should show outside the terminal when the connection is made. Lastly, when stripping flex of its insulation, take care not to sever any of the fine strands. The gauge of the flex will be reduced and therefore also its current capacity.

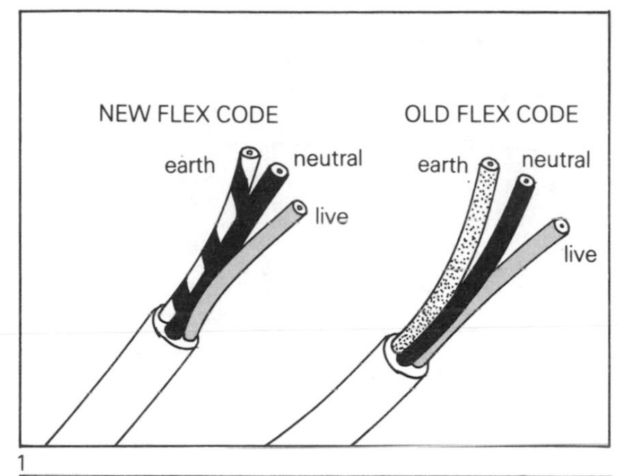

1

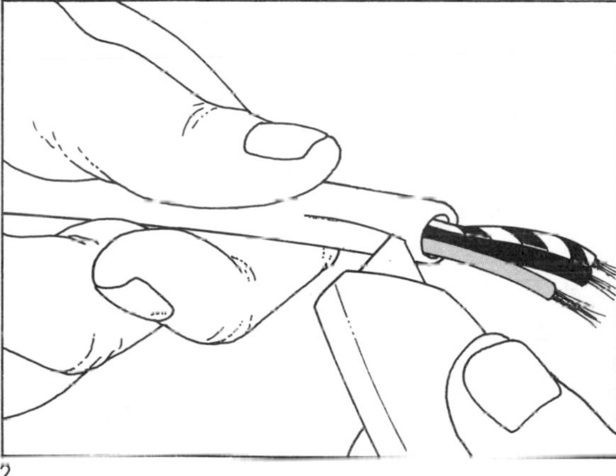

2

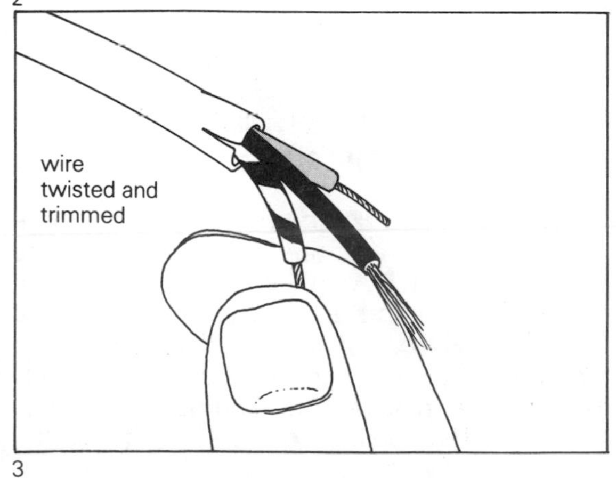

3

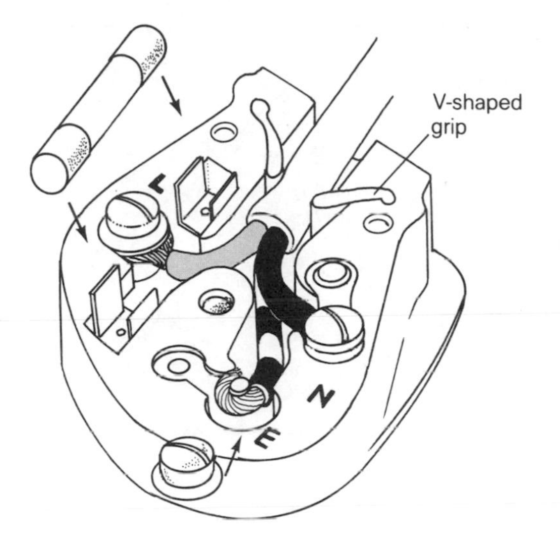

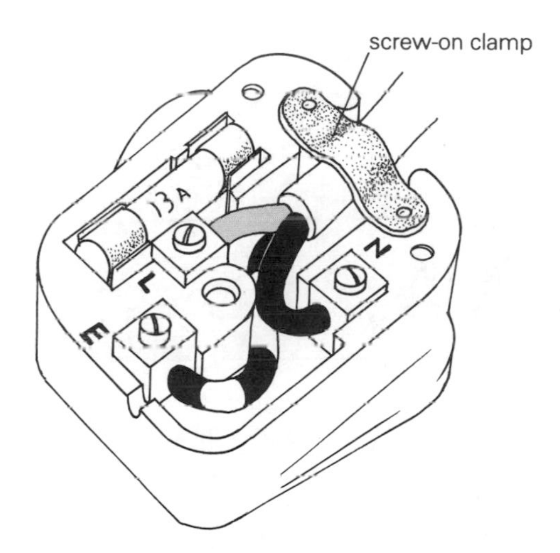

Top left: Colour coding for live, neutral and earth – old and new; Centre left: Use a trimming knife with care when stripping back the insulation – not only for the sake of the wiring but also for your fingers!; Left: It's important not to have straggling wires and for the insulation to go right up to the terminals
Above: Two kinds of plug with different clamps and terminals

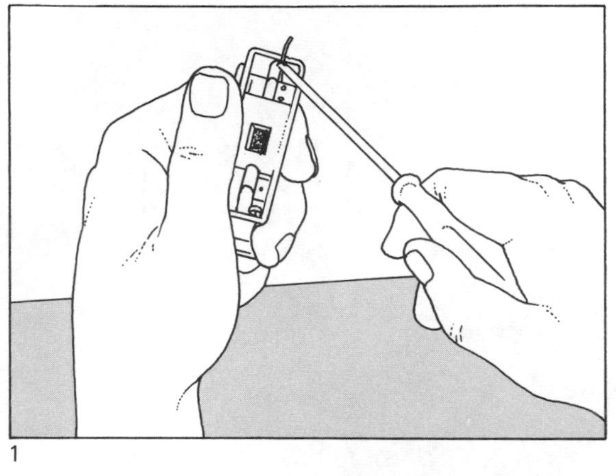
1

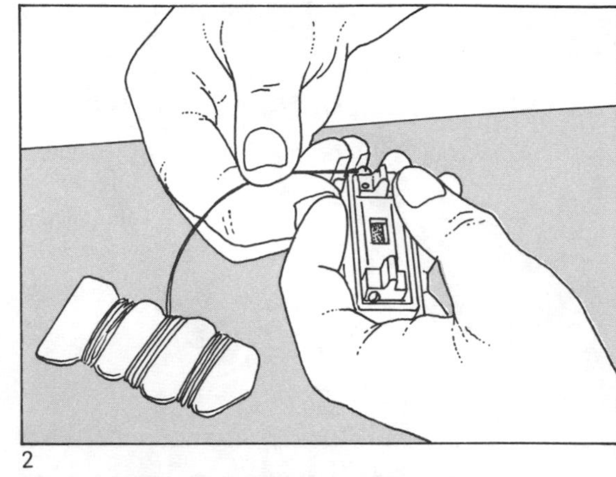
2

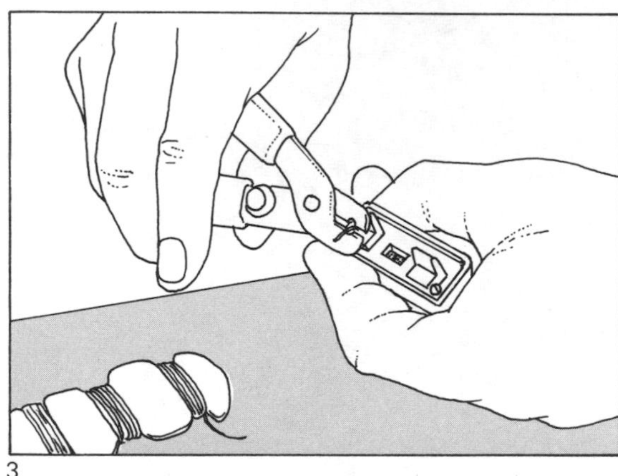
3

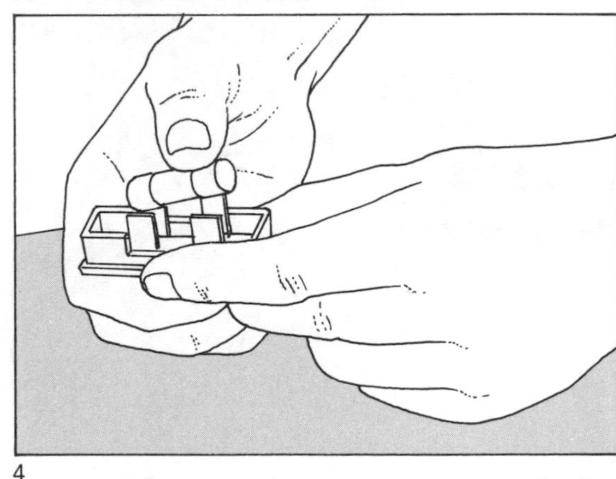
4

also cause a fuse to blow; it simply gets old!

Before repairing any fuse, switch off the power. The main switch could be on the consumer unit or on a separate switch-box nearby.

Each separate circuit in the house has a separate fuse. These are housed in a consumer unit or fuse box close to the electricity company's meter. You could have one of two main types of fuse: either a rewirable fuse or a cartridge.

Rewirable Fuse

This type has been in use for years and has a fuse wire stretched along a channel in a porcelain holder. Two screws hold the wire at either end. (Always keep a card of wire near the consumer unit; fuse wire is inexpensive and comes in three ratings, 5 amp, 15 amp, and 30 amp.) Pull out the fuse carriers one by one until you find the blown fuse, then slacken the screws, remove the old fuse wire and clean off any charring. Choose the fuse wire of the correct rating, secure the ends round the terminal and tighten up the screws. Two important points: don't over-tighten the wire and always cut off loose ends.

Above: Repairing and replacing fuses. 1. Clean out old wire; 2. Wind correctly-rated wire around terminals; 3. Trim off neatly; 4. Cartridge fuses are simply pressed into place

Cartridge Fuses

Once you've located the blown cartridge fuse and removed it, it has to be replaced, not rewired. Fortunately it is impossible to fit the wrong master cartridge fuse because each amp rating has a different size cartridge. You'll find them colour coded too: 45 amp is green; 30 amp is red; 20 amp is yellow; 15 amp is blue and 5 amp is white.

A more sophisticated system used in some domestic consumer units is a Miniature Circuit Breaker (MCB). If a fault occurs or a circuit is overloaded, these automatically switch themselves off. They are very sensitive to faults. When you have found and corrected the fault, the circuit can be reconnected simply by flicking the switch on the circuit breaker.

Labelling the Consumer Unit

Pulling out a number of fuse-carriers to locate a blown fuse is tedious and unnecessary. Most consumer units have a numbered panel, which corresponds with the number of fuse carriers in the box, so it makes sense to label each carrier indicating exactly what circuit it controls. For example, 'upstairs lights'; 'immersion heater'; 'ground-floor ring-main'; and so on. If the upstairs lights have gone out, you'll immediately know which fuse carrier to go to.

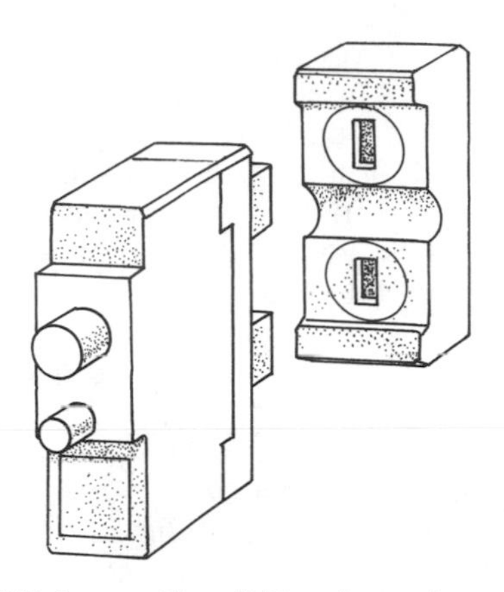

Above: Miniature Circuit Breakers give greater protection to your home

KEEPING AN EYE ON THE COST

You can check just how much one unit of electricity costs, either from the electricity company or from your electricity bill. Storage heaters on a separate circuit cost less. Every time that you flick a switch to light up something, cook something or heat something, units of electricity are ticking up on your meter. If you turn on an electric fire for one hour and the fire is 1 kW (or 1000 watts), you will have used one unit of electricity.

APPLIANCE	*WATTAGE*	*UNITS PER WEEK (approx)*
Electric blanket	100	1
Food mixer	400	1
Freezer *(thermostatically controlled)*	300	7
Hair-dryer	350	2
Electric fire	2000	30
Immersion heater *(lagged and thermostatically controlled)*	3000	50
Electric iron	1000	4
Kettle	2500	5
Five electric lights	100 each	7
Colour television	350	7
Toaster	1000	1
Vacuum cleaner	500	5
Washing machine	2500	10

Having checked on your electricity bill the cost per unit, you'll know exactly how much you're paying for one hour's heat. If you knew the wattage of all fittings and appliances that you use and approximately for how long you use them in a week, you could then begin to calculate your electricity costs.

Compare the number of watts of the appliances in the chart. The average number of units used in a week is shown in the last column. Let's take, for example, five electric lights burning five 100-watt light bulbs for two hours each night; remember that 1000 watts burning for one hour is one unit of electricity. 500 watts burning for two hours, therefore, is also one unit's consumption (that is, 1 kW). For seven days, the equivalent is seven units (7 kW). Multiply seven units by the cost per unit and you have the total cost of the lighting. It's as simple as that!

If you have a digital meter, it's very easy to check your electricity consumption over a period of a week or a month. Make a note of the numbers over a certain period and subtract them to find how much electricity you have used in units, then multiply that number by the cost per unit as shown on your electricity bill. Working from the appliance/unit chart, you will then be able to assess where the most electricity is consumed.

DIMMER SWITCHES

You can easily and cheaply improve the lighting effects in your home by the addition of a dimmer switch, which enables you to change your lighting effects from subtle to bright at the touch of a button. Stairways, landings and nurseries can have low-key lighting for long periods at very little cost. You don't have to go to a specialist electrical store to buy a dimmer switch: most DIY outlets have a large selection of the best on the market. You buy them as a simple kit with full, illustrated instructions. All you have to do to install one is to replace your present switch cover with the same size dimmer switch cover. Behind each cover are wires screwed into terminals – your job is to switch them over. Before you do that, you've got to make yourself familiar with the colours of the wires (i.e. the colour coding) and the letters stamped on the terminals.

There are two popular types of dimmer switch. The more sophisticated and expensive type is the 'touch control' dimmer. It appears to have no switch but, as the name suggests, the square switch-plate is sensitive to the touch and the light is controlled simply by putting your finger on it. The on/off is operated simply by touching it and you then vary the amount of light by the pressure on the flat control panel.

The cheaper and more popular type is the 'rotary' dimmer. This is turned off and on by turning the central knob: turning the knob further increases the brightness of the light. Some manufacturers provide an on and off switch at the side of the dimmer control knob.

One important point for you to consider, however, is the mode of lighting in that room. Most dimmer switches are not suitable for controlling fluorescent lights; they are only suitable for normal tungsten light bulbs. Manufacturers supply DIY stores with leaflets telling you all about dimmer switches; all essential installation details are included, as well as loading information. (Loading refers to the number of watts – the usual maximum loading for a dimmer switch is 400 watts, but it can vary.)

Dimmer switches are ideal for changing the lighting effects and atmosphere in bedrooms, sitting-rooms and dining-rooms. It is perhaps inadvisable to use them in workshops, separate WCs, bathrooms and kitchens. Note that you can only use one dimmer switch to control each set of lights. If, however, you want to be ultra-sophisticated and make use of advanced technology, there are some amazing innovations on the market. Lights can be dimmed with remote control units by installing an infra-red beam system; time-delay switches are available which will dim the lights at a set time. There are also dimmer switches which can be fixed to plugs, so that standard and table lamps can also be controlled. The ultimate model is one that incorporates an automatically-timed fading device. Its soporific effect must make it ideal for a bedroom when children are going to sleep!

Installing a Dimmer Switch

Most modern switch plates are held to a wall-mounted box by two screws. The size of plate and the screws are standard, making replacement with a dimmer switch quite simple. A single standard switch must, of course, be replaced by a single dimmer switch: a single dimmer switch cannot be used in place of a double or multiple switch.

Firstly, switch off the power. If each lighting circuit is marked in your consumer unit, it's easy to isolate just that circuit, so you still have power and light in the rest of the house. (Always double check that you've removed the correct fuse.) A circuit tester will show you that it's safe to get on with the job.

Take out the two retaining screws of the switch and you'll find that the plate hangs down 2 or 3 inches (5 or 7.5 cm) on the cables. Have the dimmer switch instructions in front of you, alongside the dimmer switch (face down). Refer to the instructions and double check that you know which cable goes to which terminal. The markings on the dimmer switch will be similar to those on a normal switch, although they could be in a slightly different position. Before you disconnect the wires to take off the existing switch plate, check you've understood which is live and which is switched. Make a little sketch of the plate and terminals so that you won't forget. The live conductor is red and connected to the 'common' terminal marked 'C'; the switched conductor is black with a red sleeve and is connected to the terminal marked 'L2'. Loosen the screws and take off the plate. Look at the instructions, and look at the back of the dimmer plate. Make another little sketch showing which wire goes to which terminal. Loosen the terminal screws (but not too much or they'll fall out and you'll loose them) and connect the red live conductor to the common terminal and the black with red sleeved conductor to the other terminal. Make sure the end of each wire is not damaged, with no stray bits sticking out. Tighten the terminal screws and then give a little tug at each wire, just enough to ensure that the wire is trapped. Lastly, if there is a fuse in the dimmer switch and it's more than 3 amp, change it. Gently ease the back of the dimmer switch into the box, pop in the retaining screws and tighten up. All you have to do now is to replace the lighting circuit fuse (or switch on the power) and wait until evening to show off the atmospheric modification and dramatic improvement to your lighting!

Some additional points. When you first take off the existing switch plate and look inside the box, you might find two cables connected to the switch. This means that the switch is wired into a second switch. One cable will have three cores and the other one four. The four core will be: a

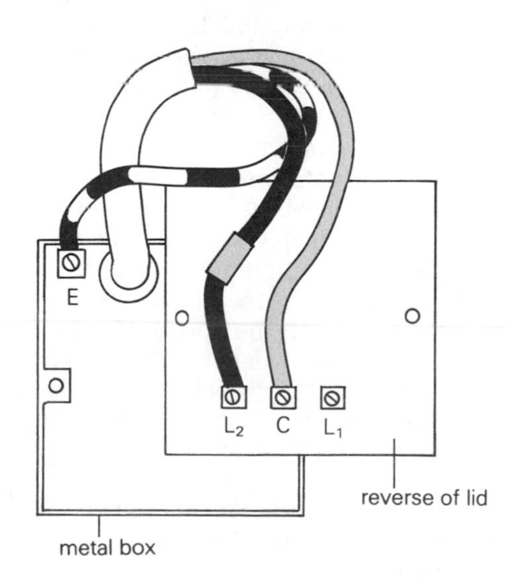

Right: Installing a dimmer switch. Switch off supply before taking faceplate off switch. Connect existing wires as indicated on dimmer switch instructions

red live conductor; one blue and a yellow conductor and a green and yellow earth conductor. It is obviously slightly more complex than the simple dimmer switch wiring and you must refer to the specific manufacturer's instructions for two-way wiring. A standard wiring diagram does not exist, since there are variations from dimmer to dimmer. Never make the cardinal error of thinking that you'll get it right, without double checking everything! Only by following the manufacturer's instructions will you do it properly and safely.

ADDITIONAL CEILING LIGHTS & SWITCHES

A number of favourable conditions have to exist, in order for you to add an extra ceiling light and a wall switch. Ideally you should be able to lift the upstairs floor coverings and floorboards and get to the ceiling joists. If you can accomplish that with little difficulty then you're over the first hurdle. It now means that you have easy access to an existing ceiling rose. Since the 1960s, the lighting circuit in electrical installations has been the loop-in system, where the cable only goes as far as the last light on the circuit and does not return to the consumer unit (as a ring-main to the power points does). This makes it very easy to add an extra light by taking the supply from an existing ceiling rose. Older houses that have been rewired should conform to this system.

The Installation in Detail

You'll need to drill two ½-inch (1-cm) holes in the ceiling, one at the new light position and one immediately above the new switch position. Find the appropriate fuse or switch in the consumer unit to turn off the power. (Double check with a circuit tester.) Use 1 mm (min) two core and earth PVC sheathed cable for your extra ceiling light installation. Unscrew the ceiling rose and let the cover slip down.

Right: The correct wiring for adding an extra light and switch, showing new wires taken from existing ceiling rose

Now make a sketch of the fitting showing the coloured wires and the terminals. From above, push about 9 inches (23 cm) of cable down through the hole in the ceiling that you'll find at the existing lighting point. Drill holes through each joist about 2 inches (5 cm) down (so that nails can't go through the cable) and thread the cable through the holes to the new light position. Leave about 12 inches (30.5 cm) of cable hanging down through the hole.

Next, push a separate piece of cable up through the hole above the switch position. Leave sufficient cable to connect to the new switch and have enough cable above the ceiling to go through the drilled holes in the joists and to

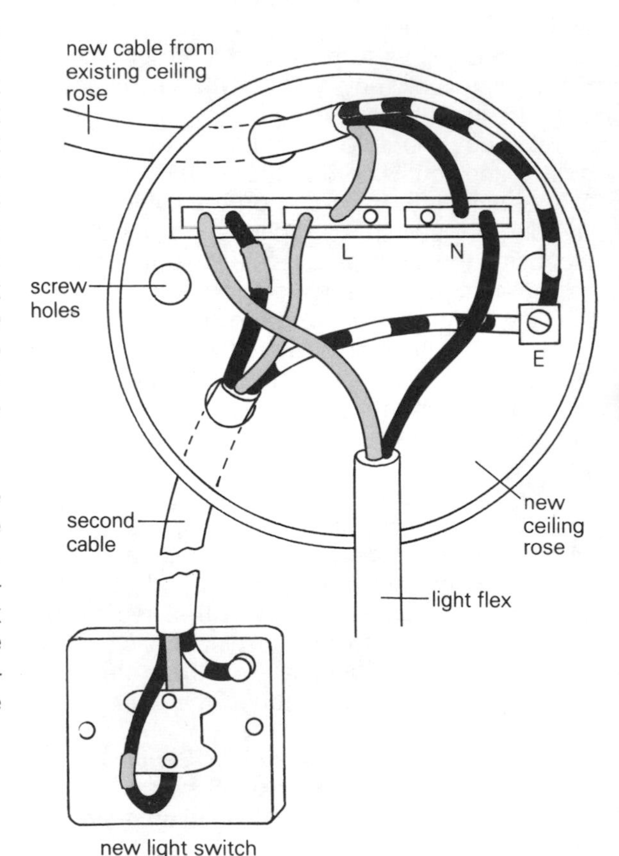

leave about 12 inches (30.5 cm) hanging down through the hole at the new lighting point position. Make sure that your new light position coincides with a timber or joist to which you can screw a new ceiling rose. You might need to knock out a little bit of plastic in the base of the ceiling rose through which you can push the wires. Fix the rose to the ceiling with screws that are long enough to go into the ceiling joist.

Remove about 2 inches (5 cm) of the outer sheath from the end of the new cable (which comes from the existing light position). It's a good idea to mark the first wire with tape before you start. You'll have a red and a black wire exposed after taking off the outer insulation. Remove about ¼ inch (6 mm) of the insulation from the ends of the red and the black wires.

Inside the new ceiling rose you'll find a terminal block. Hold the end of the red wire in one of the terminal holes in the centre of the terminal block marked 'L' and tighten the screw. The black wire is screwed in the middle hole (there are usually three) of the neutral terminal marked 'N'. Push the slack cable back into the ceiling through the hole. The second cable has to be prepared in the same way. Connect the red wire into one of the other two holes in the terminal marked 'L'. You must now cut a short piece of red PVC sleeving and slip it over the black wire. (This is a statutory regulation.) The black wire now has to go into the inner hole of the two-hole terminal block. More sleeving is wanted, but green this time, to be slipped over the bare earth wires, covering them completely. Connect the wires to the terminal marked 'E'.

You will have prepared a lamp-holder with a length of flex to match the existing light in the room. The flex now has to be connected to the new ceiling rose terminal block. Strip about 3 inches (7.5 cm) of insulation from the two core flex which goes through the cover first. Take off about ¼ inch (6 mm) of insulation from the brown and blue wires. Connect the brown to the outer hole of the switch wire terminal and the blue to the outer hole of the neutral terminal marked 'N'. Go back over all the terminal screws to make certain they are securely holding the wires. Little anchor pieces will take the weight off the lamp-holder when the flex is hooked over them. Offer up the ceiling rose cover and tighten it to its base.

If this is your first attempt at electrical wiring, it should give you a lot of confidence to tackle the rest of the job: the switch is next!

Surface-Mounted Switch. This is far easier to fix than the flush-mounted type. If the switch is to be flush you must use a metal knockout box (with ready-made holes for feeding cable through) sunk into the plaster. As for the cable from the ceiling to the switch, you have a choice of either mounting it on the surface using plastic cable clips or cutting a channel in the plaster and burying it in a plastic conduit. Hold the switch box in position against the wall and mark the screw holes. Drill, plug and screw to fix it in place. Strip the end of the cable as you did for the ceiling rose. The red wire is connected to the common terminal. A short piece of red PVC sleeving must enclose the black wire, which is connected to the other terminal. For safety, the earth wire must be enclosed in a full length of green PVC sleeving and is connected not to the switch top but to the earth terminal in the mounting box. Two screws will hold the switch top to the box.

Connecting to the Existing Ceiling Rose. Remove the outer insulation and prepare the ends of the wires of the new cable, as you did for the ceiling rose. Connect the red wire to the centre terminal, the black wire to the neutral terminal and the earth wire, with its green sleeving in place, to the earth terminal. If an existing earth wire is unsleeved, disconnect it and sleeve it before reconnecting. Now make sure that the lamp-holder flex is secured. The brown goes to the outer hole of the switch-wire terminal and the blue to the outer hole of the neutral terminal. Be certain that the other ends of the cable are secure in the lamp-holder. Screw back the ceiling rose cover.

Put back any floorboards or carpets you might have removed in the room above and then restore the power. You can now bask in the extra illumination supplied by your very own efforts.

TELEVISION AERIALS & SOCKETS

The sight of television aerials sprouting from roof tops is common all over the UK. The television set is an accepted part of our furniture. There is no need, however, for a great number of those aerials to be on the roof. It could be an unnecessary expense to hire a professional aerial rigger, if the reception in your area is excellent. There are a number of sources for you to check on how good the signal is where you live. The BBC and the IBA each have an information department to help you with your enquiries. Local television dealers are also a source of information concerning television reception. Another indication of the strength of the signal locally is the number of aerials which you can see on the roofs in your district.

If the reception in your area is outstanding, you're in luck: you need only buy an indoor aerial which sits on the top of the set. Your local television dealer will advise you on the make and type of aerial best suited to your set. You could find that the quality of reception in your area does not call for a roof-top aerial, but isn't good enough to produce a good picture using a room aerial either. In this case you have two alternatives, each one a DIY job. Either fit an aerial beneath the eaves of the house, which is capable of providing very good reception, or in the loft. In either case you'll need advice as to the type of aerial needed to achieve the best picture.

The advantages of siting an aerial in the loft yourself are numerous. In most cases, you'll get almost as good a reception as if the aerial were high on the roof; you'll have no outside maintenance costs, no expensive charges to meet for a professional rigger, and no cables to replace when high winds cause them to chafe and lose their outer insulation. The aerial and the cable can be fixed inside the house where you choose.

Fixing Up the Cable

The shortest possible run of cable between the aerial and the set is the best. The cable is not cheap and besides, the less cable the better the

Right: Cable connector; Below: Coaxial cable for aerials; Bottom: Braid clamp and plug

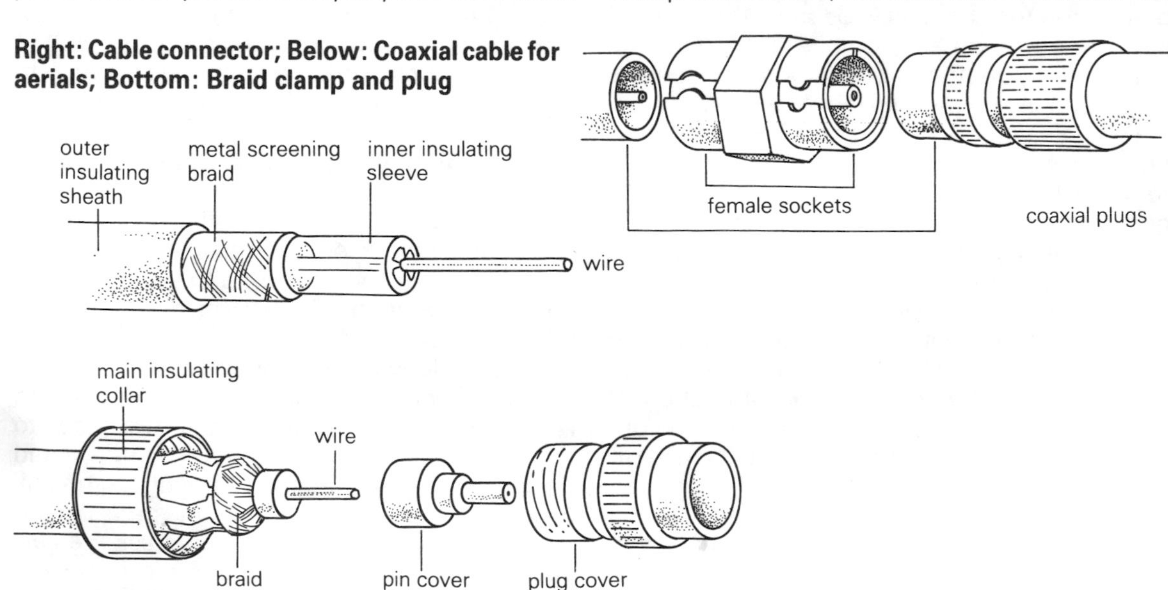

picture, so when you've chosen the best positions for the television set and the aerial, you must then measure the distance between them. Choose an inconspicuous run for the cable – you can run it in plastic conduit or fix it to walls or door frames with cable clips. When you buy the cable, ask for a low-loss coaxial cable. This is made up of an outer covering and with a metal screening braid inside that. An inner insulating sleeve surrounds the signal-carrying wire. When holding or laying the cable, make sure that you don't bend it sharply or you will ruin your picture.

As well as having bought the cable and cable clips, you'll need the plug which connects the cable to the back of the television set. Allow sufficient cable near the television set to be connected without kinks or sharp bends. Carefully cut off about 1½ inches (3.5 cm) of the outer insulating sheath. Take care not to cut through the braid but fold it back to leave about ¾ inch (2 cm) of the inner insulating sleeve clear. Very carefully cut off about ½ inch (1 cm) of this inner insulation. Next separate the parts of the plug and push the end of the cable through the plug collar, so that the braid clamp tightens onto the folded-back braid. Thread the thin inner wire carefully into the pin unit, so that the inner insulation slips inside the pin unit body. Ease on the other end of the plug, screwing it into the plug collar. The other end of the cable has to be connected to a junction box on the aerial. Allow sufficient cable to be able to move the aerial around in order to get the best picture. If the aerial is in your loft, take it to the highest position that you can. Cold-water storage tanks made of galvanised steel have been known to deflect signals, so if you have one in the loft take the aerial as far as possible away from it.

Wiring up the Junction Box

Strip the end of the cable and prepare it exactly as you did for the plug. The cable now has to be connected to the junction box of the aerial, so find the hole in the side of the junction box protected by a rubber seal. The seal will have a hole through which you push the cable. Directly opposite the opening is a terminal with a small screw. Thread the inner wire into the terminal and tighten the screw. The exposed braid must be held securely by the metal clamp which is adjacent to the rubber grommet. Check there are no loose screws and replace the cover. You are now ready to establish the correct position for the aerial. You need to talk to the Television Engineering Information Service to discover the location of your nearest television transmitter. This is important because you have to point the aerial so that the shortest element, or cross piece, is the one nearest to the transmitter. Switch on the set and you'll get a picture. Now you need help from one of the family to establish the best picture. Whilst you are directing the aerial to the best position possible, you can be told by the other person when the best and clearest picture appears. Fix the aerial in that position, so that it won't move.

BURGLAR ALARMS

In practically every police station in the UK a Crime Prevention Officer is available to give free advice – not only on crime prevention but more especially on the system of home-security most suitable for your home. They will visit you by appointment and spend time looking around the inside and the outside of your property. Their advice and knowledge of all security devices will prove invaluable, and when you consider that a million homes a year are broken into, it is certainly worth considering a burglar alarm kit suitable for a DIY installation. The CPO will have pamphlets illustrating how any possible entry points can be protected. Before you consider any type of installation the officer might ask you to take into account the following considerations. A burglar alarm system that you install yourself is not likely to be acceptable by your insurance company. Do you have a cat or a dog who is normally left indoors whilst you're away? If so, your pet could accidentally trigger off the system. Are you happy to have to secure all the doors and windows every time you go out, even for a short while? Are you willing for a neighbour to hold spare keys of the alarm and of your house? If nobody does, bells could ring for long periods unnecessarily. The local police, of course, must have your (and your neighbour's) addresses and telephone numbers.

Your Choice of System

By the time you are ready to make your choice of the system most suitable to your own home, be it a house or a flat, you will have assessed all the available information. Either you fit a wired circuit into the mains electricity supply or you fit separate home security – internal electronic door and window alarms.

The mains circuit alarm system has a number of components: an outside bell; an inside bell; a control box; a number of activating sensors and a separate panic button. When the key is turned and the alarm is set, an intruder will disturb one of the sensors and the alarm will sound. (It is also possible to link the system direct to a police station.)

The security of your home can also be assured by fitting internal electronic door alarms. This separate system gives you great flexibility in that you can choose door alarms suitable for any door in the house. There is also a very wide range of door and window locks available, door security bolts, window stay locks, lockable window handles, door-chains and push bolts. Full instructions are printed on the packets of each of these devices. The instructions are easy to follow, the locks and alarms simple to fit. From your basic tool kit you'll need a drill, a hammer, a bradawl and a screwdriver.

The Electronic Door Alarm

This alarm is suitable for interior doors and flush fitting windows and it is well designed and unobtrusive when fitted. The two parts are simply fixed by four screws. When switched on, the loud eighty decibel battery-operated alarm will be activated if the door is forced open. Even if an intruder closes the door the alarm will continue to sound. To stop the alarm, the switch has to be turned off.

For added security to internal and external wooden doors, strong brass security bolts can be fitted. A door push-bolt is ideal for french windows. In addition to the door alarm on your front door, a door-chain or door 'limiter' will give you added security and a very useful device is the door viewer, which enables you to view a visitor without being seen yourself. The latter's use, however, is limited to daylight hours, unless you have an exterior light-fitting.

The Wired Circuit System

Tiny magnetic pads are fixed to doors, windows and frames. These are magnetic switches, the most popular device for use in a wired circuit system. The alarm sounds when the system is switched on and the door or windows are opened. This is the type of burglar alarm most popular with the DIY installer. One advantage of using magnetic switches between a door and its frame is that the two surface contacts can be as far apart as ½ inch (1 cm), and even movement or rattling of a window by the wind will not break the contact. (Once switched on, the alarm system will be activated whether a door is opened accidentally or by force, so it is important that all catches on doors and windows fitted with surface contacts can be securely closed.)

Contacts can also be put under carpets or mats, where an intruder might have to step to get into a room. (Obviously if your pet dog is used to sleeping at the foot of the stairs, you'll have to take this into account!)

All alarm systems carry full fitting instructions. Read them as many times as you need, so that you know exactly how and where to fix. A panic button, for example, can be fixed by your bedside, although you might consider it more important to have the panic button close to the front door. If you do have an unwanted visitor, a door-chain will bar entry for enough time to allow you to make full use of the panic button. When you're fixing the wiring, take extra care with the connections. Loose wires or faulty connections result in false alarms. The contacts placed under carpets must have no wires showing and the

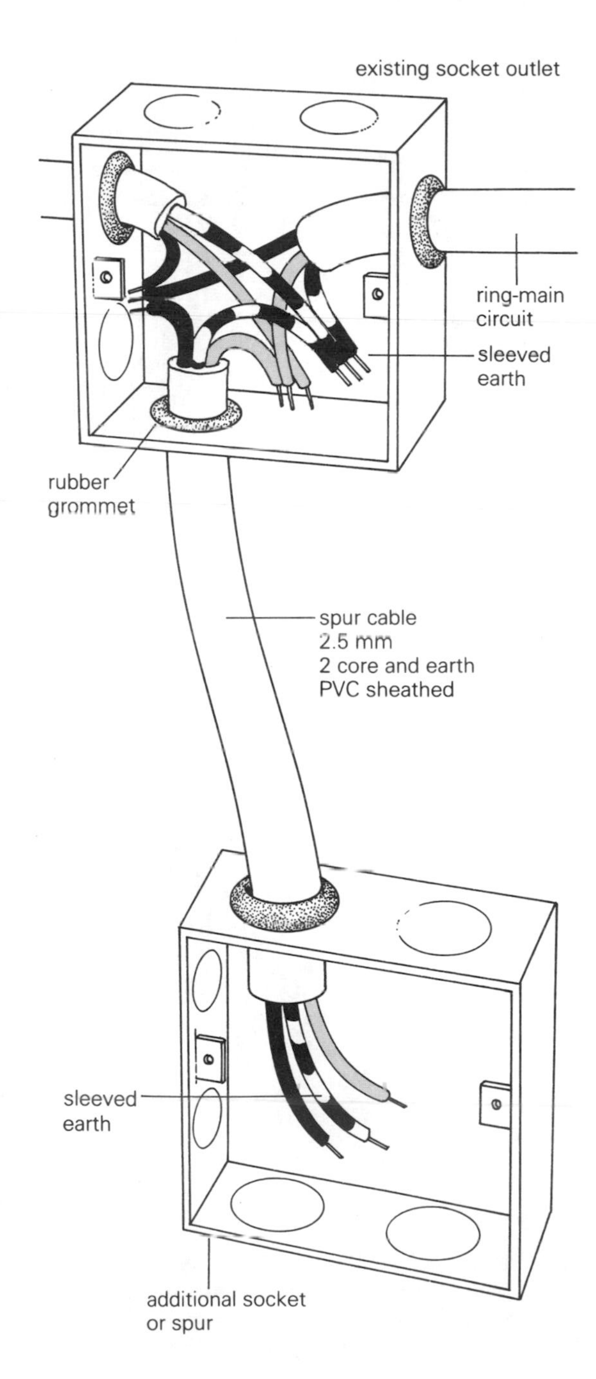

wires and the contacts must not be allowed to move. You can secure the mats with double-sided sticky-tape. Hide the control box so that it is not immediately visible, but is easily accessible to you. The outside bell should, of course, be on view to everyone.

AN ADDITIONAL POWER POINT

If this is the first additional power point that you've installed, your best plan is to add a single power point to an existing single power point and use the shortest possible run of cable. Make certain that there are no pipes or wires buried in the wall. The easiest socket to mount is one that is screwed to the surface of the wall. There are removable small discs in the socket box knock one out to push the 2.5 mm cable through. Fix the new socket in place and run the cable in first. Release the screws on the new socket terminals (which will be marked 'E' for earth, 'N' for neutral, and 'L' for Live). See page 69 for colour coding.

Strip back the correct length of the outer insulation with the wire-strippers at the correct gauge. Remove about ⅜ inch (just under 1 cm) of insulation from the cores. Use a green and yellow PVC sheath on the earth wire before connecting it. Check that the cores are into the correct terminals and that the insulation goes as far as the terminal holes. Screw the socket plate to its box. Either surface-mount the cable using cable clips or run the cable through conduit chased (or embedded) in the plaster. Leave sufficient cable to make the connection to the existing power point.

The branch or 'spur' that you now have in position has to be connected to the electricity supply via a convenient socket. The socket will be on a ring-main circuit. At the consumer unit, switch off the power to this ring-main.

Left: Siting an extra socket. Try to use an existing socket on the same floor as the spur: this avoids confusion at consumer unit

(You might, of course, live in an old house that does not have a consumer unit and a ring-main circuit. In this case it is not possible to add a power point to what is probably a radial circuit. This is where round pin plugs are to be found!)

If any spurs have already been added to the ring-main circuit, you must find out how many. You cannot add more than four spurs.

Wiring to the Ring-Main

On opening up the existing socket, you should find two cables entering the box (if there's only one, it'll already be a spur). Your new cable can enter the box by removing a 'knockout'. Remove the outer insulation and the coloured insulation to the cores as previously indicated. Release the screws in the terminals to allow another wire of the same colour to be added to each terminal. Sleeve the earth wire with a green and yellow sheath. Double check that the terminal screws are holding the three wires firmly and that the three wires are not twisted together as they go into the terminal. You need to push the connections inside the box without having to force them in with the socket plate. Fix the plate with the retaining screws. Now switch on at the mains.

SHAVER SOCKETS

Even though it's called a 'shaver socket', it can be connected to the lighting circuit. There are two types of unit into which a shaver can be plugged. A shaver supply-unit has a transformer and is meant to be installed in a bathroom. A shaver socket-outlet is for use in bedrooms. All electric razors have two-pin plugs and will not fit into an ordinary socket outlet. You'll notice also that the plug is an integral part of the core cable. The reason for this is the obvious one of safety and for that reason too you must never ever consider fitting an ordinary socket in a bathroom.

Installing the Shaver Socket Outlet

As well as the shaver socket outlet, you'll need sufficient 1 mm two-core and earth PVC sheathed cable to run from the outlet, down the wall and under the floorboards to the point above

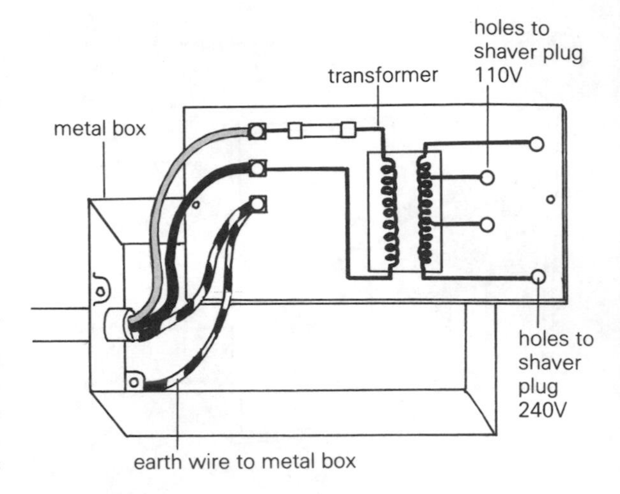

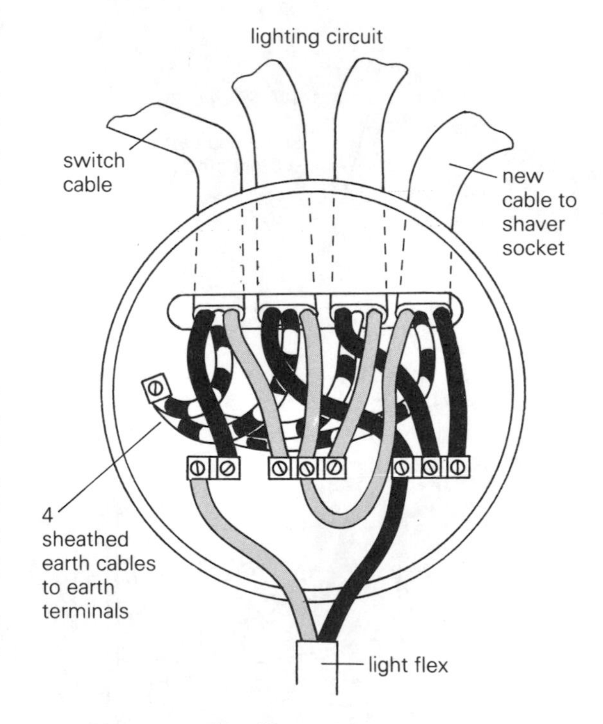

Top: Shaver socket. Never install anything other than a shaver supply unit in a bathroom; Above: Detail of ceiling rose, showing new cable for shaver socket. Use with a 'loop-in' system

the nearest light in the room below. Hopefully the carpet and floorboards will come up quite easily. If you're lucky, the cable will run in the same direction as the joists. If not, you'll have to drill about 2 inches (5 cm) below the surface of each joist and thread the cable through the holes. This is to ensure that no floor brads or nails pierce the cables. The shaver outlet can be screwed to the wall fairly low down, to save too much disturbance of the decorations. Strip the insulation and wire the shaver socket as before. Fix the shaver socket to the wall. Either surface mount it or chase it into the plaster. Run the cable down behind the skirting board and across the ceiling. Now switch off the power.

From the room below, open up the ceiling rose. Pull the shaver socket cable through a convenient hole in the rose. Strip off sufficient insulation so that the black wire can be fed into a spare terminal marked 'N', the red into a spare terminal marked 'L' and the earth wire (sheathed) into the earth terminal. Double check that those and all the other screws are holding firmly. Replace the ceiling rose, plug in, switch on and smile!

OUTDOOR LIGHTS

The increased visibility and the dramatic effect created by a covered front door light or a patio light is certainly worth the effort of installing one. First of all, find the best position to give you the most light on a dark evening. That position should also be convenient to a lighting point indoors. You'll need a light-fitting that is specially manufactured for use out of doors and it must be earthed. Instructions for wiring an exterior light are printed on the packaging. Unless advised otherwise, the easiest method of installing one is to run a length of 1 mm twin core and PVC sheathed cable from it to the hall light by connecting to the terminals matching the coloured wires. Somewhere you'll have to drill through the wall and you should try and find the most inconspicuous run for the cable. You might drill in a position just above the floor upstairs and be

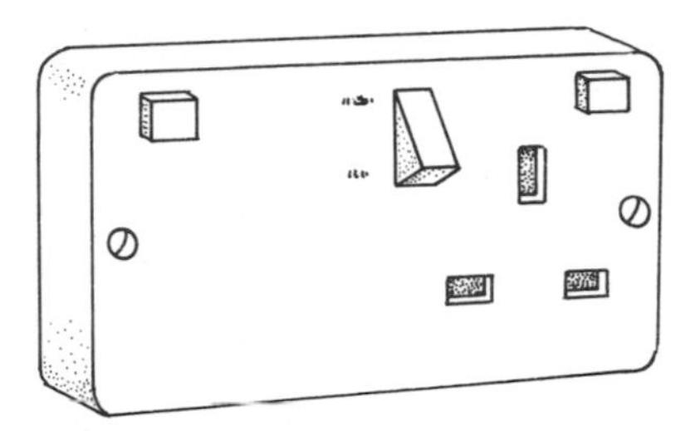

Above: Socket protected with an RCCB

able to pull the cable to the ceiling rose position under the floorboards. Now switch off the power. Thread the cable down through the ceiling rose and make your connections as follows: sleeve the earth wire and connect to 'E'; the red wire should go to the outer two-terminal block; the black wire to the outer three-terminal block marked 'N'. You've now made the necessary connections so that your new light can be switched with the existing hall light. This has saved the introduction of a terminal joint box, extra cable, an extra switch and a great deal of disturbance of decorations. You'll have to carry out exactly the same operation if you want to put a light at the back of the house.

If you're thinking of running an extension lead for a temporary light in the garden, don't! Cables for all external leads must be of the correct size and suitable for outside use. Plugs and sockets used outside must be sealed and manufactured especially for that purpose and you can buy garden lights that can be moved around. The specially-sealed fitting has a non-conducting spike on the end of it to secure it into the earth. If you use such lights, or external lights at Christmas time, then the power supply must be protected by an RCCB (Residual Current Circuit Breaker) which switches off the electrical current in a fraction of a second if a current leakage occurs. Small submersible pumps, which power a fountain, are inexpensive and very popular. These too must be protected by an RCCB. To safeguard you and your family and pets you must have read the instructions and fully understood them before any installation work.

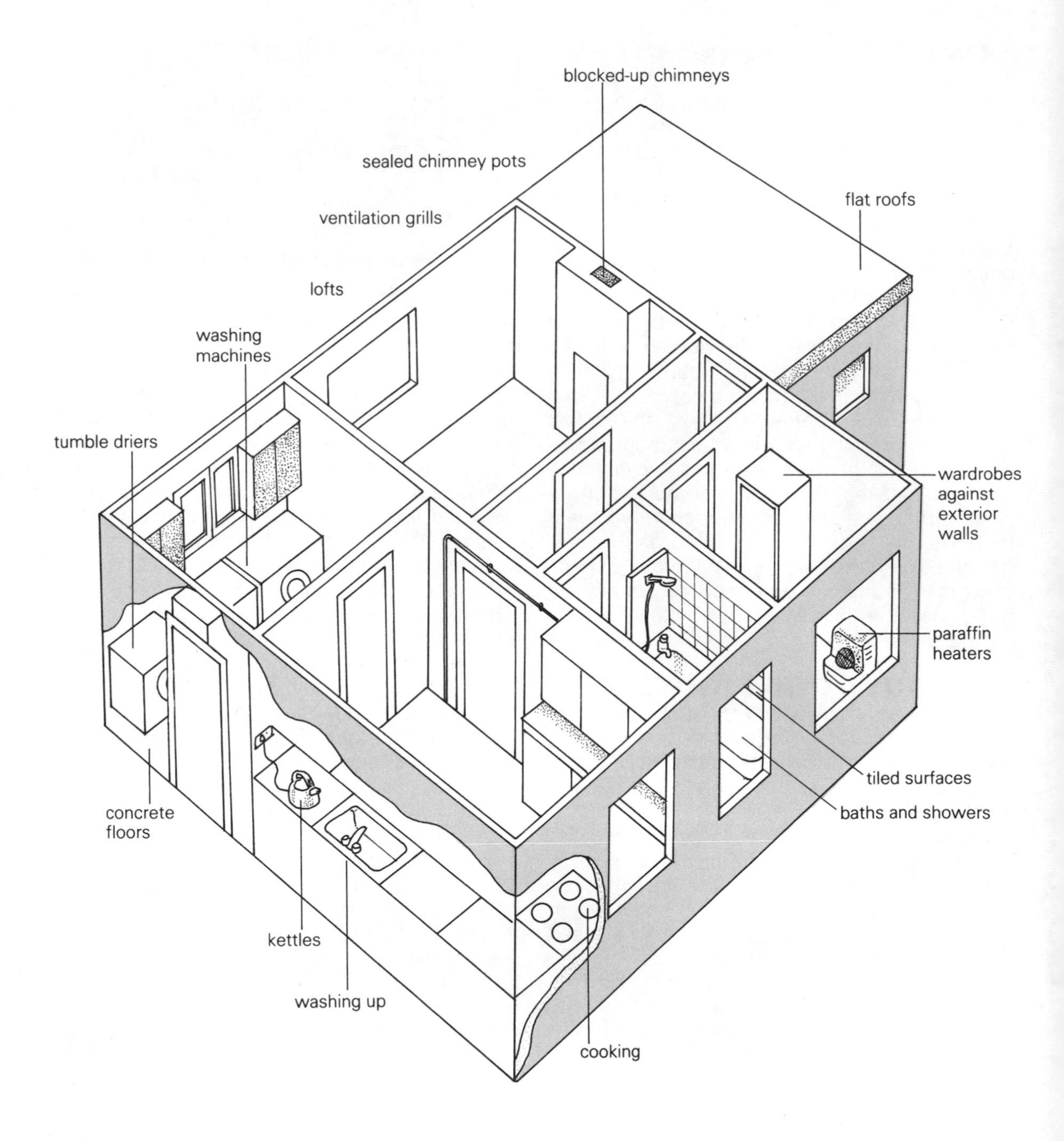
blocked-up chimneys
sealed chimney pots
flat roofs
ventilation grills
lofts
washing machines
tumble driers
wardrobes against exterior walls
paraffin heaters
tiled surfaces
baths and showers
concrete floors
kettles
washing up
cooking

INSULATION, HEATING & VENTILATION 5

CONDENSATION

As winter approaches, most householders begin to think about a damp condition that attacks the fabric of all our homes: condensation. The cause is simply water-vapour; the effect is steamy ceilings, misted-up windows and rivers of water on walls. But there are cures if you understand the main factors involved: heating, ventilation and insulation. In the average household, water-vapour is produced at a phenomenal rate. Up to 4 gallons (18 litres) can be produced every day by an average family, through the ordinary activities of washing, cooking and just breathing! Did you know, for example, that if you use a paraffin heater a gallon (4.5 litres) of water-vapour will be produced for each gallon of paraffin burned?

The air around us always contains water in the form of vapour. We can neither see it nor feel it and when we are out of doors we are not aware of its effects. Indoors though, where the damp air comes into contact with a cold surface, some of the water-vapour will condense into water, resulting in visible condensation. The amount of water-vapour that air can hold depends on its temperature. Warm air can hold much more than cold air, so it follows that because we keep our rooms warmed we run the risk of increased condensation. We've all been encouraged to try and improve the insulation of our homes. This, combined with the use of central heating, means higher temperatures in all our rooms. In turn, warmer air means the amount of water-vapour present is increased. Without adequate ventilation your home will almost certainly suffer from condensation.

It's a pity that so many new houses are being built without chimneys which help provide ventilation. Even in older houses many DIY enthusiasts have neatly blocked off the fire opening without providing an alternative means of ventilation, such as a grille fitted on the chimney breast. Double-glazing and modern PVC windows, when installed, also prevent ventilation.

Damp in a corner of a room at a low level is not necessarily rising damp. If it happens on an exposed external wall, especially a solid wall or one with no wall insulation, it may be caused by condensation. The air in a room is cooler at a lower level, so that condensation takes place in that area only. If the damp is accompanied by mould growth, it is very likely to be condensation. A similar condition can be found in ground-floor flats, especially if the block is steel-framed with concrete infill.

To help cure condensation you must think in terms of (a) reducing water-vapour, (b) warming up your home if it's too cold and (c) providing adequate ventilation. Most water-vapour in the home is produced in the kitchen area. If you don't use a saucepan lid, for example, twenty minutes of boiling potatoes can produce enough steam to ruin your decorations and promote black marks between your kitchen tiles! To prevent that excessive water-vapour from reaching the rest of the house simply close the door. To expel it from the kitchen, install an extractor.

Opposite page: Condensation, some potential sites and causes. Water-vapour can penetrate the most unlikely places, especially if the home is draught-proofed. Vapour can then be drawn into the roof void, cavity walls and ceilings

VENTILATION

The simplest method of ventilating our homes is to open windows and doors regularly. But this is not always desirable so it may be more practical to install vents, fans or extractor fans in kitchens and bathrooms. An extractor fan must be installed as close to the vapour source as possible. It's a pointless exercise to install an extractor fan if you don't use it immediately steam is being produced. However, what you also have to consider is that when you are extracting the steam you are also extracting heat! If you find that you are losing a great deal of heat you should investigate the possibilities of installing an electric dehumidifier. One of these small units costs about the same as a small cooker and plugs into the mains electricity supply. It will run for ten hours for the cost of one unit of electricity. It is highly efficient and can extract up to 3 or 4 gallons (13.5 or 18 litres) of water per day from the internal air of a house.

If you find you have blocked-off fireplaces in your house, you must check that the flue is ventilated. If you intend to block up a fire opening then you must provide permanent ventilation by means of a grille at the point of blocking. You must also leave an opening at the stack or chimney pot.

What you are doing, in effect, is creating movement of air in the flue. This will ensure that any damp air is carried away before it can condense.

If a flue is blocked-up and not ventilated, the effects of the interstitial dampness could be disastrous. In an older house, the bricks and mortar would certainly absorb any moisture produced. They would continue to do so over a very long period. The result would be black, sooty patches on the chimney breast. The wet soot is sucked through the permeable bricks creating a very serious problem.

INSULATION

Do we really need to insulate our homes and what does it do for us? Think of it this way: how much more comfortable and warm one is on a chilly winter's day when wearing a hat, overcoat, gloves and warm boots. What we're doing is keeping in our body heat by insulating ourselves. Do the same with your house and the insulation keeps in warm air. Clothing your house in appropriate insulating material will ensure a more comfortable atmosphere.

When your gas, electric or other fuel bill arrives after the winter has passed, it's a useful exercise to check just how much you've spent on heating the house. If your roof is not insulated, a quarter of your fuel bill was spent on heating the outside air! If your house has cavity wall construction without insulation, you needlessly paid a third too much on your bill. One-tenth of heat went through the doors, one-fifth through the windows and one-sixth through the floors. Insulation will not prevent all the heat escaping (there has to be ventilation, of course) but it will cut down the amount. At the same time it will cut down the size of your fuel bill. If you can devote a couple of evenings and a couple of weekends to insulating your home you'll enjoy greater comfort, noticeably warmer rooms and, just as important, a radical reduction in the winter fuel bill. There is no form of insulation that most householders cannot easily tackle, except perhaps injecting the cavity wall.

Forms of insulation and types of materials differ considerably. Various Ministries and Local Governments prepare information pamphlets which give advice on insulating the home. Your DIY store will supply you with helpful literature about every form of insulation from the simple rubber-strip draught excluder to insulating-boards for lining walls, and fibreglass for the loft. Start by insulating the loft because this is where the greatest amount of heat is lost. It is also one of the easiest of all DIY jobs, where minimum expertise is called for. Full instructions for measuring, cutting and fitting are supplied on the

Opposite page: Some cures for condensation on the ground floor and in the roof

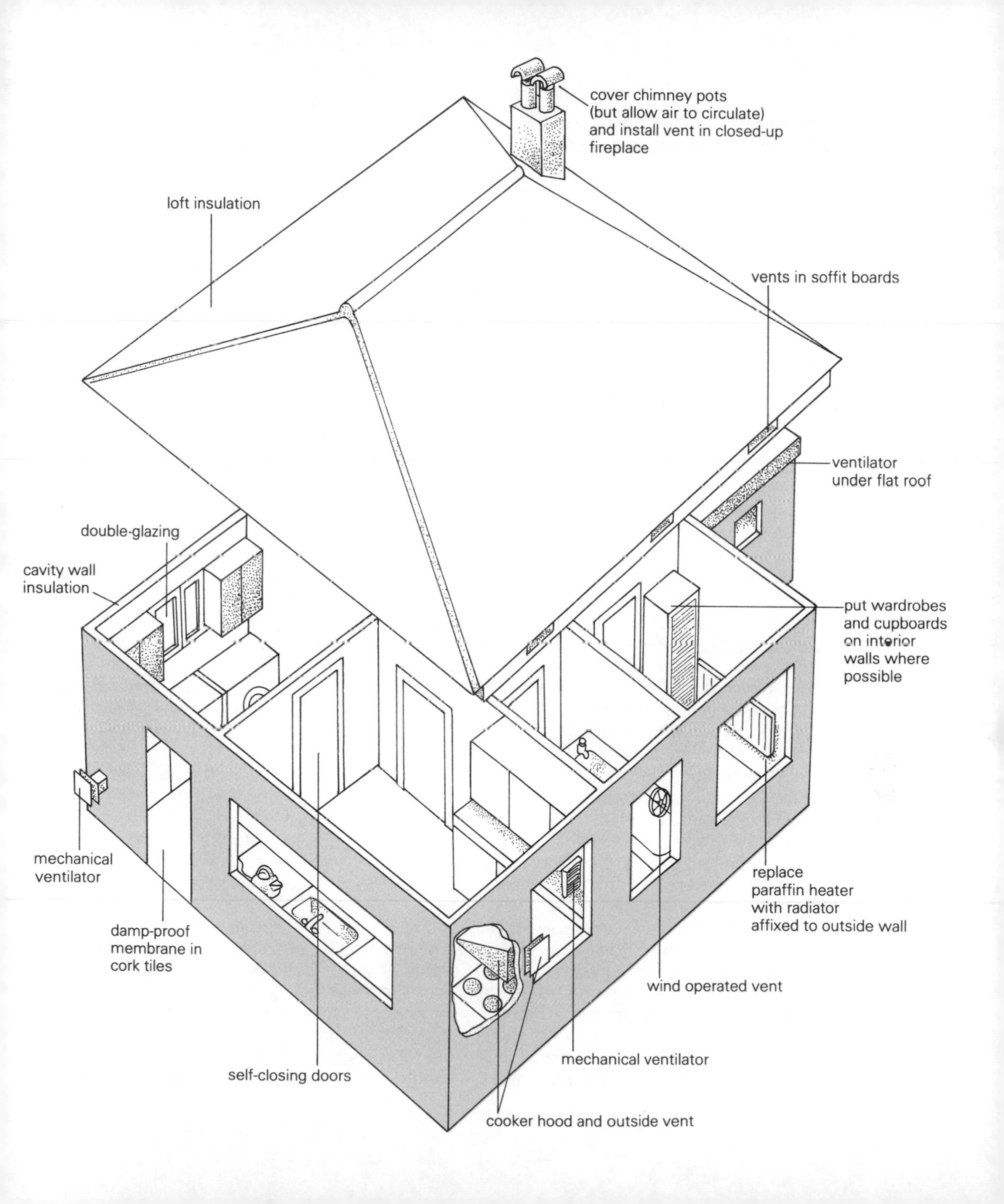
cover chimney pots
(but allow air to circulate)
and install vent in closed-up
fireplace
loft insulation
vents in soffit boards
ventilator
under flat roof
double-glazing
cavity wall
insulation
put wardrobes
and cupboards
on interior
walls where
possible
mechanical
ventilator
replace
paraffin heater
with radiator
affixed to outside wall
damp-proof
membrane in
cork tiles
wind operated vent
mechanical ventilator
self-closing doors
cooker hood and outside vent

Right: Insulate with 'bonded' fibreglass, it's easier to handle. Allow for expansion pipe

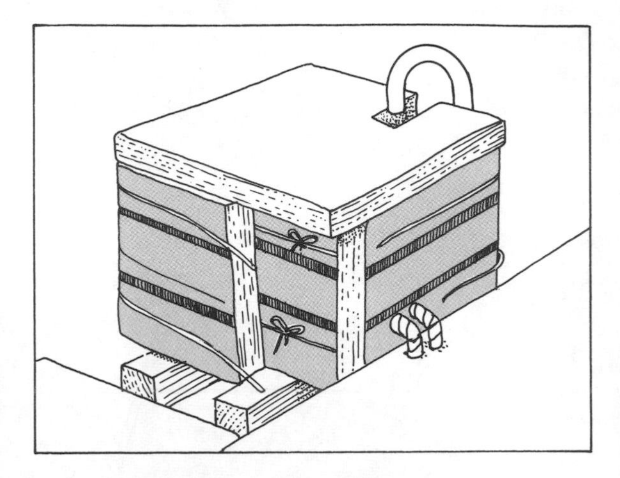

wrapping of the product. Your DIY store will give you a pamphlet with advice on protective clothing and how to crawl about safely in the attic. Don't forget to insulate the back of the board covering the attic opening, and also use foam-strip on the ledge on which it sits. If you've had a cold attic over a long period, once it's insulated you'll notice the warmth on the landing and in the bedrooms. The change is quite dramatic.

After you've measured and purchased the necessary amount of fibreglass insulation or bags of loose-fill, make sure you've got a working light in the attic. You'll also need a couple of boards to lay across the joists, a knife or scissors for cutting and trimming the fibreglass and a broom for pushing it into awkward corners. When handling glass fibre or mineral-wool, it is advisable to wear gloves, a dust mask and goggles. Wear old clothes that can be shaken out and easily washed. You might come across electric cables and plumbing runs in the attic. Copper pipes may either be covered over by the insulating material or separately lagged. Electric cables must not be covered with insulation, however, so either secure them to the side of the joists, using cable clips, or lay them on the top of the insulating material.

The alternative to fibreglass is loose-fill insulation (granules of insulating material). One disadvantage of this material is that the granules can flow down inside a cavity wall. To avoid this, block off each gap where the joists meet the rafters in the narrowest part of the roof void. The granules are very lightweight and tend to fly about very easily, but they are very easy to lay. Spread them evenly with a board notched either end to run along the tops of the joists.

Government building regulations stipulate that there must be ventilation in attics. Pamphlets which contain the details are obtainable from your local council. However, ventilation will not prevent the insulating material doing its work because it takes place at the eaves, outside the area covered by the glass fibre, mineral-wool or loose-fill material.

To prevent the water in the cold-water storage tank freezing in winter, the tank must be insulated. Either use sheets of expanded polystyrene, 2 inches (50 mm) thick, or buy a ready-made tank-cover. If you choose polystyrene the pieces can either be skewered together or fastened with tape or string. Whichever method you choose, don't insulate under the tank, as this will prevent heat rising from the house which helps to stop the water freezing.

Lag every pipe in the attic. There are various forms of insulation for this purpose: mineral-fibre rolls, strips of blanket insulation or foam tubes. If you use foam tubes do be certain that the tubes fit the pipe. It's useless putting a ½-inch (12-mm) tube on to a ¾-inch (20-mm) pipe.

If you live in a particularly windy area, an amazing amount of cold air is driven in between slates or tiles. These winds also carry soot and dust. To help overcome these problems you might consider stapling 'tiler's felt' to the underside of the rafters. If you do this, always start at the top of either slope. Overlap each piece by about 4 inches (10 mm). Then any water

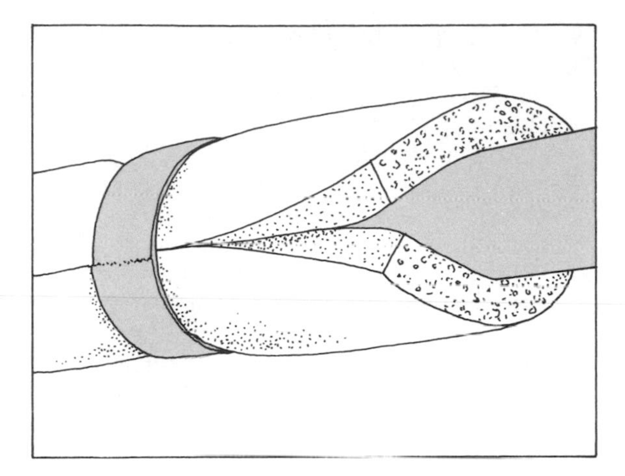

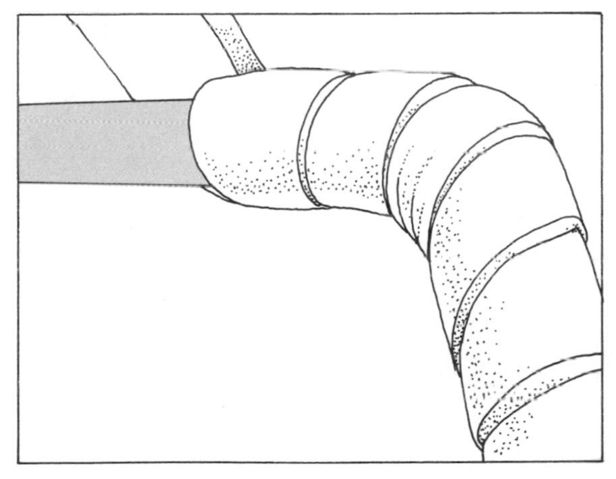

Left: Foam plastic tubing; Below left: Felt lagging (overlap well, especially at bends)

penetration will not fall into the attic but will be carried away down to the eaves. A staple-gun is inexpensive and certainly worth buying if you're undertaking this job. Knocking in nails to hold felt on to the underside of rafters can cause breakage and damage to tiles and slates.

Insulating Doors and Windows

You can sometimes actually hear wind whistling in through gaps around doors and windows! The cold air entering through these gaps can be eliminated by one of the cheapest forms of draught excluders: the plastic foam-strip with an adhesive backing. It is extremely simple to use, will last for a whole year and is easily replaced if you redecorate. If the door or window is uneven or the gap is wide, two strips can be used. The only tool that you'll need when fitting this is a pair of scissors. If you want to choose a more permanent draught excluder for your door, the choice is either plastic-strip or sprung metal-strip. Both these are fixed to the door through ready-punched clearance holes with tacks. The pack will provide the tacks and instructions for placing and fixing the strip. (For further detail on insulating doors and windows, see Chapter 2.)

Underdoor Draughts

There are on the market a number of underdoor draught excluders to deal with any situation. Obviously, there has to be a small gap at the bottom of the door to allow it to open properly but there are many cleverly designed excluders available which will fill that gap and prevent draughts. You must read the instructions to find the one best suited to your particular problem. External doors need weatherproof materials as they have to exclude rain as well as wind.

One of the simplest forms of excluders for an internal door is a flexible rubber or plastic strip screwed to the bottom of the door. A 'rise and fall' automatic device can be fitted to an internal door. A spring mechanism operates when the door is closed, forcing a vinyl flap down against the threshold giving a very effective seal. Another type is the metal plate with the brush strip attached. The brush strip rides gently over a carpet but provides a good seal. For suitable exterior doors, one type comes in two halves which interlock when the door is closed.

Floor Insulation

Draughty floors usually have bare floorboards and are at ground level. If you have wooden floors that have gaps between the boards, you'll be losing a great deal of heat. Floorboards are fixed to strong timbers called joists and it's at this level that you'll find ventilating grilles on the outside wall of the house. This source of fresh air is essential to maintain the fabric of the house beneath the floor level and to prevent rot, but you have to stop that cold air entering the room through the floorboards.

Remove as much furniture from the room as possible in order to check as many of the boards as you can for splits and cracks. Lever up one or two of the boards to examine the wood underneath and the joists. Any sign of woodworm must be treated immediately. If the flooring is made of tongue and grooved timber, draughts are more likely to be present because the tongues have split, the timber has shrunk to give oversized gaps or there are splits in the timber itself. Check also around the skirting boards where you might find undulating gaps caused by movement of separate floorboards. You may find one long gap along the whole length of the floor. This could be caused by the floor dropping or by shrinkage in the skirting board.

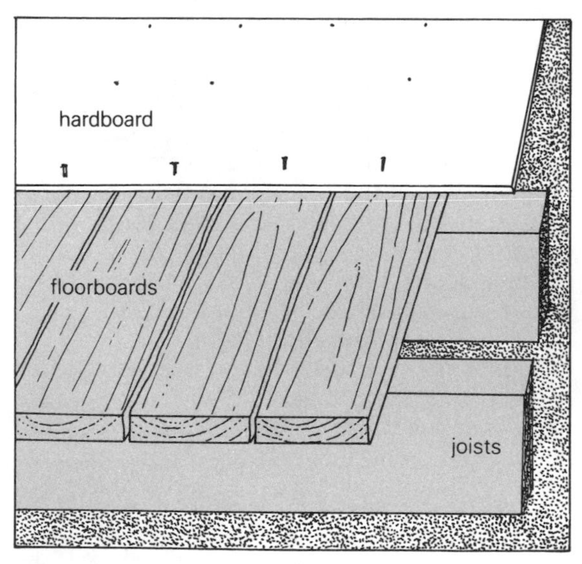

If your floor is sanded and sealed then a mixture of sawdust and transparent wood adhesive can be made into a very good filler for gaps. Press the mixture into the gaps, leave to dry and then sand down. Then apply another coat of seal which will run into the joints and seal them.

Large gaps in a floor that is to be covered over can be filled in two ways. If the gaps are the same width along the floor, glue in beading to form a tight fit. The joists crossing the floorboards will prevent the beading from slipping down underneath the floor. If the gaps are not of a constant width, cut your own slivers of wood from scrap timber. The alternative is to make a mix of shredded newspapers and glue. All schoolchildren know about making papier-mâché by tearing newspapers into shreds, adding flour and water and boiling in a saucepan! If the gaps between the boards are oversized, either slivers of wood placed beneath the surface or rolled newspapers stuffed in tightly will do as a base for the papier-mâché pulp.

This treatment is particularly suitable if you are going to cover the floor with hardboard. This is an excellent base for most forms of floor coverings because it helps to level out any unevenness in the floor. You must remember to adjust doors to allow for the hardboard.

Hardboard should be dampened before fitting. Damp it with a sponge and leave it overnight

Above left: You can fill large gaps between floorboards with papier-mâché; Left: Fill gaps between boards before laying hardboard and underfelt, vinyl or tiles

lying flat. Cut the hardboard to cover the entire floor making tight joints. Use only hardboard pins, nailing them in at 6-inch (15-cm) intervals. If you have a very large area to cover, hire a good staple-gun. The staples are ¾ inch (20 mm) long and designed for just such a purpose. If you wish to lay underfelt for a carpet on the boards later, tape the joints of the hardboard after the boards have dried. If a gap still remains at the skirting board a small wooden bead is the answer. Press it hard down to the floor with a piece of wood but don't nail it to the floor. Use panel pins to fix it instead to the skirting board.

If you live in a house with a cavity wall construction, it is possible that you'll suffer from draughts through gaps in floorboards on the first floor. You can carry out exactly the same treatment as for the ground floor. Don't be tempted to use anything but hardboard pins because longer panel pins or nails might pierce cables or pipes.

Another possible source of irritating draughts is where a power point has been fitted in a cavity wall construction. When chopping out the blockwork to fit in the metal box, carelessness can result in a chisel piercing through to the cavity. An ill-fitting box and cover can allow cold air to penetrate the room.

Window Insulation

There are three reasons for heat-loss through a window. Glass is so thin that it is responsible for a certain amount of heat being lost through the material. Ill-fitting windows can also cause a great deal of discomfort by allowing in piercing draughts. The greatest nuisance, however, is condensation. This is caused by the warm, moist air in the room coming into contact with cold glass and has been dealt with earlier in this chapter.

There is always movement in wood. Doors and windows can shrink and warp leaving gaps between them and their frames. The easiest and cheapest method of excluding draughts from an ill-fitting window is to use foam-backed strip. Before any such strip can be stuck to the frame all traces of dirt must be wiped off and then the surface dried.

Draught-Proofing a Sash Window

To seal a sash window effectively you need a combination of different forms of draught excluders. At the sides of the sashes you need a sprung strip but on the meeting rails of the windows you need a self-adhesive brush strip. For

Left: Draught-proofing a sash window

the bottom of the window you should fix foam-strip or a sprung strip to the bottom of the sash. At the top, foam-strip or a sprung strip should be fixed to the frame.

Double-Glazing

If you choose to fit secondary windows or a proprietary brand of double-glazing, then make sure you consider one essential factor. In the event of an emergency, you might have to get through that window very quickly. With double-glazing fitted you're making it more difficult for an intruder to get in but you could be making it doubly difficult for you to get out. The cost of paying a firm to fit double-glazing is fairly high. You must be realistic and accept that in terms of cost-effectiveness it will take years to recoup the cost, but if your criteria are immediate warmth and comfort, then it's well worth having double-glazing fitted.

Insulating by double-glazing simply means that you are buffeted against the outside, cold air by a layer of warm and dry air between two sheets of glass. It is possible to buy 'sealed units' which are factory made and mean that the two sheets of glass are completely sealed around the edges. The sealed units are then secured into the window frames. You can pay a firm to do this or you can, of course, carry out an effective double-glazing operation yourself. If you intend fitting a proprietary brand of double-glazing, you must buy the best that you can afford. Manufacturers give you a choice of UPVC or aluminium double-glazing. Shop around your DIY store and you'll find the best that suits your house and your pocket. Look at the manufacturers' leaflets which will tell you everything you need to know to select the right system for your house. The best manufacturers use only first-class materials and their products are manufactured to rigorous quality standards. The market for double-glazing is so competitive that the manufacturers are continually improving materials and installation methods, and bringing down costs as a result.

Some pamphlets refer to the 'U-value' for single or double glazing. Don't be puzzled, the only thing you need to know is that the U-value is 1 for single glazing and 0.5 for sealed units. Technically, the U-value of a material is the number of BTUs (British Thermal Units) it will allow through 1 square foot (30.5 cm), in one hour, for each degree fahrenheit difference in temperature from one side to the other.

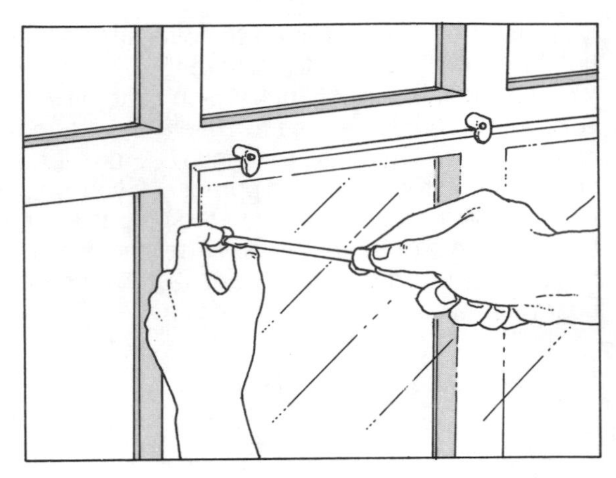

Above: Fitting clips for double-glazing; Opposite page: Using fixed double-glazing and hinged double-glazing. Surprisingly easy to fit and well worth the effort

A simple and effective DIY system of double-glazing allows for a separate pane of glass to be fitted in an aluminium frame inside the existing window. It can match the quality, looks and performance of a similar, professionally-installed system of double-glazing at a fraction of the cost. You don't need to be a DIY expert to install this type of double-glazing as the systems fit quite easily inside your existing window opening. You don't even have to cut mitred corners when you buy a package as the sections come pre-drilled. An accompanying pamphlet gives you easy-to-follow, illustrated step-by-step instructions.

The ideal material for this system of double-glazing is either aluminium or UPVC and is increasingly used in place of wood. It won't rust, chip or flake and is corrosion-proof. With the rigid

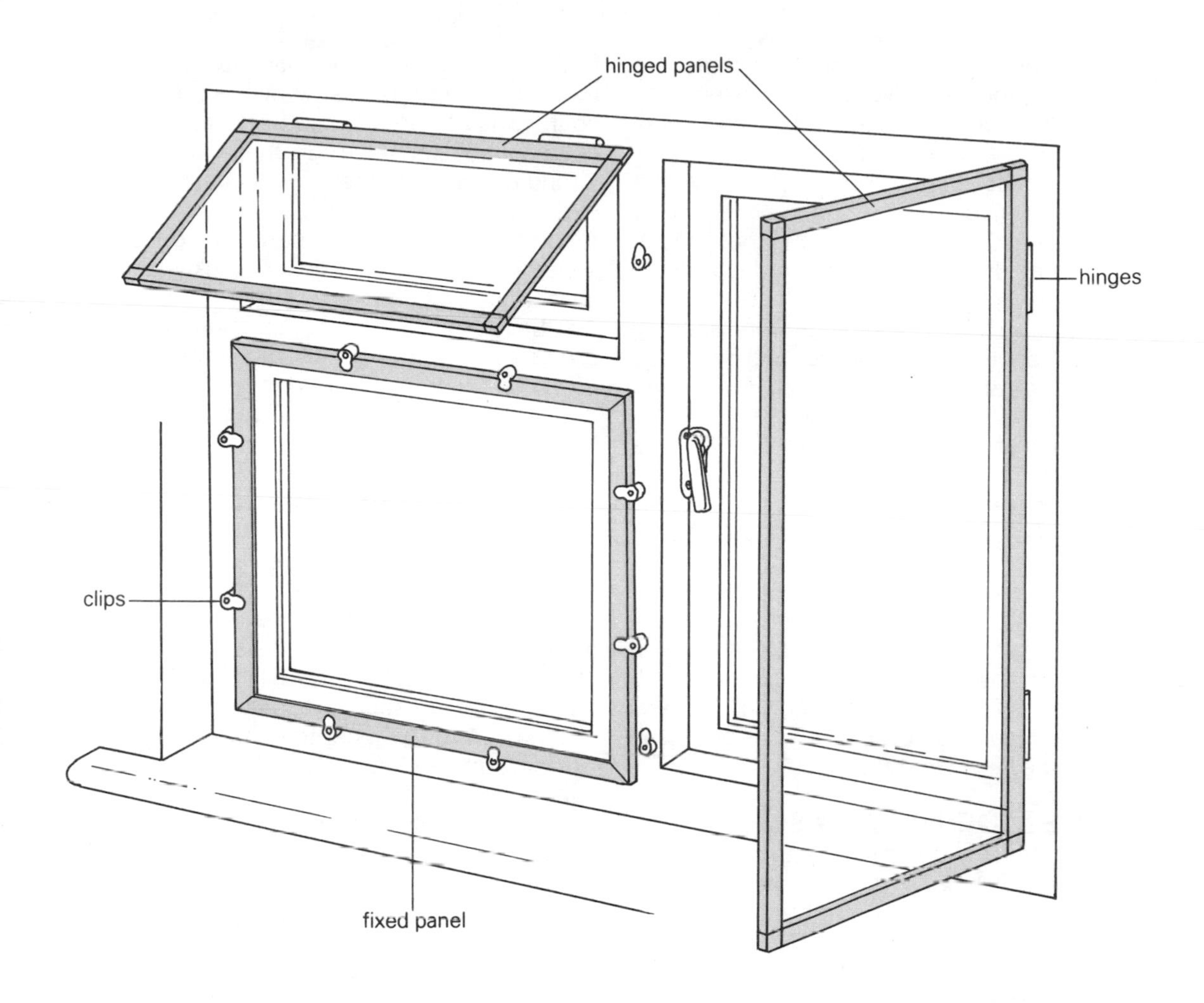

UPVC sections you can double-glaze casement windows up to 6 feet (2 m) high or sash windows up to 8 feet (2.5 m) high. The systems are surprisingly simple to put together, and easy to cut with a junior hacksaw.

First measure the height and width of your window recess. (The parts for the height and the width of the window come separately. Remember to overestimate the lengths you need. The tracks to fit the recess are now cut to size and fixed into place. It's only at this point that you measure for glass, which you buy separately from your local glazier. Choose the thicker 4 mm glass for a better result. You might consider using some safety material if the window is close to the floor or if children are likely to be playing close to it. There are various materials available including acrylic sheet.

You must measure accurately for fitting the glass and allow for the protective frame to be fitted to the glass. The plastic channelling is easily cut with a junior hacksaw and fits snugly over the glass. Ease the framed glass into the top channel, which has enough clearance to allow you to drop it into the bottom channel. As the separate panes are slid into the closed position, the inner uprights interlock giving extra strength and an effective seal.

If you are budget-conscious and only want a cheaper form of double-glazing for the winter period there is a system for you: one that you put together yourself. All that is required is a roll of double-sided sticky-tape and a sheet of heavy-duty plastic. This is suitable for opening casements, or hinged windows, and what are called fixed lights.

Clean and dry the inside of the glass and the glazing bars. Cut the plastic film to size. Using a hair-dryer, warm up the whole of the frame. This will ensure that after you've stuck on the plastic film the air trapped inside will be as dry as possible. It is dry air that is the most effective. Stick the film to the frames using pieces of sticky-tape about half the width of the sash frames, overlapping them at the corners. Be certain that no air bubbles are trapped under the sticky-tape and that there are no folds in the plastic film. You will have wasted your time entirely if you don't have a complete seal.

FUEL COMPARISONS

Running costs for a central heating system can easily be assessed at the end of the year. To make genuine comparisons between different types, however, is not easy because each home is unique. The amount of insulation present, the occupiers' demands for heat and the construction of the building make comparisons difficult. Factors to be considered when choosing a particular fuel for your central heating system include availability, storage and dependability as well as cost. As far as cost is concerned, prices for the available fuels differ very little up and down the UK, certainly not enough to favour one system rather than another on a geographical basis.

Solid Fuel

There are various types of solid fuel available and you should find that the makers of your particular boiler will recommend the appropriate grade of fuel to use. One of the disadvantages of solid fuel is that it creates ash which is messy and, of course, has to be disposed of. Fires and boilers have to be cleaned regularly and there is no letting-up on the need for constant attention, even with hopper-type boilers, as regular topping-up with fuel is needed. The inability to switch off a solid-fuel boiler quickly is perhaps another disadvantage.

A boiler for an average-sized house will burn between two and three tons of central heating fuel per year so you'll need to buy in bulk to get a better price. However, it is often inconvenient or impossible to provide storage facilities for bulk buying. During the summer months, when solid-fuel boilers are not normally used but hot water is still needed, it is necessary to have the use of an electric immersion heater.

Gas

Mains gas is available in most towns and urban areas in the UK but rural areas have to depend upon bottled gas. Large, refillable containers can be installed in such areas to store sufficient bottled gas to run a central heating system.

Mains gas is clean, doesn't have to be stored, and there is no waste. A flue is necessary, however, to discharge the gases created by burning the gas. Pipes can be run around the house, mostly hidden from view. Whatever appliance is connected to a gas run, whether it's a cooker, fire or boiler, it can be controlled with great precision simply by turning a knob. Gas boilers are designed to fit aesthetically into the décor of a well-designed kitchen.

Oil

Oil has to be both stored and paid for in bulk. A 600-gallon tank is normal for an average-sized house. The tank must be sited out of doors and in a convenient position for deliveries. Before committing yourself to an oil-fired central heating system you should ensure that local oil deliveries are dependable.

One of the advantages of using oil is that there is no waste material to dispose of. Oil burners are small, quiet and efficient.

Electricity

Electricity comes into our homes as energy, used to light, heat, and operate appliances. If you choose to use electricity to heat your home, your local electricity board will give you full details of the cheaper, night-rate electricity tariff. Night-storage heaters, as they are called, can be placed in any room in the home. Wiring from them is taken to the Electricity Board's separate meter located near your consumer unit. The charge for each unit of electricity consumed on this special-rate tariff is considerably less than the normal rate. The heaters are slim and unobtrusive and can be bought in colours to match your décor.

CENTRAL HEATING SYSTEMS

All central heating systems are made of materials that can become corroded. Where pressed-steel radiators are used in conjunction with copper-tubing a form of electrolytic corrosion can take place and this results in sludge and 'air' in the system. (The 'air' is actually hydrogen gas.) The pump may eventually fail and leaks may develop in the radiators. To prevent corrosion, fit what is called a 'sacrificial magnesium anode'

into the domestic hot-water tank. To remove the sludge, drain the system and introduce a special solvent into the feed and expansion tank. A chemical corrosion-proofer is not the same as the special solvent for removing sludge. It is best to introduce the corrosion-proofer when the system is first installed but it can be carried out at any time. It will not, however, correct any damage already done.

If there is sludge in the system you must remove that with a special solvent before introducing the corrosion-proofer. Full instructions are supplied with each product.

Venting the Radiator

By turning a key you can rid a radiator of an air-lock which will prevent the water circulating. If you put your hand on the inlet pipe and feel that it's hot but then find that the top of the radiator is cold, the water is not being allowed to circulate. A key with a square hole is usually supplied with the radiator. On one side of the top of the radiator, you'll find a hole with a square peg inside. Simply release the peg with a few turns of the key, but don't turn too much! Hold it open until the bubbling of gas has stopped and water begins to escape. You'll need to hold a towel or a container to catch the water. At this point turn the key to close the valve. If you have continually to vent a radiator in your central heating system, it's probable that corrosion is taking place. But before introducing a special solvent to remove possible sludge and air, make a simple test. Hold a lighted taper to the air escaping when you vent the radiator. When corrosion takes place hydrogen gas is formed within the system, so if the escaping gas burns with a blue flame the chances are you have got corrosion, because hydrogen gas is present. Remove curtains and other inflammable materials when you carry out this test, although it is quite safe if you take normal precautions.

Left: Venting a radiator. Also known as 'bleeding' a radiator, this process is crucial in avoiding unnecessary heat loss

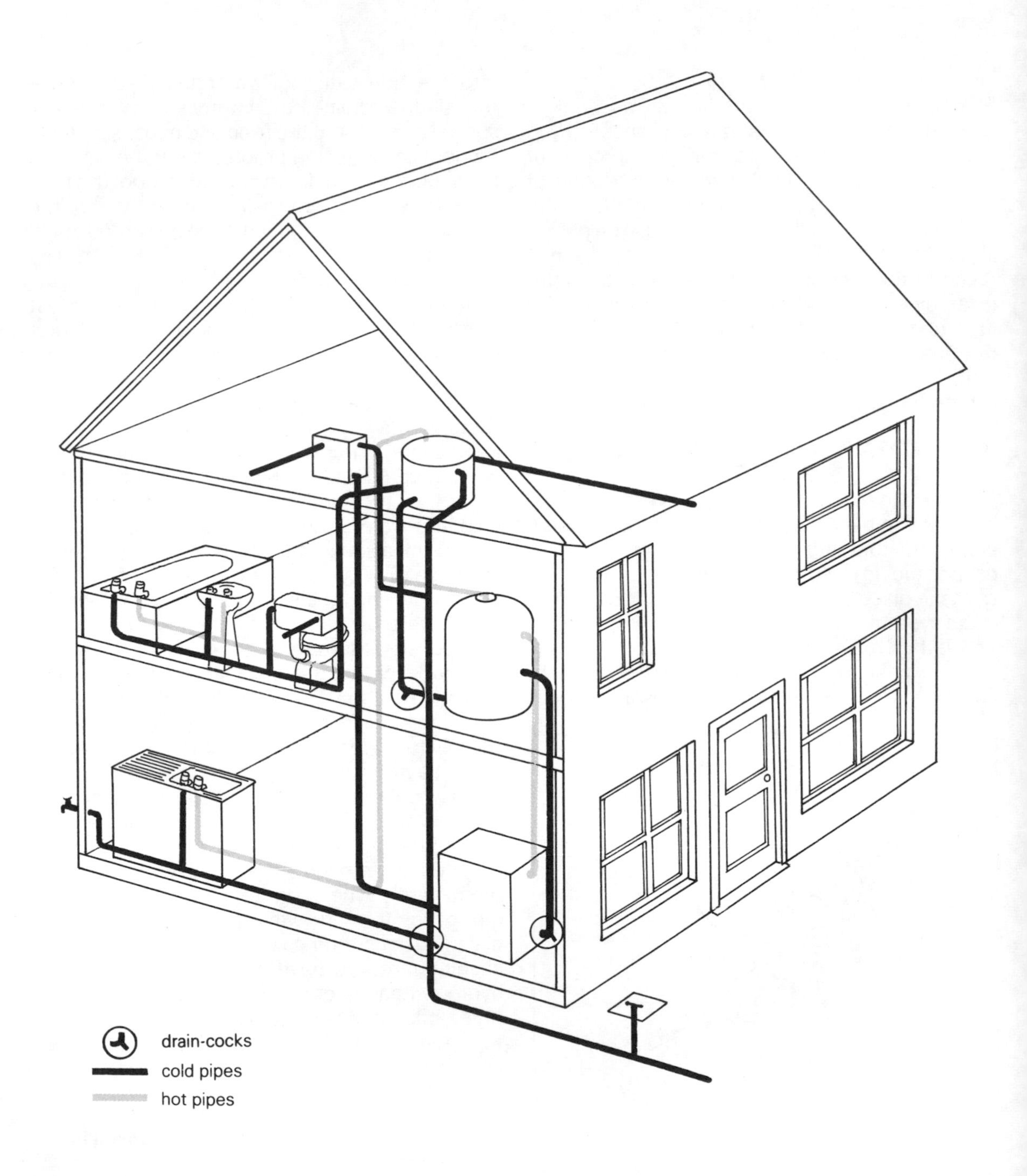
drain-cocks
cold pipes
hot pipes

Draining Down the System

If you leave your house for any length of time it's advisable to drain down the central heating system, especially during winter. The boiler and the radiators are supplied by water from the expansion tank. Therefore if you stop the supply to the expansion tank, you can drain all the water out of the system. The means of escape for the water in the system is always at its lowest point. Either you will find a drain-cock at the base of the boiler or you will see that one has been provided at the lowest point of the run inside or outside the house. If it's outside the house, make sure that the water has a clear run to a gully.

Find the expansion tank which will probably be high up in the attic. Turn off its stop-cock, which will shut off the supply of mains water to the tank. Then go to the drain-cock. If it is inside the house, you'll find it has a hose-connector as part of it. Insert the end of a hose into a jubilee-clip before pushing it on to the hose-connector. Tighten the jubilee-clip to prevent accidents as the hose takes the water to the nearest gully! Turn on the drain-cock and wait while the system drains out. This will take a little time. You can seal off any switches to the central heating system with sticky-tape. Make a note of what you've done, so that when you have to refill the system you do things in reverse order. When you return from holiday, do check that the boiler and immersion heater are still switched off before refilling the system. You'll probably find a certain amount of air in the radiators. Use the vent key to allow this to escape.

Leaking Radiators

A leaking radiator is unlikely to be cured by any of the proprietary brands of sealants. A sealant might block a split or a hole for a short time but once rust has penetrated the metal it is virtually impossible to eliminate it completely. It really is better to replace a radiator if it has sprung a leak. By closing both valves it's possible to undo the compression joints and lift the radiator off its brackets. Some water might be left in the radiator, so you'll need to tilt it to run the water into a bucket or onto a plastic sheet. Make certain that you replace the radiator with one of the same make, type and size. Do not try to reuse the air-vent valve or the union connectors from the old radiator and use special tape known as PTFE on the compression joints. Reverse the process of removing the radiator and make certain that you tighten all union connectors and valve unions. After undoing the control valve, check all joints to make certain there's no seepage of water. Unscrew the air-vent valve at the top of the radiator with the key and once water begins to flow out close the valve.

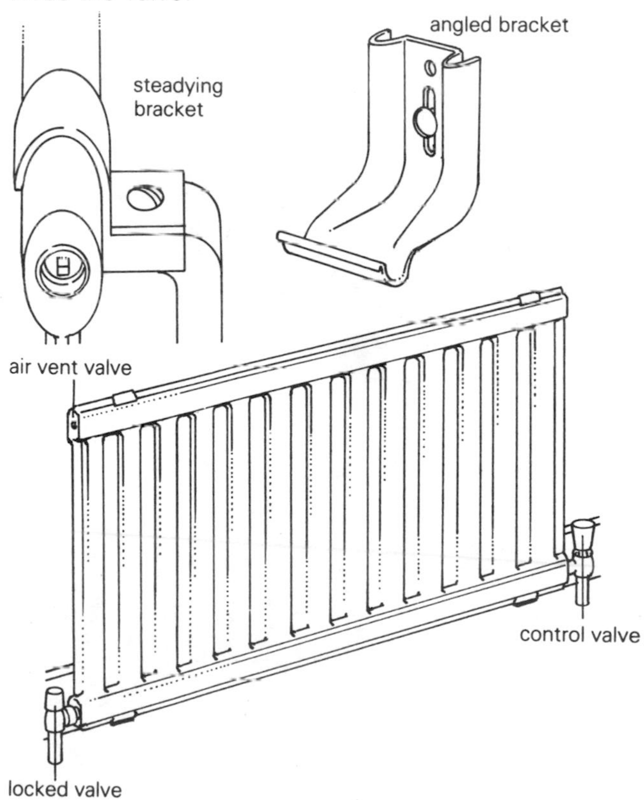

Opposite page: Draining down the system. The main stop-cock outside the house should be accessible and easily turned in case of an emergency; Right: Panel radiator and brackets

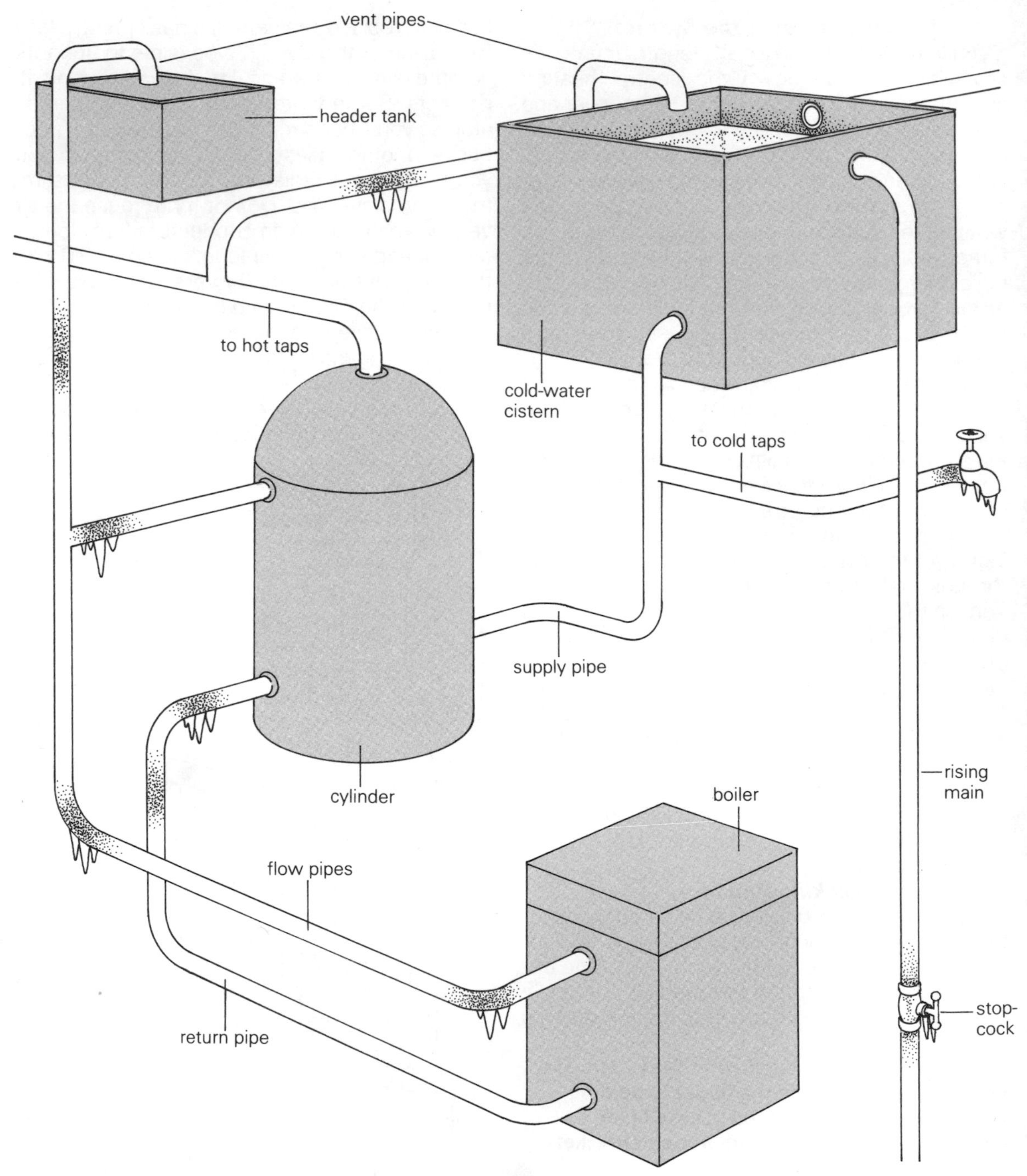
vent pipes
header tank
to hot taps
cold-water
cistern
to cold taps
supply pipe
cylinder
boiler
rising
main
flow pipes
return pipe
stop-
cock

PLUMBING

6

In the case of plumbing and drainage a little knowledge is not a dangerous thing! For example, knowing where your main stop-cock is located means that you can turn the whole of the supply to the house off in the event of an emergency. Make sure the stop-cock is in working order and, if it's deep down, keep a long-handled turn-key close by. Get to know something about the drainage system. Find out where all the inspection chambers are and how to use a set of drain rods. These you can hire for half a day at a nominal cost.

The Water Authority has a statutory duty to supply all domestic properties with drinking water. As cars and lorries trundle over the main roads, our drinking water is flowing along pipes under those roads and into our homes – but water is flowing the other way too! Soil water and waste products are taken from our houses by means of soil pipes which connect to the main drainage system. This in turn connects to a network of sewers underneath our roads.

Once clean mains-water has passed the main stop-cock and entered the house, it passes through pipes direct to the drinking tap in the kitchen and to the cold-water storage tank in the attic. From the storage tank water is drawn off at baths, hand basins, bidets and WCs.

All waste water and waste products flow to a manhole just outside the house and then into the main sewers. The largest pipe that you'll see

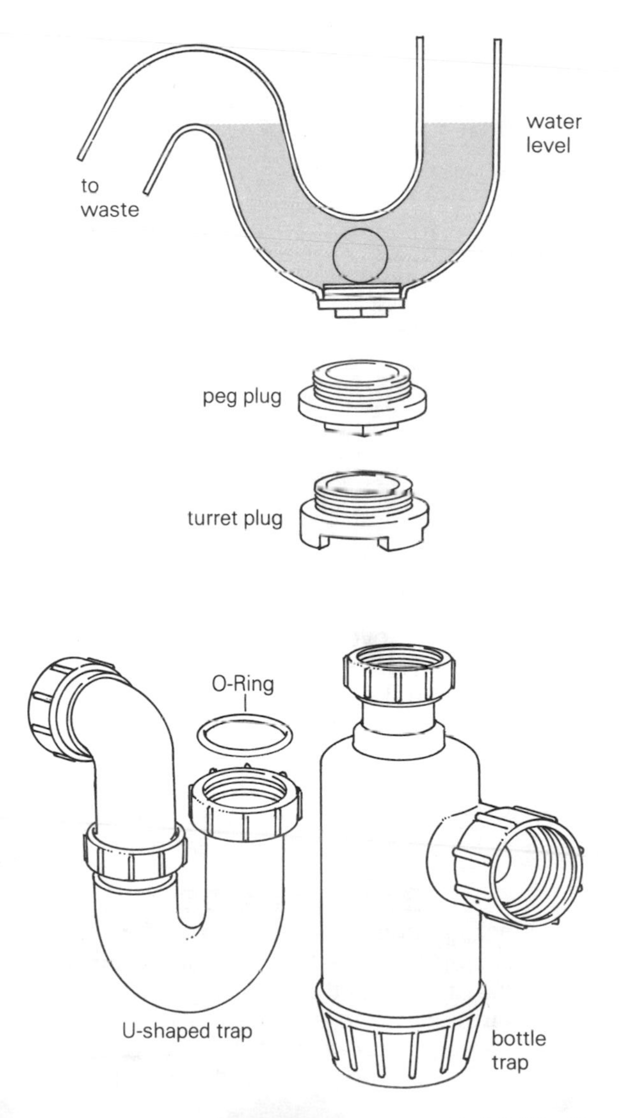

Opposite page: Likely danger spots for frozen pipes; Above right: A one-piece trap and alternative plugs; Right: A two-piece U-shaped trap and a bottle trap, both easily dismantled

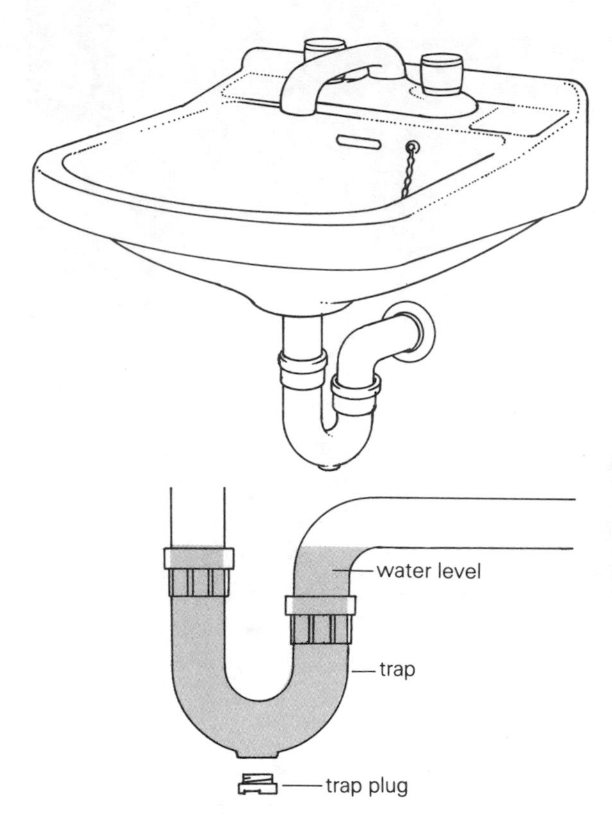

outside the building is the soil vent pipe which finishes well above the eaves. This is a ventilation pipe which allows air into the drainage system. Without it, if a lavatory was flushed the down rush of water would suck water out of the traps of basins and baths. The traps, or U-bends, are the bends underneath basins and baths and are designed to hold water to prevent unpleasant smells from entering the house.

BLOCKAGES

If a blockage occurs in a trap beneath a sink or hand basin there are two very quick and easy methods of clearing the blockage. A handle with a rubber cup on the end, called a force-cup or sink-waste plunger, is a useful gadget to keep under the sink. Run a little water into the basin and hold a damp cloth against the overflow outlet. Push the plunger up and down over the waste outlet hole a couple of times. This will displace the blockage and allow the water to run freely. If, however, the blockage is simply moved along the pipe, run more water into the basin and keep on plunging. Eventually, you'll move the material into the soil pipe.

An alternative device, which can be purchased very cheaply, is a strong flexible wire which can be threaded down the pipe and around bends to clear blockages.

A third method is to gain access to the trap itself. Traps either have a screw-in seal near their base or sections which can be unscrewed by hand. Whichever you have, it's fairly easy to gain

Left: Basin and detail of trap. If suction from a plunger won't clear a blockage, unscrew trap plug and prod with wire to pull out obstruction; Below: S-trap section of lavatory pan, showing water level

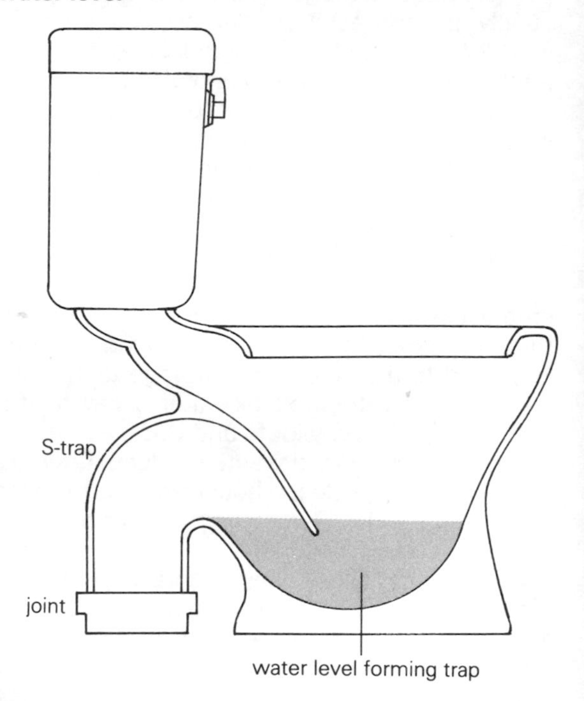

access to the inside of the trap and extract the blockage material with a piece of wire. Because the trap contains water put a bucket underneath the trap before you open it.

If the water level in the lavatory pan rises to the rim when you flush it, there is some sort of obstruction which you'll need to clear. A DIY plunger, such as a scrap of cloth wrapped round a stick, can be effective! If, however, you have drain rods, a 4-inch (100-mm) diameter rubber disc can be purchased which is screwed on to the end of a rod. This makes an ideal plunger for clearing the bend in a lavatory pan. You can also buy flexible wires manufactured expressly for this purpose. In all cases, you'll need water, bleach and rubber gloves to carry out this operation hygienically.

In the unlikely event of a manhole close to the house becoming blocked, water will begin to back up to the house. If you find that a lavatory on the ground floor is not discharging its waste the cause could be a manhole blockage. After removing the manhole cover and rodding the drain, allow plenty of fresh water, to which disinfectant has been added, into the drainage system to clear the smell of the bacteria.

WINTER PROTECTION

Long before winter comes make sure that your house is protected in every way against severe frost and sealed against the harshest weather. It's best to check your exterior defences early on in the autumn, so that you don't have to carry out repairs to chimneys, roofs and burst pipes in the middle of winter.

Make a check-list and refer to it each autumn. Start with the mains water pipe. After leaving the main stop-cock the pipe has to enter the house somewhere and it's usually 2 feet (61 cm) down in the ground! Even once it's behind the front wall it could be inadequately protected from the cold weather. It may run close to a cold exterior wall or even change course under the eaves. It's out of sight underneath the tiles or slates but it is as vulnerable there to the frosty air as if it were outside. Check once and for all that all plumbing pipes are fully insulated and protected. Even though the roof void has to be ventilated, pipes, tanks and fittings can and must be properly insulated. Often overlooked is the overflow pipe for the water tank, which should not face prevailing winds. Attach a plastic bend to the overflow pipe so that the bend dips into the water. This prevents freezing air entering the tank. Pipes should not be lagged with material that holds water. If

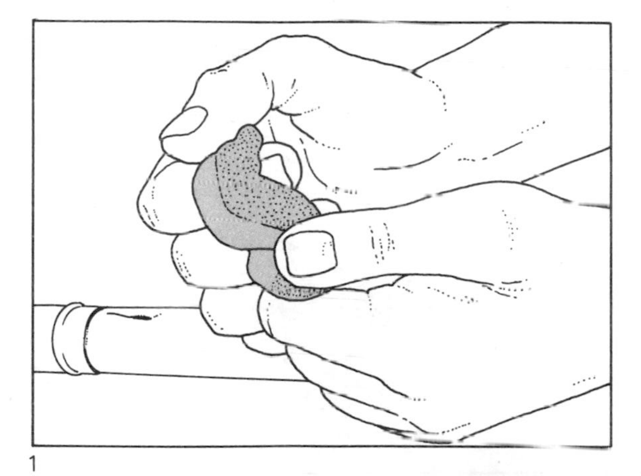

1

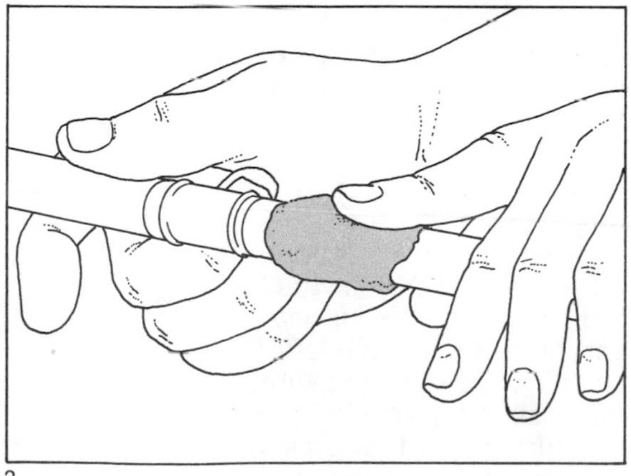

2

Above right and right: Using plastic putty. Epoxy resin plastic putty is easy to use: just follow the instructions

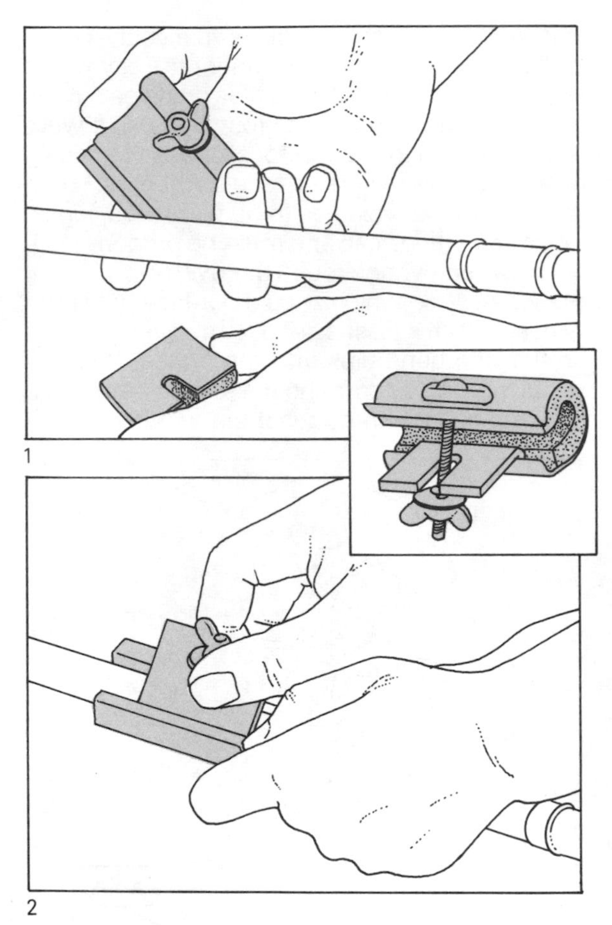

Top and above: Using a pipe clamp, a repair aid which can be re-used on different sizes of pipe; Inset: Detail of clamp showing rubber gasket

they are it could add to the potential freezing problems.

If winter conditions are so bad that you're unlucky enough to have a burst pipe, the most likely place for this to happen is in the coldest part of the house, the loft. Go to the main stop-cock immediately and turn it off. At the same time ask everybody in the house to go to a tap and turn it on. This drains the entire system, reducing the damage to the pipes and the decorations. The leak won't be difficult to find! A plug of ice in a copper pipe will easily split the pipe or force open the joint. Use a small length of copper and two compression joints and you will have a permanent repair. For a temporary repair, resin repair-kits are available and so, too, are steel clamps that have a rubber gasket to seal over the split. Full instructions are supplied with both these kits, which are available from plumbers' merchants. If, however, the compression joint itself needs to be replaced, all you need is a junior hacksaw and either a shifting spanner (which can be adjusted to fit) or a wrench.

DRIPPING TAPS

The incessant drip, drip, of a bath tap is just as unpleasant as the nasty brown stains left on the surface of the bath. Proprietary brands of bath cleaner are available to solve the latter problem and you will find that the hardest part of this cleaning operation is going out and buying a tube of the stuff! You simply paint it on and wash off.

The cause of the dripping is a worn washer. Before opening up the tap and replacing the washer you'll need to stop the supply of water to the tap. (Supataps, however, can be re-washered in a very short time, without the need to stop the water supply, and are dealt with later in this chapter.) If the bath tap does not have a stop-cock serving it, then the supply of water to the tap from the cold-water storage tank must be stopped. If there's a valve available and easily accessible, turn it off. Otherwise, tie up the arm of the ball-valve serving the storage tank and open all bathroom taps and the hot tap in the kitchen to drain the water.

On conventional pillar-type taps (which are the most common sort in use) you will, after stopping the supply of water to the tap, need to remove the shield or protective cover. Some can be removed by hand; some have a hexagonal base which will take a spanner; others need you to use a pipe wrench or a strap wrench. The only danger is possible damage to the chrome. Once the shield is loose, the whole of the head-gear

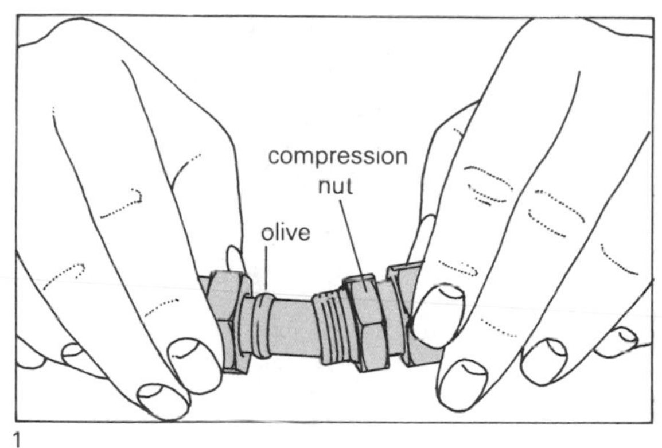

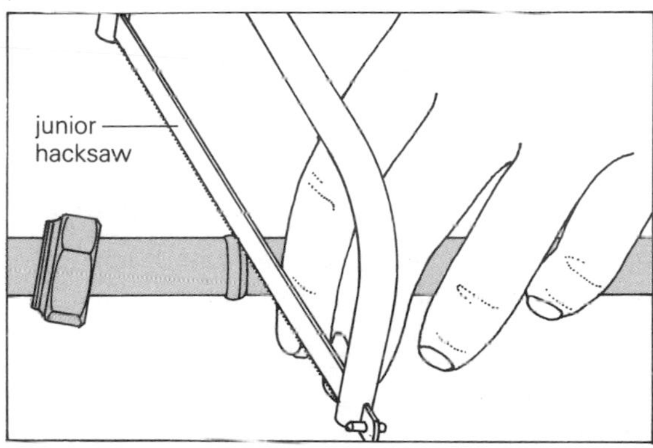

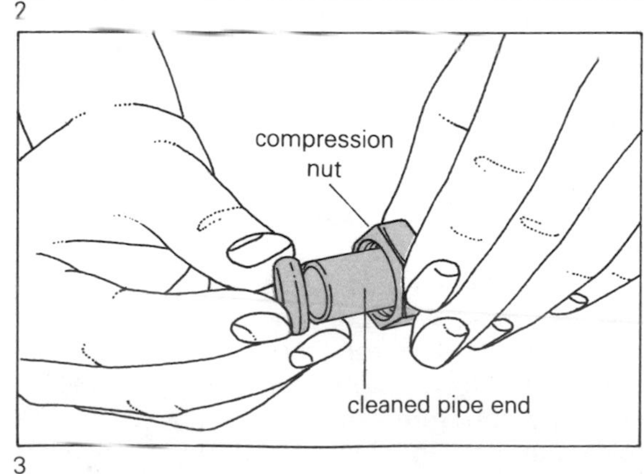

Above: Repairing a compression joint. 1. Unscrew cap-nut and pull pipe from casing. 2. If olive is damaged, remove with hacksaw. 3. Clean ends with steel wool and apply new olive

can be removed by unscrewing the head-gear nut with an adjustable spanner. After removing the 'jumper' to which the washer is screwed, it should be a simple job to undo the retaining nut and take off the damaged washer. Take care not to damage the jumper spindle if you have to hold it in a tool. Rub it with emery cloth to remove any burr, replace the jumper with the new, correct-sized washer in position and reassemble the tap.

An updated type of pillar tap is the shrouded-head tap. Instead of the traditional capstan-head, this tap has a neatly designed cover which does not conduct heat. The cover is normally held to the head-gear by a small retaining screw underneath the label disc. If this is not the case in your tap you'll find a tiny screw in the side similar to the retaining screw on a pillar tap. Once you've removed the cover, the head-gear is easily unscrewed and the procedure is then exactly the same as for the pillar tap. At the top of the head-gear of a tap is a gland nut and gland packing. Some modern shrouded head taps have a rubber 'O' ring seal instead of a conventional gland. They are designed to be trouble free but if there is any water escaping up the spindle, renew the ring.

The sight of water coming from the top of a tap can be disconcerting. If the tap can also be turned on and off very easily with, as it were, a spin of the fingers, then the cause is certain to be gland failure. It's most common on a conventional tap and can often be stopped just by tightening a nut.

To do this, take off the capstan-head by removing the retaining screw. The shield or protective cover of the tap must come off next. The adjusting nut, which you need to tighten, will be the first nut through which the spindle of the tap passes. Trial and error will give you the correct adjustment. If all the allowance for adjustment has already been taken up then you'll have to remove the gland packing and renew it. Take off the nut completely to remove the greased packing material. Repack the void with string or wool and Vaseline: fill completely before replacing the

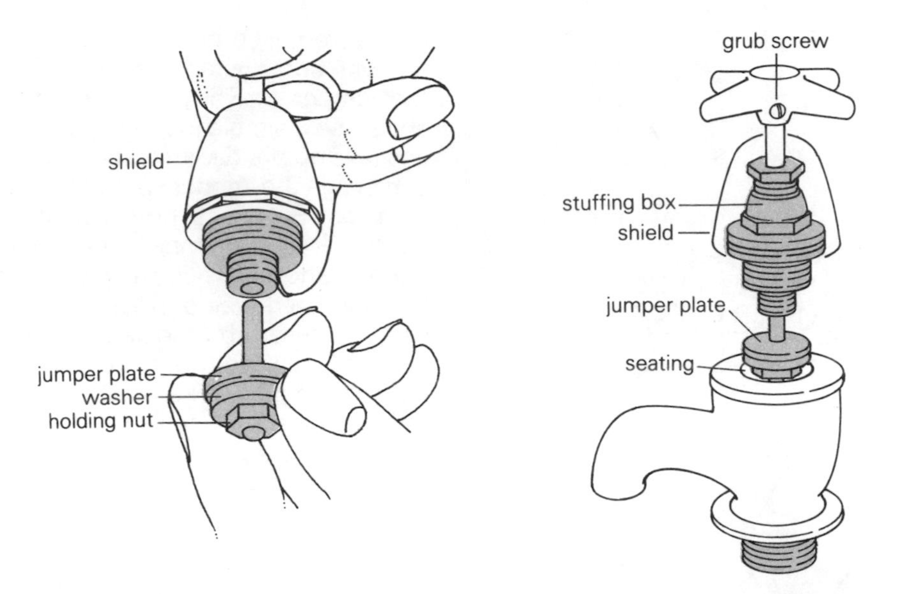

Above: Replacing a tap washer; Above left: Detail of jumper plate and holding nut

nut. Reassemble the tap, open the stop-cock and you've successfully completed yet another DIY job.

Don't feel that you've been a failure if a tap continues to drip after you've fitted a new washer! It probably isn't your fault at all but suggests that the valve-seating might be scratched, so even fitting a new washer is not going to result in a watertight seal. Although there are reseating tools available, the cheapest and quickest way to deal with this problem is to use a seating kit with a new nylon washer. Instructions are supplied with the kit. The nylon seating is placed onto the scratched brass seating, and a new washer and jumper are inserted into the head-gear of the tap. When screwed down, the valve seating is forced into position. Don't try to change the seating on Supataps without using a special reseating tool, available from the manufacturer.

You don't need to turn off the water supply to rewasher a Supatap. Loosen the top by opening the tap slightly and undo the retaining nut at the top of the nozzle. Let more water out of the tap until, surprisingly, the water stops. This indicates that the check valve inside has fallen into position. You'll then find that the nozzle will come off in your hand. The washer and jumper are fixed into an anti-splash device. After a couple of light bangs the anti-splash device will come away. You can then prise between the plate and the anti-splash device to remove the washer and jumper. Pop in the new one and replace the anti-splash device in the nozzle, which screws back on with a left-hand thread.

WATER LEVELS

The two most common faults that occur in a cold-water storage tank or a WC system are water overflowing or not filling properly. Regularly check that the level of water in the cold-water storage tank and the WC flushing system is maintained at a constant level. The mechanism to achieve this is a float fixed to a movable arm which, in turn, pushes a washer to seal off the water supply. When water is drawn off, the float falls and the arm opens the valve.

Water rushes in and, of course, the float raises the arm which pushes the washer into position again. This constant moving up and down produces wear and so from time to time parts have to be replaced. Modern float-valves are small and non-corrosive but the older types of ball-valve have a washered metal-plug to control the flow of water. Over the years the washer loses its strength, causing leaks. If more pressure on the washer does not cure the leak you'll have to replace it. If you do find water dripping from the overflow or warning pipe, it means that the water level is too high which indicates a worn washer. First of all, try bending the arm down at the float end. This should keep the level of the water about 1 inch (2.5 cm) below the overflow pipe outlet in a cold-water storage tank and ½ inch (1 cm) below the outlet in a WC cistern.

If the washer is too worn, the water will still rise and you'll need to change the ball-valve washer. The Croydon and Portsmouth types of ball-valves are the most commonly found and have easily-replaced washers. First, close the water supply by turning off the stop-cock. Some valves have a screw-on cap at the arm end and this must be removed. Holding the float arm to the body of the valve is a little split pin. Pull it out and then ease out the cranked end of the float arm which has been sitting in a slot in the plug. Push out the plug, which you'll see has two parts. The plug moves horizontally in the Portsmouth ball-valve and you'll see the old washer held in place by a retaining cap. By holding a screwdriver through the slot in the plug you should be able to unscrew the cap with a pair of pliers. Replace the washer and screw back the retaining cap. It must lie flat under the flange. If you can't unscrew the retaining cap, just pick out the old washer with a sharp skewer. You can then wriggle the new one underneath the flange of the retaining cap. Clean all the parts before reassembling with fine emery paper. There are two more things to do: renew the split pin and

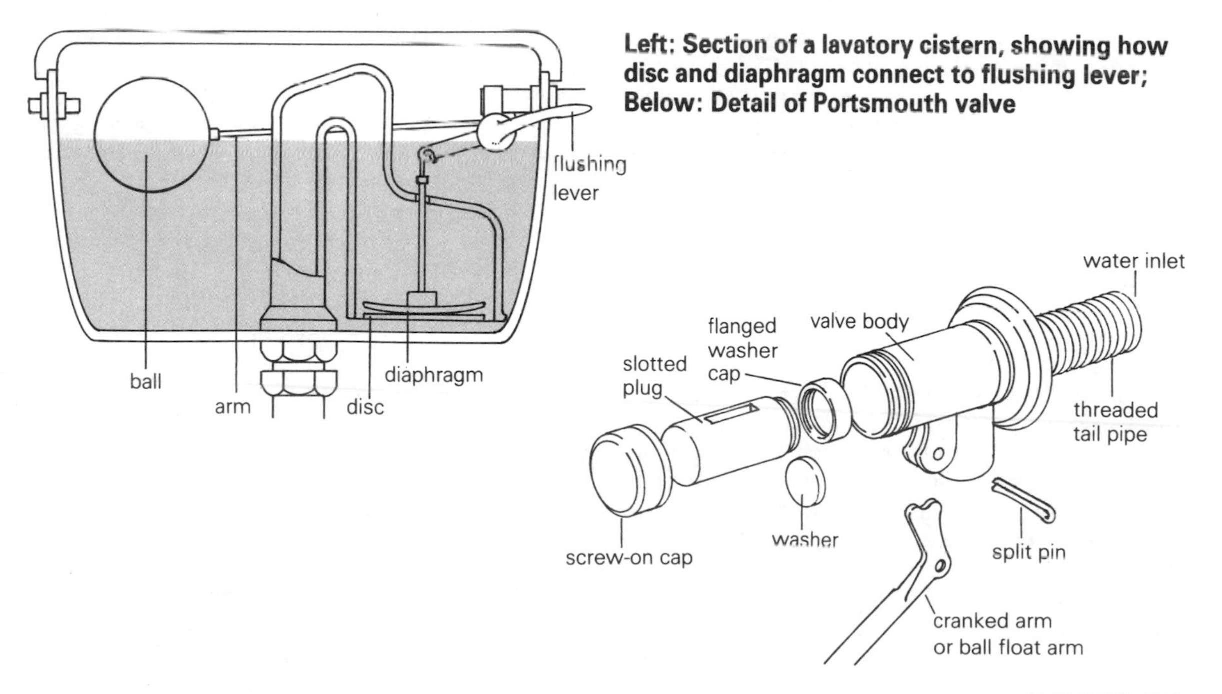

Left: Section of a lavatory cistern, showing how disc and diaphragm connect to flushing lever; Below: Detail of Portsmouth valve

smear the plug lightly with Vaseline before popping it back.

A simpler and more effective valve is the diaphragm ball-valve. This more modern valve is simple in design and has only one moving part, the plug. The cone-shaped nylon-nozzle is closed by a rubber diaphragm against which the plug presses firmly as the water level rises. If the diaphragm jams, the result would be a poor flow of water. If this happens, cut off the water supply to the system and dismantle the valve. Unscrew the large 'knurled' retaining-nut and pick out the diaphragm. You'll probably find that some debris has caused the diaphragm to jam. Clean it out and reassemble.

Should you want to adjust the water level in the cistern you'll find a small screw with a large slot near the valve end of the arm. This screw controls the raising or lowering of the float arm and by experimenting you should be able to set it to achieve the water level you want.

STOP-COCKS & GATE-VALVES

Because stop-cocks are opened and closed infrequently the washers rarely need changing. If you do have to change a stop-cock washer, tackle it in the same way as for a tap. First, stop the supply of water along the mains by closing down the Water Authority's stop-cock. This is usually just outdoors in a small, especially-constructed pit 2 feet (61 cm) deep. Drain the rising main, as far as possible, from the cold tap over the sink and from the drain-cock if there is one incorporated in your stop-cock. If you have to replace a stop-cock, make sure it's the same size as the pipe into which it is to be fitted. Just as important, check that the stop-cock is fitted the right way round. An arrow (in relief, on the body) must point in the same direction as the flow of water. Unscrew and take off the compression cap nuts and the olives from the stop-cock. The olive is the ring that you find when you remove the cap nut. Clean off the ends of the copper pipe. Push the first nut and an olive over one of the pipes to be joined. Do the same thing on the other piece of pipe. The ends of the two pipes when sprung into the body of the stop-cock must sit snugly against the shoulders inside. A little bit of waterproofing compound on the pipe ends and on the olives will help make a good seal when the nuts are tightened onto the stop-cock. The olive will be compressed in the joint.

In order to carry out repairs and maintenance swiftly and safely, all appliances and plumbed fittings should have either a stop-cock or a gate-valve. They enable you to isolate any one appliance quickly. A smaller stop-cock called a mini-valve is usually fitted just before a ball-valve or a bath or basin tap. A screwdriver or a coin can be used to turn the slotted screw. When closed, the water supply to the tap or ball-valve is interrupted so that you can replace washers without affecting any other part of the plumbing.

Where it is necessary to have an uninterrupted flow of water and where the water pressure is low, a gate-valve can be used. They are ideal for bathroom cold-water taps, especially when located immediately below the cold-water storage tank. The gate-valve can be identified by the wheel which is used to close the valve. Gate-valves are not directional, as stop-cocks are, so you can fit them either way round. However, they must be the same size as the pipe into which they are fitted. Always keep a gate-valve fully open. Often an air-lock in a hot-water cylinder is caused by a gate-valve on the supply pipe (from the cold-water system) not being fully opened.

There are two places in a house where it is essential to use only a screw-down stop-cock. The first location is the main internal stop-cock just above the point at which the mains water pipe enters the house. You often find this underneath the kitchen sink. It is set into the rising

Opposite page: Plumbing in a washing machine, a straightforward operation if you identify the supply pipes and waste pipes correctly

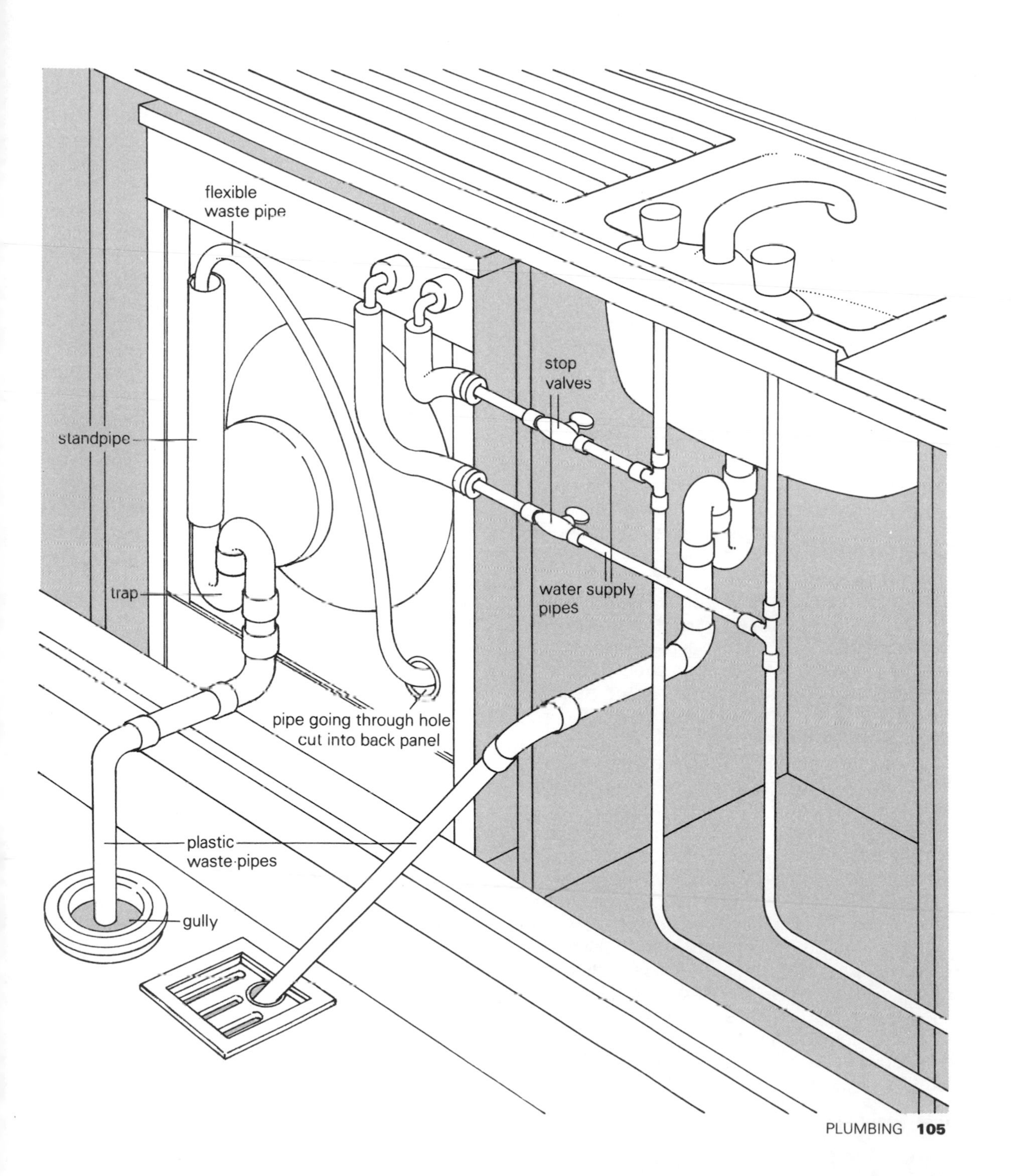
flexible
waste pipe
stop
valves
standpipe
trap
water supply
pipes
pipe going through hole
cut into back panel
plastic
waste pipes
gully

main and normally kept fully open. As with many other taps, to close it you turn the handle or head in a clockwise direction. The second location where a screw-down stop-cock is vital is just inside the house on the mains-supply to an outside source such as a garage or a garden tap.

PLUMBING IN APPLIANCES

Plumbing in a kitchen appliance sounds tricky. 'Plumbing' suggests a big bag of plumber's tools, pipe benders and blow-torches. But when you think about it, all you're doing is pushing a self-contained box-of-tricks into a space beside the sink! All you have to do is, first, connect up a water supply, as you would a garden hose; second, help the dirty water out to the gully; and third, plug into the power supply, set the automatic controls and switch on. Manufacturers of washing machines and dishwashers supply illustrated instructions for the installation of their machines. The information is easy to follow and the illustrations show the simplest methods of making connections.

Check first of all the size of the available space in your kitchen and compare it with the limits recommended by the manufacturer for the machine and the fittings. Then check where you will take the water supply from. Some machines take hot and cold water, so you must be certain that there is sufficient pressure in the hot-supply to match the cold. If the machine takes only cold water, is it to be supplied from the domestic cold-water system or from the mains?

Find a convenient pipe from which to take the supply and turn off the stop-cock, so that you can drain the water from the supply pipe. A section of about ¾ inch (2 cm) long needs to be cut from the ½-inch (12-mm) copper pipe and a compression tee-joint put in its place. Make sure that the cut ends are square, clean the pipe ends and the olives with steel wool. Put on the cap nut and then the olive. The olive has a long and a short slope to each side and the short side should face the cap nut. Before inserting the pipe into the joint, apply boss white to the pipe ends and the olives. Make certain that the pipe ends are against the shoulders inside the fitting. Thread on the caps and tighten up but do not use strong-arm tactics! From the outlet of the tee connect a short length of ½-inch (12-mm) pipe and a special washing machine hose-attachment called a 'running tap'. (There are also washing-machine stop-cocks available which have back-plates that can secure your pipework to the kitchen wall.) The inlet hose from the appliance has a screwed connector and, with the washer in place, tighten up the compression joint to the running tap. Keep the machine's control knob in the 'off' position until you turn on the main stop-cock again.

A flexible hose at the back of the appliance takes away the waste water. You can, if it's convenient, hook it over a sink to discharge the water. It is neater to install a stand-pipe outlet and keep the hose hooked permanently into it. The stand-pipe should be larger in diameter than the outlet hose from the machine. A trap at the base will ensure that no smells come back into the room. The plastic tube from the trap is taken through the wall of the house to discharge outside.

You'll probably use one of two methods to join the plastic pipe: solvent welding is cheaper but push-fit jointing is easier. In either case, to obtain a square cut on the pipe itself, first of all wrap a sheet of paper round the pipe to overlap squarely. The top of the paper forms your square cutting line. Use a junior hacksaw to cut through the pipe. With a fine file, chamfer the end of the pipe so that it pushes into a joint easily. For solvent welding roughen the end of the pipe and the inside of the fitting. Clean off all dust and apply the solvent cement to the end of the pipe and to the inside of the fitting, using a small brush. After gently pushing the pipe into the fitting add a smear of cement around the joint. In less than a minute it will have bonded.

When using a push-fit joint roughen the pipe as for solvent welding. A rubber seal between the fitting and the pipe completes the joint. Use a recommended lubricant on the end of the pipe so that it slides into the fitting without damaging the sealing ring. Push it fully home and then ease it back about ⅛ inch (3 mm) to allow for expansion when hot water flows through the pipe.

SEALANTS

It's not difficult to trace the cause of many damp problems when one can see cracks and gaps appearing between materials, allowing water to seep in. Where there is bound to be some flexing of materials, for example, at gutter joints and at a bath edge, remedial work using unsuitable hard materials will only make the problem worse. As the filler sets hard, slight shrinkage can occur and more water penetration takes place. Spores settle in the cracks and mould begins to grow.

Now at any DIY store we can buy modern sealants which have transformed the cracks and the gaps situation! Generally, there are two types of sealants: silicone sealants, which are very flexible and long-lasting, and oil-based sealants, which form a tough skin but remain soft underneath and which are mainly used outside the house. A silicone sealant provides a strong, rubbery, waterproof barrier, which is why it is suitable for joints in bathrooms and kitchens. You can buy a bath sealant in a small, easily-held plastic syringe with a plunger. The bath sealant cartridge has a nozzle tip with two neat little wings which smooth the sealant as it's applied, giving a very neat finish to the joint between the bath and the tiles. When you cut a cartridge nozzle to suit the gap to be filled, always cut the aperture slightly smaller than you think the gap is. If you cut the aperture too big you'll make a mess of the joint but if you cut it too small you can always cut away a little more.

Before using the sealant, carry out all your remedial treatment to grouting and tiles. Old sealant must be removed completely. Renew the grouting between the tiles: you will find this gives a remarkable face-lift to the look of the bathroom. Any black mould must be scraped away and the grouting removed to a depth of

Above: Cement pointing can be dislodged through movement of building or frame. A flexible mastic will prevent draughts

at least ⅛ inch (3 mm). Work the grouting material over the surface of the tiles with a rubber scraper and gently clean it off with a chamois leather or a soft, wet cloth. When dry, a film of powder will cover the tiles. This is easily removed with a dry cloth and it helps to polish the tiles.

Before applying the sealant, rub the edge of the bath and the tiles until they are absolutely dry and clean. Then dust off the surfaces and apply the sealant. Read what the manufacturers say about the sealant and how to apply it. A gentle, firm and continuous movement is better than a slow, hesitant one which might result in ridges and bumps. Finishing off with a damp cloth wrapped around the end of your forefinger will give a remarkably clean and neat line to the edge of the bath.

One manufacturer produces twelve colours of sealant to match most popular colours of bathroom décor. It also guarantees its product for ten years against drying out and crumbling.

A sealant that also acts as an adhesive will effectively seal a hand basin to a work-top. It is especially formulated for bedding down hand basins and surface-level sink tops. The sealants

Right: Plastic guttering is always clipped into position and is easy to dismantle. Rainwater pipes are pushed into sockets and can be lifted apart

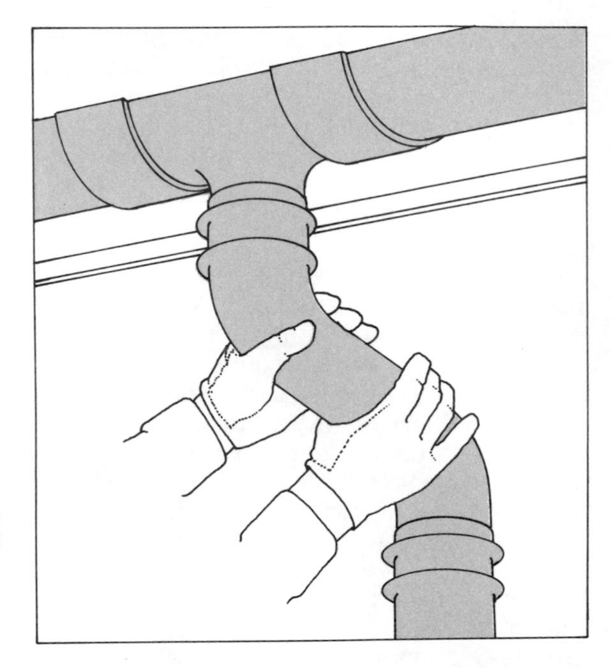

contain a special fungicide which helps prevent most mould growth.

Sealants are supplied in two types of packs. Bath sealants usually come in a plastic syringe-type cartridge which holds enough to seal completely around one bath. Larger cartridges are designed to be put into a simple, trigger-operated gun. The gun is a very simple device, lightweight to handle and very inexpensive. It can also be used for other sealing jobs around the house such as sealing gaps round window and door frames.

A ten-minute job with the cartridge gun can prevent rain being blown in that can rot the frames from inside. Sealing those gaps outside prevents uncomfortable draughts inside and, of course, loss of heat. Work from the top with a steady, sliding movement and an even pressure on the gun trigger.

Leaking joints in guttering and rainwater pipes can lead to all sorts of problems. Special gutter sealant can be bought at your DIY store. Use it as soon as you spot a leak. If you can open up the leaking joint to clean it out so much the better. The sealant will stick to both dry metal and plastic surfaces. Full instructions are supplied with the gutter sealant.

ROUTINE MAINTENANCE 7

TOOL KIT

We spend a great deal of our time as householders repairing, installing and decorating. We should do more, we should set aside a certain amount of time each month for routine maintenance of the structure of our homes, contents and the tools with which we carry out our repair and renovation work. You'll find that one of the more pleasurable aspects of a drawn-out DIY job in the home is to approach a clean work area each time with tools sharpened and orderly. Nails and screws should have separate containers; brushes should be clean and ready for immediate use; tools should be in their proper place ready for action.

Professional tradespeople depend upon their tools for their livelihoods. The motor mechanic, the plasterer, the doctor, the graphic artist and so on, all have a vested interest in maintaining the tools of their trade in tiptop condition. We must adopt the same outlook. For a very small outlay you can buy a couple of slotted plastic covers for your saws, a number of plastic caps to cover the cutting edges of your chisels and some plastic boxes with lids in which to keep drill bits, bradawl and small screwdrivers.

At some time you must organise the storage of your basic tool kit. Wherever possible keep the tools that are most often used in a tool rack. Nearby, keep a piece of oiled felt pad in a shallow tray or a pressurised container of penetrating oil so that when tools are finished with you can give them a thin film of oil to prevent rust. Children should not be allowed to play with tools. You should have a small bag or box in which to carry tools to the work area. Make a rule always to have spare blades for your coping saw, hacksaw, and hand saw. Never be without the popular sizes of drill bits.

Regular use of your tool kit should evoke memories of woodwork lessons at school. The rules learned then should still be part of your basic routine:

1 Planes when not in use should always rest on their sides to avoid damaging the blade.
2 Store metal tools in a dry place to stop them rusting.
3 Never use a chisel as a screwdriver or for lifting things; the cutting edge will be chipped and ruined.
4 Keep hammer heads clean and free of any traces of paint, sealant or adhesive.
5 Frequently rub the hammer face squarely with a piece of fine glasspaper wrapped round a block of wood.
6 Never tolerate loose heads of hammers. Wedging pins for holding hammer heads in place are cheap.
7 You'll never lose the key of an electric drill if you tie it to the lead with string.
8 Always hang up saws and protect the teeth.
9 A damaged measuring steel tape is useless, never leave it extended for this to happen.

There are two small tools, a saw-sharpener and a saw-set, that will keep your saws sharp and set and will pay for themselves over a short period. A saw-sharpener is simple to use, maintains the correct depth of teeth and gives the accurate filing angle. After sharpening a saw use a saw-set to ensure a clean, easy cut. A saw-set will guarantee that every tooth tip is properly angled out on either side of the blade. Sending out saws to be sharpened is an expensive business so learning to maintain your own saws in prime condition is well worth the trouble. Easy-to-follow instructions are supplied with both these simple tools.

Chisels and plane blades should always be kept sharp. Two angles form a cutting edge: the ground angle at 25° and the honed angle at 30°. The honed angle is formed and maintained by rubbing on an oilstone to give it a razor-sharp edge. A honing guide is an ideal aid for maintaining the cutting edges of these blades. It only takes a few minutes to achieve a sharp cutting edge and this will be reflected in the quality of your work.

We are so often tempted to use a screwdriver to open a tin of paint but we should resist the temptation! A screwdriver is used more often than any other tool; unfortunately it is also the most commonly abused tool. A screwdriver should fit exactly into the slot in a screw head. If the blade is too wide, it will damage the wood. One that is too narrow takes the edge off the slot and makes it impossible to drive the screw in. When using a screwdriver think of it as part of the screw and keep it in a straight line with the screw. This is particularly true of the pump screwdriver. An important part of the action is to make sure that the blade is squarely on the screw and lined up with it before pushing down to start the rotary action. If you don't take care, a pump screwdriver tends to slip off the screw while you're pushing and because you have to exert force you can damage the surrounding surface of the wood.

DRAWERS WHICH STICK

Drawers made of plastic or laminated materials which slide in a plastic groove or channel don't usually stick. Wooden drawers, however, do, because they and the wooden carcass holding the drawers can expand and contract. It can also be caused by considerable wear on the runners, if the drawers are in constant use.

Check that the joints at each corner of a drawer are tight with no movement. If not, it's a simple matter to apply some wood glue and tap the joint back home. A couple of small panel pins will hold the joint until the glue is set. If the drawers are sticking at the sides, a brisk rub with sandpaper wrapped round a block will often solve the problem. If more drastic action is required, use a smoothing plane or a Surform tool. Plane in from the corners, otherwise you'll split the end grain at the joints.

A drawer sticking at the top and bottom is usually easier to fix. The top of a drawer is finely squared and polished, so any easing should be done from underneath. In any case, the bottom of the drawer is set higher than the runners so either sandpaper or plane along the runners themselves. A candle rubbed over the bottom of the drawer runners will also help to ease the running of all drawers. Sometimes an older piece of furniture will have runners so worn that the drawer rocks. In this case, level the bottom of the drawer and then, if you have room, stick on a piece of lipped plastic edging strip using a contact adhesive.

You don't usually have to work inside the carcass but occasionally the drawer supports will drop or the drawer stop will have disappeared. These are minor carpentry repairs using glue and pins or screws. If the front of a drawer disappears inside the chest, you'll need to replace the little block of wood called the stop. Measure accurately the depth of the drawer, and transfer that measurement in order to position the new drawer stop.

Whilst working on the drawers give the front a face-lift too. Take off the knobs or handles and clean or rub down the whole of the outside. Either polish or paint and then replace with new handles or knobs.

REPOINTING

One day you might look up at the front elevation of your house and be aware that some repointing is necessary. If it's brick or stone and the mortar shows signs of wear or crumbling think about

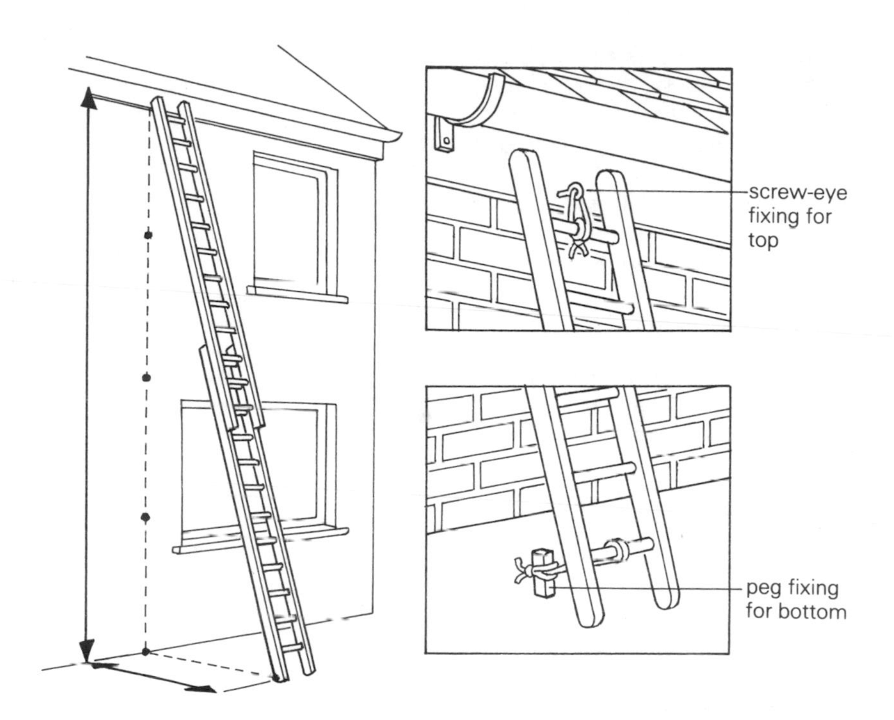

tackling it yourself. It might appear daunting and difficult but it's not. Pointing is an easy art to acquire and very rewarding because it's going to be there for years.

Generally, bricks and stone do not deteriorate and are maintenance-free. The joints between the bricks, however, may suffer from weathering, show signs of decay and then need attention. Structural movement in a building can also cause the mortar to crack. Sulphates in polluted air will attack the mortar and cause deterioration. Once any of these things has happened, rain can penetrate the mortar and, in cold weather, the water will freeze, expand and break up the surface even further.

Check the surface of the wall for moss or growth of any sort. Scrape off and kill any such growth with a mix of one part bleach to four parts water. (Do take care to protect your skin from splashes.) Rake out the mortar to a depth of about ½ inch (1 cm) from the whole of the area you are going to repoint. A small cold chisel, a plugging chisel, and a 2-lb club hammer are the tools necessary for this part of the operation. You must leave a squared-off recess between the bricks otherwise the mortar will fall out. Brush off all dust particles and dampen the brickwork with some water before you begin repointing.

Above: Extension ladder and fixings. (For safety reasons, distance along ground from wall to foot of ladder should be one quarter of height from base of wall to top of ladder.)

Mix just enough mortar to use in one session. Each mix should be exactly the same as the previous one in order to maintain the colour of the mortar throughout the whole of the repointing job. On a clean, dry surface mix together the cement, lime and washed builder's sand in the following proportions: one shovel-full of cement, one of lime and six of sand. Mix the constituents dry to begin with as this helps to achieve a constant colour. Scoop out a hollow in the centre and add water gradually. Continue to add water to the mix until you find it easy to pick up a trowel-full of the mix and then slide it easily off the trowel. If the mix is too watery it will flop out of the joints. If the batch begins to dry out before you've finished the section of repointing then throw it away. Never add water to try to restore the cement mix because the structure of the mortar will be weakened.

Use a hawk (a square of wood about 12 inches by 12 inches (305 mm by 305 mm) with a small wooden handle centrally underneath) to hold about a fistful of mortar each time. Form a small pyramid of the mortar in the centre of the hawk. With the back of the trowel facing away from you, take off about ½ inch (1 cm) of mortar from the lower edge of the pyramid. Tilt the trowel to keep the mortar uppermost and gently ease it into the upright recess. Try out a patch of a foot (30.5 cm) square to start. Force the mortar into all the uprights first, easing the mortar in with a stroking motion. Don't worry at this stage about excess mortar. Then point all the horizontals; you'll find this easier! As you stroke along the horizontals the ends of the verticals will be 'struck'.

Go on to the next patch, making this one slightly larger. You should eventually be able to cover about a square yard at a time. Then go back to the original patch to remove the excess mortar. There are various ways of finishing the pointing but try to match the existing pointing, unless you are repointing the entire wall.

A 'weathered' joint is an angled joint to throw off the rainwater and is formed very simply by pushing the trowel blade into the top of the joint and stroking it along at an angle. A 'flush' joint is formed when the new mortar is level with the face of the brickwork. A 'tooled' joint is concave in contour and is made by drawing along a rounded piece of timber or a rounded handle from a discarded bucket. A 'recessed' joint is formed by raking into the mortar with a squared piece of timber the exact width of the mortar joint. Whichever method you choose, when the mortar is still 'green' and flexible brush off unwanted mortar from the face of the brickwork with a fine brush. Years later you'll still look at your work with a great deal of pleasure!

RISING DAMP

The results of rising damp in the walls of a house are far from pleasant; they can be seen, felt and smelt. There are several causes of rising damp and often the problem could be avoided if one was aware of certain principles of building.

About 6 inches (15 cm) above the outside ground level, inside the walls, is an impervious layer of material. This is the damp-course sandwiched between the brickwork. It can be made of slate, a bitumen-based material or a specially-formulated plastic material. It's built into the house to prevent moisture in the ground from penetrating the main structure of the building. Structural movement in the building can sometimes cause a breakdown of this damp-course, but a more common cause is when earth or other material is piled up against the house and breaches the damp-course.

Each year you might be tempted to build up your rose border outside the house until, without realising it, the earth is well above the damp-course level. The bricks above the damp-course will then suck in moisture from the earth and pass it to the inside walls of the house. Similarly, a patio or a path can be built at the side or front of the house, higher than the level of the damp-course. This will permanently feed moisture to the inner walls of the house and result in rising damp. If your house is rendered with a sand and cement mix the lower level should stop above the damp-course. If the rendering goes lower and covers over the damp-course it will act like blotting paper sucking up water and dispersing it throughout the wall area. Sometimes the cause of rising damp can only be discovered by removing a brick at damp-course level from the outside of the house. This will show whether mortar has been allowed to drop inside the cavity to a height above the damp-course, thus bridging it. Laying a new solid floor on the inside of the house can also cause damp problems, if it's laid at the wrong level.

If the cause of rising damp is earth breaching the damp-course, then it's easily curable. External rendering carried too low can be cut back to the correct level. Inside plaster which inadvertently touches a solid-floor concrete slab can also be chopped back.

If no damp-proof course exists or rising damp persists because of a breakdown in the damp-proof course, the problem can be stopped by the injection of a water-repellent silicone solution. Holes are drilled at intervals around the wall and the solution injected under pressure. The whole layer of the wall is thus impregnated and provides an impervious barrier. Tools and plant can be hired and the silicone solution purchased. It's not the easiest of DIY jobs but it is possible to do. A booklet giving details of how to tackle this job is supplied when the liquid is purchased.

FIRE-EXTINGUISHERS

When you take into account the potential damage and loss caused by any fire in the home, then the relatively small cost of a fire-extinguisher must make it worthwhile having one, if not two, in the home. One should certainly be kept in the kitchen and, ideally, one on each floor of the house. You must take every precaution to protect yourself, your family and your property. There are various types of fire-extinguisher available for controlling different types of fire as well as other devices to help you to escape from any part of the house. To reassure yourself, telephone or visit your local fire-station and ask for advice.

Fire-extinguishers are not as unwieldly and confusing to use as they might at first appear. Go to your local DIY store and ask the staff to help you decide which is the best and the most effective for your own purposes. They'll have easy-to-follow pamphlets which will tell you all you need to know about siting, handling and safety.

After ensuring you have extinguishers of the correct capacity and rating, the speed with

Right: Fire-extinguishers are classified according to their capacity and intended use. Choose the one or ones most suited to your home

CHECKLIST: EXTERIOR MAINTENANCE

1 **Chimneys**: if any pots have tilted, the *flaunching* (the cement which holds the chimney pots to the chimney stack) has cracked and needs replacing. If smoke escapes through cracks in the *pointing*, there may have been serious movement in the stack – this is dangerous and needs to be corrected immediately. The *flashing* (lead or zinc seal between the chimney stack and sloping tiles or slates) is a vulnerable area for water penetration. Make sure it is sound and tight on all sides. The lead *apron*, which fits into a mortar course within the stack and overlaps with the top layer of tiles or slates, must be well sealed on all sides and not allow water to penetrate the brickwork behind.

2 **Cement fillets**: the fillets of cement used for sealing the joint between the pitch of a roof and the wall must be completely clean and smooth if they are to stop rainwater entering the house. Any green in the mortar between the ridge tiles (at the apex of the roof) indicates either the presence of water or that the mortar is perished.

3 **Tiles and slates**: check for any which are cracked, loose or missing – and replace as soon as possible. If a roof has been 'turnerised' (bitumin felt has been laid on top) it will be difficult to check if something is wrong with the tiles or slates.

4 **Gutters**: if yours are iron, check they aren't rusty; if plastic, that they're intact. The bottom of a rainwater pipe should have a 'shoe' (a piece of pipe set at an angle) directed so that the water discharges into a gully.

5 **Soil vent pipes**: the top of these should always be at least 3 feet (1 m) above the highest window in the house. Make sure the joints are sound and that the back of the pipe (usually unprotected by paint) isn't split, especially at ground level.

6 **Barge boards** (protective boards under the overhanging roof): always worth checking, as are **facia boards** (on which gutters and pipes are screwed) and **soffit boards** (underneath facia boards).

7 **Door and window frames**: door and window openings can let in huge amounts of wind and rain, especially between the frame itself and the brickwork of the opening in the wall. Also check putties and cracks in the glazing, and check metal frames for rust.

8 **Window sills**: see that they're all in one piece, free of rot and have a 'drip' (or ridge) underneath the front face.

9 **Pointing**: if pointing is discoloured anywhere, bits will probably come out with some gentle prodding. Make sure the pointing hasn't been given a cosmetic job, so that the surface looks fine but the underneath is perished.

10 **Paintwork**: blistering or flaking paintwork will not protect anything from the harsh elements, and neglect may, therefore, lead to more extensive maintenance later on.

11 **Damp-course**: this must meet the statutory requirements (it must reach 6 inches above the outside ground level, for instance) and you must take care nothing is stacked up or built against the wall which might allow moisture to penetrate the wall above the damp course.

12 **Rendered walls**: any pebble dash or rendering on exterior walls should stop at the damp-course. If timbered, the timbering will need preservative and should be checked each year.

13 Applying the kind of scrutiny used in all the above points, do a regular check to see that any paths, patios, drives, fences, gates or out-buildings are in good condition. The sooner you act upon what you see, the less work you'll have to do!

which you attack a fire is the next most important factor to think about. All extinguishers have simple operating instructions printed large enough to be read easily even by the short-sighted. Make yourself read through the instructions until you are thoroughly familiar with them. Test each member of the family, so that they know and understand the operating instructions. A valuable half-minute can be lost trying to find out how to operate the extinguisher in the event of an emergency.

If a fire, even a small one, occurs in your home or if you smell burning, dial 999 and summon the Fire Brigade. Having an extinguisher in the home is no substitute for the professionals but don't under-rate the fire-extinguisher which, if used quickly and properly, can keep damage and loss to a minimum. If the fire is too large to tackle yourself then leave the house as quickly as you can and wait for the Fire Brigade. Your first consideration must be to save lives. Fire can be prevented from spreading too quickly by shutting all doors and windows. If there is dense smoke and it is difficult to see or breathe, get away as speedily as you can by crawling. Often, the air near the floor is easier to breathe and the smoke will be less dense.

There are added precautionary measures that you can take. A smoke detector is a small device no larger than a saucer. It has no external wires and can be simply screwed to ceilings in hallways and landings, and so on. It reacts to the first signs of smoke and combustion and will immediately sound a warning.

A personal fire-extinguisher is small enough to be carried around and simplicity itself to operate. You will have your own reasons for carrying one in any particular situation, but it is particularly useful when near or working with inflammable liquids.

If you keep inflammable liquids in a store or in a garage then a woven glass-fibre blanket in a flat wall-pack should be hung close by. The type on a hanger is released in a second by pulling at the tapes. The bottom of the blanket should be about 4 or 5 feet (1.2 or 1.5 m) above floor level and at the side of the inflammable material.

A fire-blanket is also ideal to smother a hot-fat fire on a stove and it is sensible to keep one in the kitchen. Never ever use water if your chip pan catches fire or if electricity is the cause of a fire. Hot fat is the commonest cause of fires in the kitchen. There are some simple precautions to take: the heat should never be turned full up nor should you ever tip wet food into fat. If you leave oil or fat in a pan unattended, it will start smoking and burst into flames. Don't be tempted to move it but smother it immediately with a fire-blanket.

If an electrical appliance catches fire switch off the source of power. If you can't get to the socket, switch off at the fuse box or consumer unit. The most suitable extinguisher for use on a fire caused by electricity will contain dry powder, inert gas and vaporising liquid. The contents of all extinguishers are very clearly marked and by reading the pamphlets from your DIY store, reading the labels on the extinguishers and by talking to the professionals you'll be able to find out which sort of extinguisher to use on which sort of fire.

INDEX

Page numbers in *italic* refer to illustrations